Visions

of the

Night

SUNY series in Dream Studies
Robert L. Van de Castle, editor

Visions

of the

Dreams, Religion, and Psychology

Kelly Bulkeley

State University of New York Press

Published by
State University of New York Press, Albany

For information, address State University of New York Press,
State University Plaza, Albany, N.Y., 12246

Production by Marilyn P. Semerad
Marketing by Nancy Farrell

Library of Congress Cataloging-in-Publication Data

Bulkeley, Kelly, 1962–
    Visions of the night : dreams, religion, and psychology / Kelly
Bulkeley.
        p.   cm. — (SUNY series in dream studies)
    Includes bibliographical references and index.
    ISBN 0–7914–4283–7 (alk. paper). — ISBN 0–7914–4284–5 (pbk. :
alk. paper)
    1. Dreams.   2. Dreams—Religious aspects.   3. Dream
interpretation.   I. Title.   II. Series.
BF1091.B94   1999
154.6'3—dc21   98–53601
                                                                     CIP

10 9 8 7 6 5 4 3 2 1

To the Sleeping Lady

Contents

Acknowledgments

This book has emerged directly out of many years of wonderful conversations with friends, teachers, students, and family members. It is by far the most social work I've ever written, and in every chapter I try my best to describe what I've learned from those happy conversations and what I hope others will learn from them, too. I would like to thank, in no particular order, some of the colleagues with whom I've enjoyed especially good dialogues: Ron Rebholz, Bert Cohler, Peter Homans, Wendy Doniger, Don Browning, George Cattermole, John MacAloon, Ernest Hartmann, the late Alan Moffitt, Carol Shreier Rupprecht, Jeremy Taylor, Jane White Lewis, Lewis Rambo, Diane Jonte-Pace, John McDargh, Robert Van de Castle, Hendrika Vande Kemp, and the members of the Association for the Study of Dreams and the Person, Culture and Religion Group of the American Academy of Religion. I would also like to express my appreciation for the work of the staff at SUNY Press, especially James Peltz, Marilyn Semerad, and Nancy Farrell, and for the assistance of Ed Kelley, Cecily Freyeremouth, and Gary Isaacs in designing the book's cover. And to my family, Hilary, Dylan, Maya, and Conor, once again I thank you for all your love and support.

For God speaks in one way,
and in two, though man does not perceive it.
In a dream, in a vision of the night,
when deep sleep falls upon men,
while they slumber on their beds,
then he opens the ears of men,
and terrifies them with warnings,
that he may turn man aside from his deed,
and cut off pride from man;
he keeps back his soul from the Pit,
his life from perishing by the sword.

—Job 33:14–18

Introduction: The Varieties of Religious Dream Experience

The subtitle of this introduction refers, of course, to William James's *The Varieties of Religious Experience*, which was based on the Gifford Lectures he delivered at the University of Edinburgh in the fall of 1901 and winter of 1902. In these lectures James developed a distinctive new method of studying religion. He used new research in the relatively young discipline of psychology to analyze and explain certain phenomena found in virtually all the world's religious traditions—phenomena like mysticism, asceticism, prayer, saintliness, conversion, and sacrifice. James, who was himself one of the preeminent psychologists of his day, approached religion just as he would any other expression of human mental life. He made careful, detailed observations of people's religious experiences in all their colorful diversity, and he gave very sensitive attention to the personal meanings different kinds of experiences had for different kinds of people. James rejected the stubborn skepticism toward religion held by many of his scientific colleagues, and he argued that the ultimate standard to use in making a psychological evaluation of a religious experience was to look at its practical effects on the individual's life—"by their fruits ye shall know them" (James 1958, 34).

However, just as much as James was interested in seeing what psychology could teach us about religion, he also wanted to explore what religion could teach us about psychology. Toward the end of the Gifford Lectures James brought the concept of the subconscious into his analysis, and he concluded that in psychological terms religious experiences are expressions of subconscious feelings, thoughts, energies, and desires. "[I]n religion," James said, "we have a department of human nature with unusually close relations to the transmarginal or

subliminal region [of the mind]. . . . In persons deep in the religious
life—and this is my conclusion—the door into this region seems unusually wide open; at any rate, experiences making their entrance
through that door have had emphatic influence in shaping religious
history" (James 1958, 366). What this means, James suggested, is that
the further development of psychological knowledge will require us to
explore experiential realms that have traditionally been regarded as religious or spiritual in nature. If we truly want to expand our psychological understanding of the human mind we must continue to examine in
a careful and respectful fashion what the world's religious traditions
have taught about those mysteriously nonvolitional, nonconscious
powers that have guided, inspired, and sometimes radically transformed people's lives.

In the twenty lectures he gave at the University of Edinburgh
James mentioned the subject of dreams but once, noting only that they
are one of the most common expressions of that subconscious realm of
the mind where religion and psychology come together (James 1958,
366). I imagine, though, that James might have devoted more attention
to dreams if he had given the Gifford Lectures a few years later, after
having what he described as "one of the most intensely peculiar experiences of my whole life":

> San Francisco, Feb. 14th 1906. The night before last, in my bed at Stan-
> ford University, I woke at 7:30 a.m., from a quiet dream of some sort, and
> whilst "gathering my waking wits," seemed suddenly to get mixed up
> with reminiscences of a dream of an entirely different sort, which seemed
> to telescope, as it were, into the first one, a dream very elaborate, of lions,
> and tragic. I concluded this to have been a previous dream of the same
> sleep; but the apparent mingling of two dreams was something very
> queer, which I had never before experienced.
>   On the following night (Feb. 12–13) I awoke suddenly from my first
> sleep, which appeared to have been very heavy, in the middle of a dream,
> in thinking of which I became suddenly confused by the contents of two
> other dreams that shuffled themselves abruptly in between the parts of
> the first dream, and of which I couldn't grasp the origin. Whence come
> *these dreams?* I asked. They were close to *me*, and fresh, as if I had just
> dreamed them; and yet they were far away *from the first dream.* The con-
> tents of the three had absolutely no connection. One had a cockney at-
> mosphere, it happened to someone in London. The other two were
> American. One involved the trying on of a coat (was this the dream I
> seemed to wake from?) the other was a sort of nightmare and had to do
> with soldiers. Each had a wholly distinct emotional atmosphere that
> made its individuality discontinuous with that of the others. And yet, in
> a moment, as these three dreams alternately telescoped into and out of

each other, and I seemed to myself to have been their common dreamer, they seemed quite as distinctly *not* to have been dreamed in succession, in that one sleep. *When*, then? Not on a previous night, either. *When*, then, and *which* was the one out of which I had just awakened? *I could no longer tell*: one was as close to me as the others, and yet they entirely repelled each other, and I seemed thus to belong to three different dream-systems at once, no one of which would connect itself either with the others or with my waking life. I began to feel curiously confused and *scared*, and tried to wake myself up wider, but I seemed already wide-awake. Presently cold shivers of dread ran over me: *Am I getting into other people's dreams?* Is this a "telepathic" experience? Or an invasion of double (or treble) personality? Or is it a thrombus in a cortical artery? and the beginning of a general mental "confusion" and disorientation which is going on to develop who knows how far?

Decidedly I was losing hold of my "self," and making acquaintance with a quality of mental distress that I had never known before, its nearest analogue being the sinking, giddying anxiety that one may have when, in the woods, one discovers that one is really "lost." Most human troubles look towards a terminus. Most fears point in a direction and concentrate towards a climax. Most assaults of the evil one may be met by bracing oneself against something, one's principles, one's courage, one's will, one's pride. But in this experience all was diffusion from a centre, and footholds swept away, the brace itself disintegrating all the faster as one needed its support more direly. Meanwhile vivid perception (or remembrance) of the various dreams kept coming over me in alternation. Whose? *whose? WHOSE? Unless I can attach them*, I am swept out to sea with no horizon and no bond, getting *lost*.

The idea aroused the "creeps" again, and with it the fear of again falling asleep and renewing the process. It had begun the previous night, but then the confusion had only gone one step, and had seemed simply curious. *This* was the second step—where might I be after a third step had been taken? (James 1910, 88–89, italics in original)

What strikes James more than anything else here is the terrifying conceptual dizziness induced by the dream, the effect it has of profoundly shaking his understanding of the ordinary structures of consciousness and personality. James provides few details about the dreams themselves, and no particular associations to the images of the lions, the cockney atmosphere, the coat, or the soldiers. Rather, it is the dizzying *plurality* of the dreams that unsettles him so deeply. Each of the dreams engages him in a vivid and distinct reality of its own, and yet he does not see any means of relating the dream realities to each other or to his daily life. James's "self," the customary center of his highly cultured and brilliantly intelligent waking-life identity, is incapable of making sense of these dreaming experiences. The dreams carry him some place far beyond the boundaries, the "braces," that have always defined and protected his selfhood.

I find many things to admire and wonder at in James's narrative. One is his ability simply to describe what has happened to him. Despite the frightening confusion he feels, he still manages to write an evocative portrait of an experience that is utterly alien to ordinary rational thought. I'm particularly taken with his comparison of the dream experiences to the feeling of being "really lost" in the woods, as I too have been drawn to wilderness metaphors when trying to describe the more extraordinary aspects of dreaming. Another remarkable element here is James's willingness to consider a variety of possible explanations for the dreams. They could be telepathic interactions with other people's dreams, they could be products of a physiological malfunction in the cerebral cortex, they could be the beginnings of a mental breakdown, they could, perhaps, be an opening toward a kind of mystical insight or revelation. James isn't sure *what* exactly has happened to him. And although no single explanation seems to fit, James clearly feels a strong impulse to understand the experience, to "attach" the dreams to someone or something.

More than anything, I marvel at James's ability to live with the exquisitely sharp emotional tension generated by his dreams. He rejects the seductive simplicity of quick, reductionistic answers, and he chooses instead to hold all the different possibilities open, hoping that with time a better understanding will emerge that will do full justice to the mysterious complexity of his experience.

Visions of the Night is not intended to be a "Jamesian" analysis of dreaming. For one thing, I am interested not only in further developing the dialogue between religion and psychology but also in expanding that dialogue to include voices from the fields of philosophy, anthropology, sociology, neurophysiology, history, literature, and film criticism. For another thing, I am motivated in my research by somewhat different questions than those guiding James in his investigations. My primary concerns can be briefly stated as follows:

1. What is the role of dreaming in human development, particularly in the development of our capacity for imaginative play? Given that all humans are "hard-wired" with a psychophysiological need to dream, what can or should a society do to educate its members (particularly its children) about the nature and the potentials of dreaming experience?

2. Why do certain dreams respond so directly and so creatively to waking-life experiences of crisis, trauma, suffering, and loss? How have different cultural traditions made practical use of these "healing powers" of dreaming?

3. What is the relationship of dreaming to politics, authority, and rebellion? In what ways do dreams both reflect and challenge the structures of power that govern a dreamer's life (at psychological, political, and cosmic/theological levels)?

4. Is it ever possible to know *with certainty* if our dreams are revealing valuable spiritual truths or are simply deceiving us with alluring but vain fantasies? Can we develop trustworthy hermeneutic principles to guide us through the epistemologically confounding process of dream interpretation?

These four broad questions are woven throughout the thirteen chapters of this book. Although each particular chapter uses a different interdisciplinary framework to study a different set of issues, all of the chapters are efforts to develop new perspectives on these four concerns. Readers who expect a book to have a precise linear argument, marching point by point toward a specific concluding destination, may be disappointed by the kaleidoscopic array of views presented in this work. Again, I can only appeal to the infinitely diverse nature of dreaming itself, and suggest that the best way to increase our understanding of dreaming is to engage in the kind of free-ranging interdisciplinary dialogue offered in the following chapters.

The specific focus of the first three chapters is on different ways of interpreting the religious or spiritual dimensions of dreaming. Most contemporary scholarship on dreams, even if it is friendly to religious issues and concerns, relies on conceptual models of religion that are narrow at best and erroneous at worst. In these three chapters I draw on resources from contemporary theology, the history of religions, depth psychology, and hermeneutic philosophy to promote a more sophisticated understanding of the numinous power and rich spiritual diversity of human dream life. In chapters 4 to 6 I consider the ways in which dreams relate not only to the dreamer's personal life but to his or her social world as well. These chapters show how dreams reflect significant features of the dreamer's cultural environment and sometimes even motivate moral and political actions that aim at the resolution of particularly troublesome problems in the dreamer's community.

In chapters 7 and 8 I respond to the dream theories of Sigmund Freud and J. Allan Hobson, both of whom share a deep but in my view misguided hostility toward religion. I suggest that their theories, despite their triumphant scientific reductionism, provide valuable resources in helping us better understand the profoundly creative nature of dreaming.

In chapters 9 through 12 I turn to the interplay of dreaming and artistic expression, and study different cultural representations of dreaming in myths, plays, and films. All of the dreams analyzed in these chapters are fictional, that is, they are all experienced by people who are characters in an artistically rendered narrative. My argument is that careful reading and interpretation of these "fictional" dreams can reveal intriguing new aspects of the "real" dreams we experience in our own lives.

I conclude the book with a personal narrative of my experiences at a dream-studies conference I attended in Moscow, a conference that by coincidence began the very day (August 19, 1991) that a group of Red Army generals tried to seize control of the country from then-Soviet leader Mikhail Gorbachev.

A postscript offers some thoughts on where *Visions of the Night* fits into the ongoing scholarly discussion about the field of religion and psychological studies, a field that is in the midst of (yet another) period of transition and reorientation. An annotated bibliography on dream research is included at the end of the book to aid readers who want to pursue the study of particular issues and themes.

1

Root Metaphor Dreams

My fascination with dreams originated in early adolescence, when I began having extremely powerful and deeply perplexing nightmares. These strangely haunting dreams were filled with terrifying monsters and darkly malevolent creatures who relentlessly attacked and pursued me no matter how fast I fled or where I tried to hide. As a child I was not raised in any particular religious tradition; my family was quite secular, and early in life I learned to prize the qualities of rationality, autonomy, and objectivity. But as I awoke each morning, shaken and exhausted from another horrible chasing nightmare, I couldn't help feeling that these dreams were trying to teach me another way of looking at the world. It seemed they were trying to make me recognize the reality of a wholly *different* realm, an "irrational" realm where my conscious self had little control and where frighteningly alien, nonhuman powers reigned.

I talked about my dreams with my family and friends, and I began reading books and attending public seminars on dreams. To my surprise and relief, I found that many other people had also experienced dreams like mine—dreams of such compelling mystery that they transformed the dreamer's whole way of understanding the world.

I began my graduate studies at the University of Chicago Divinity School with the desire to answer a basic question: What do these kinds of profoundly transformative dreams *mean*? I took two approaches to answering the question. First, I studied the role that dreams have played in world religions. In the course of this cross-cultural exploration I discovered that virtually every religious tradition throughout history has looked to dreams for revelations from the gods, for spiritual guidance, and for creative inspiration. Second, I examined modern psychological research on dreams and dreaming. Here, I found many studies showing that dreams promote psychological integration, preserve our emotional balance, and help us overcome crises, conflicts, and traumas.

My twin investigations gave me many new insights, but they didn't really answer my basic question. The problem with the history of religions material was that it used strictly religious terms and concepts to describe dreams; but my dreams, and the dreams of the other people I had met, were not always conventionally "religious" in form or content. The limitation of the modern psychological material was that it often reduced dreaming to a purely individual, intrapsychic phenomenon. But again, the kinds of dreams that I was studying were striking precisely because they seemed to lead *beyond* the individual, *beyond* the ordinary boundaries of the dreamer's personal psyche.

What I needed was somehow to bridge the fields of religious studies and psychology. My efforts to build such a bridge led me to develop the concept of *root metaphor dreams*. My hope was that this concept would not only connect and synthesize the insights of both religious and psychological approaches to dreams, but would also provide psychotherapists, pastoral counselors, and lay people with practical guidance for exploring the spiritual dimensions of dreams, either their own or their clients'.

Metaphors are descriptions of one thing in terms of another. For example, people today often use computer metaphors to describe the human brain—we speak of our brains "processing information," "storing data," and "operating" at higher or lower "efficiency." In using such metaphors, we refer to the features of something that is relatively more tangible and well-known (e.g., computers) to help us understand features of something that is more *in*tangible and *un*known to us (e.g., the nature of the human brain). Many linguistic philosophers have come to the conclusion that metaphorical thinking is the ultimate foundation of all human knowledge and understanding (See Lakoff and Johnson 1980, and Ricoeur 1970, 1974, 1981).

What I call *root* metaphors are those metaphors that help us understand the fundamental questions of human existence—questions such as, why are we born, why do we suffer, and why do we die? Is the cosmos governed by some kind of order and harmony, or is it essentially chaotic and aimless? Is there a God? What makes for a meaningful and fulfilling life? To answer these important yet mysterious questions we use special metaphors: we draw upon relatively concrete images from our ordinary experience to help us understand these supremely transcendent spiritual questions.

I use the adjective "root" to emphasize three qualities: first, that these particular metaphors reach down into the deepest issues of human existence; second, that these metaphors are uniquely alive, vital, and powerful; and third, that we need many of them to enjoy a balanced, thriving life—just as a tree needs many roots to steady and nourish it.

From this perspective, a religious or cultural tradition can be seen to revolve around a distinctive cluster of root metaphors. Mahayana Buddhists use the image of a corpse as one of their root metaphors; this tangible image metaphorically expresses the Mahayana Buddhist belief that mortal life is one of inevitable suffering, death, and decay. The image of Mother Earth serves as a root metaphor in many Native American cultures, as it portrays a person's relationship with his or her mother as a model for our spiritual relationship with the whole natural world. In contemporary Western culture the image of the "invisible hand," drawn from Adam Smith's work *The Wealth of Nations*, functions as a root metaphor in that the reassuring vision of a great, godlike hand carefully and benevolently managing our collective affairs is taken as a concrete means of understanding the powerful and pervasive effects of capitalist economics on modern society.

Many of the world's great religions have derived their root metaphors from dreams. For example, Jacob's dream in Genesis 28 of the ladder spanning heaven and earth presents a powerful root metaphor that reveals how the divine and the human realms connect with each other. A ladder (actually, the original Hebrew word suggests a temple stairway) is a simple, concrete object used to connect things at different heights. Jacob's dream uses this well-known object to express metaphorically the very mysterious and intangible question of God's connection to the human world. This dream has a powerful effect on Jacob, reassuring him that despite his anxiety and loneliness God remains a vital, nurturing presence in his life. The transformative effects of this dream are indicated by Jacob's astonishment upon awakening, by his immediate performance of a ritual of gratitude, and by his vow of eternal obedience to God (Gen. 28:16–22).

Many other dream experiences in the history of religions have these same qualities. Sufi mystics begin their lives of religious devotion after having an initiatory dream of a special spiritual advisor. The leaders of several new religious movements in Africa are inspired by a numinous dream that motivates them to found their movements. Many Australian Aborigines meet their ancestral heroes and guardian spirits in dreams (Bulkeley 1995). These religious accounts of profoundly meaningful dreams correlate very closely with the findings of several modern psychologists, who have discussed case studies in which their clients experienced vivid dreams which deeply altered their existential beliefs and radically changed their future behavior (Boss 1958, Fromm 1951, Jung 1974, Perls 1970a, Ullman and Zimmerman 1979).

Based on these dream reports from historical and contemporary sources, I developed the following definition: root metaphors are concrete images that metaphorically express our ultimate existential concerns, that are powerful and challenging, and that have deep, transformative effects on our lives. Root metaphor *dreams* are dreams that have these characteristics and effects.

At one level, then, the concept of root metaphors provides a means of understanding how certain dreams have played an important role in many of the world's religious traditions. But root metaphor dreams are not the exclusive property of people in formal religions. One of my great hopes in developing this concept was also to understand better the spiritual qualities of dreams that are not conventionally "religious" and that are experienced by people who are not members of a church or other religious institution.

The following is an example of such a "nonreligious" root metaphor dream. A man who now works in the field of natural resources (I will call him "Jim") shared this dream with a colleague:

> A number of years ago, when I was working/living in a field unrelated to the environment, forests, natural resources, etc., I had a dream. This dream opened a new door—leading me to new work and thought, to an area that *fits* my life in a way no other has. . . . This is what I remember of it:
>
> I was facing east, deep in a forest of large, old trees. The foliage was dense, perhaps there were vines or moss in the trees, adding to the depth and shades of green. Sunlight was making its way through the green— from the east (maybe an hour after sunrise). Mostly the sun made the leaves glow, some shafts pierced through. There was a communication between the trees and me—not verbal yet not ephemeral either. There was a rightness, a sureness I felt in being there, as well as an excitement, a charge.
>
> I woke with a line in my head: "That's what I do with my life—It's with the big green stuff." (The "big green stuff" is trees.)
>
> Since that time I have pursued an advanced degree, changed jobs and have "come down where I ought to be" (in the words of the Shaker hymn). (Schroeder 1996)

Jim's dream does not involve gods, angels, or other supernatural beings. However, it does have extraordinary numinous energy, a "charge" in his words, and it does speak directly to one of the key existential questions in any person's life: What is the most meaningful and fulfilling vocation for me to pursue? Jim's dream provides him with a simple yet powerful experiential answer to this question, in the form of his intimate nonverbal communion with the gloriously beautiful forest of trees. He now *knows* that the right thing to do with his life is to devote himself to caring for "the big green stuff." His reference to the Shaker religious hymn emphasizes his feeling that the dream has helped him find his true vocation, his proper place in the world. In my terms, the dream becomes a root metaphor for Jim in that it responds to an essentially spiritual question with a very tangible image that has profoundly transformative effects on his life. (It's worth noting that he shared this dream with his colleague on the condition of strict anonymity, because Jim feared that admitting the influence of a dream on his career choice would compromise his credibility as a natural resource professional.)

Another good example of a root metaphor dream without conventional religious imagery is the experience of a five-year-old boy named Ben (Siegel and Bulkeley 1998). Ben was the youngest child in his family, and as he grew up he enviously watched his two older brothers riding their bicycles up and down the driveway. Finally the day came when Ben was given his own bicycle. During this exciting time when he was first learning to ride all by himself, Ben had a dream:

> I see a golden bicycle, with glowing golden light from behind. It's a ten-speed road bike, and it *glows*.

Although this dream was very brief (as is typical among young children), its central image was extremely vivid, and Ben never forgot it. As he got older he became a bike racer, joyfully competing in motocross races with other children. Before starting college he opened his own business manufacturing specially designed bicycle brakes. Once he finished college Ben took a job working for a leading bicycle company, where he specialized in doing research and development on new, cutting-edge bicycle manufacturing technologies.

Now an adult, Ben acknowledges that his childhood dream of "the golden bicycle" served as a powerful source of inspiration, nourishing what he felt was the truly spiritual role of bicycles in his life. Bike riding opened up to him a wealth of wonderful sensations: the harmonious rhythms of pedalling and breathing, the fluid shifts of speed, weight, and balance, the freedom and independence to go wherever he wanted. Although not "religious" in any conventional sense of the term, Ben's dream gave him a powerful vision of the passionate creativity and joyful fulfillment that bicycles could bring him. Much like the special "vision quest" dreams of Native American youths, Ben's dream of the golden bicycle revealed to him a numinous image that would guide him throughout his life.

As I've already mentioned, this concept of root metaphor dreams is meant to offer more than a contribution to dream theory: it is also intended to provide practical guidance to psychotherapists, pastoral counselors, and lay people who are interested in exploring the spiritual dimensions of dreams.

In many ways, effective dream interpretation is simply a matter of asking good, stimulating questions that can open up new horizons of meaning and possibility for the dreamer. I've found that the following questions are particularly helpful in initiating spiritual reflection on a particular dream:

1. Does this dream touch on any basic existential issues in my life? For example, is it addressing my beliefs about suffering and death, about good and evil, about the reality of God? Is it giving me any insights into the most powerful, fundamental forces shaping my individual life?

2. Does this dream reveal a deeper dimension to a current life crisis or transition I am experiencing?

3. Does this dream reveal any ultimate ideals that I've forgotten, or ignored, or never been conscious of before?

4. Is this dream suggesting that I *lack* ultimate ideals to nurture and support me?

5. Is this dream presenting me with any radically *new* ways of thinking, feeling, or behaving in the world?

6. Does this dream *challenge* my current worldview? Does it show that certain beliefs may be false, or may be defensive illusions allowing me to avoid unpleasant realities?

7. Does this dream say anything about the ultimate ideals of my family, community, church, or culture? Does the dream reveal how my ideals are related to, or are in conflict with, the ideals of these social groups?

8. Is the dream prompting me to undertake any new spiritual practices, projects, or quests?

These are some of the questions that can help to initiate an exploration of the spiritual potentials of dreams. In addition to what questions we ask, there is also the matter of which dreams we ask these questions of. Which dreams are most likely to bear spiritual meanings? The immediate answer would be strikingly powerful, vivid dreams: dreams of divine or mythological beings, nightmares of heart-stopping terror, especially vivid lucid dreams, and dreams so numinous that we remember them our whole lives. Such dreams, although rare, clearly have a powerful dimension of spiritual meaning to them, and the questions listed above can help in discerning their meanings.

Another answer would be recurrent dreams. Recurrent dreams of special themes, figures, or situations are often grounded in fundamental patterns of meaning. Often these patterns of meaning reach all the way down to our most basic spiritual ideals and values. Recurrent dreams tend to reveal very clearly the deep symbolic structures that are orienting our lives and our experiences.

However, recurrent dreams and spectacular "big" dreams are not the only kinds that have spiritual potential. Root metaphor dreams are dreams that touch on the basic existential concerns of human life. Sometimes these dreams have a numinous, overwhelming power, and sometimes they are much more subtle, speaking to us in soft whispers. Insights into our spiritual concerns can often be gained from seemingly quiet, innocuous dreams, from dreams that do not appear at first sight to have any special spiritual force to them. This is not to say that *every* dream is spiritually meaningful; rather, it is to suggest that any dream *may* be spiritually meaningful, not just "big" or recurrent dreams. The only way to find out if a dream is spiritually meaningful or not is to ask questions, and to listen carefully for what answers may come.

As I reached the end of writing my doctoral dissertation, which was devoted to a scholarly explanation of this notion of root metaphor dreams, I realized that I needed to present one last dream example to help in summarizing all that I had been discussing. With a mixture of dread and curiosity I decided to use one of those strange chasing nightmares from my adolescence—a harrowing dream in which an evil, black-clad alien catches me and methodically dissects me, removing my brain, my heart, and even my DNA from my writhing, agonized body. This was by far the scariest dream of my life, and I knew that all my research was worthless if it couldn't help me make some sense of this nightmare. But for some reason, I just couldn't start writing this final section of the dissertation. I was so close to being done, and yet I kept hesitating. When I found myself obsessively reediting my footnotes I realized that my resistance had reached a truly ludicrous degree of desperation.

Then one night I had an extraordinarily vivid dream. In the dream I'm sitting at a table with a beautiful, dark-haired woman; she is a musician, and she is upset about something. I'm trying to think of a way to comfort her, when she says to me, "You don't know how much I *trust* you." When I awoke from the dream (trembling from exhaustion, bathed in a full-body sweat), I immediately felt that it formed a pair with the "evil alien" dream. If that nightmare had revealed to me the reality of something truly evil and destructive, this dream revealed something truly good and creative. With the image of this beautiful woman and her words of trust so vividly in my mind, I dove into the writing of that last section of the dissertation, and finished it two weeks later.

My dream of the woman who trusts me helped me complete my graduate work. But from another perspective, the dream showed how *in*complete my graduate work was—indeed, how incomplete any academic study of dreams must always be. I realized that if we want to understand our most profound and spiritually transformative dreams, we must let the dreams themselves be our guides.

2

Dreaming and Conversion

Dreams have played a prominent role in conversion experiences in many of the world's religious traditions. We have accounts of "conversion dreams" occurring in Buddhist, Christian, and Islamic contexts, as well as in various cargo cults, revitalization movements, and "new religions" (see Laufer 1931; O'Flaherty 1984; Ong 1985; Kelsey 1974; Jedrej and Shaw 1992; Von Grunebaum and Callois 1966; Fisher 1979; Wallace 1958; Burridge 1960; Davis 1980; Trafzer and Beach 1985). However, scholars of religion have for the most part devoted only minimal attention to these dream reports. To put it bluntly, the reports seem *fake*—most of these dreams sound like pious fictions created by the alleged dreamers or by those who recorded the dreams, fabrications intended to give an aura of heavenly sanction to decisions made for more earthly reasons. For example, the Roman Emperor Constantine allegedly dreamed in the early fourth century A.D. that Christ appeared to him and showed him a cross of light (the *labarum*). This dream, according to the early church historian Eusebius, prompted the conversion of Constantine (and thus the whole Roman Empire) to Christianity (Kelsey 1974). This remarkably convenient "dream" has aroused great skepticism among historians and theologians, who suspect that Constantine in fact made up his revelatory experience in order to expand and legitimate his political power.

Further skepticism is cast on such dream reports by the psychoanalytic theories of Sigmund Freud. In *The Interpretation of Dreams* Freud describes the dreamwork mechanism of "secondary revision," by which the original dream is subtly altered, edited, and molded to conform better to the standards of waking consciousness (Freud 1965a). Freud argues that the dreamer is often not even aware that his or her report of the dream is very different from the original dream experience. So regarding

15

reports of conversions via dreams, even if we grant that the convert has not intentionally fabricated his or her dream, we might still suspect that the dream has been unintentionally altered in the process of secondary revision—for example, to make the dream fit more smoothly into the expected patterns of the given religious tradition. This seems to be another strong reason why reports of dreams such as Constantine's should be regarded with great doubt and mistrust.

In this chapter I will question that skepticism by arguing that reports of conversions experienced through dreams are legitimate and understandable phenomena. We can never, of course, determine the "reality" of any particular dream experience; we can never know whether Constantine "really" dreamed of Christ presenting him with a cross of light. But we can determine that dreams truly do have a powerful capacity to transform a person's spiritual life, and we can develop a solid, well-reasoned understanding of that capacity. Indeed, if we use the findings of various disciplines and fields of research to guide us, we will discover that dreams give us a valuable perspective on the nature of religious experience. To put my thesis in a phrase: *dreams can bring a dreamer closer to the sacred.* Certain dreams have the power to integrate psychological, cultural, and religious elements in such a way that the dreamer is spiritually transformed; the sacred becomes a more vital, immediate presence in his or her life.

The place to start this examination is with the phenomenology of religions, where we find many rich, detailed accounts of conversion dream experiences. I will present three brief reports of such experiences, all from the Christian tradition but each from a different cultural and historical context.

1. St. Jerome, the fourth-century Christian leader who translated the Bible into the Latin Vulgate, wrote that his own religious life was deeply changed by a dream. Born into a Christian family but educated in the Greek and Roman classics, Jerome could not reconcile his Christian faith with his love of classical writers. One night, while he was extremely sick, Jerome had the following dream:

> Suddenly I was caught up in the spirit and dragged before the judgement seat of the Judge; and here the light was so bright, and those who stood around were so radiant, that I cast myself upon the ground and did not dare to look up. Asked who and what I was I replied: "I am a Christian." But he who presided said: "Thou liest, thou art a follower of Cicero and not of Christ. For where thy treasure is, there will thy heart be also." Instantly I became dumb, and amid the strokes of the lash—for He had ordered me to be scourged—I was tortured more severely still by the fire of conscience. . . . At last the bystanders, falling down before the knees of

Him who presided, prayed that He would have pity on my youth, and that He would give me space to repent of my error. He might still, they urged, inflict torture on me, should I ever again read the works of Gentiles.... Accordingly I made an oath and called upon His name, saying: "Lord, if ever again I possess worldly books, or if ever again I read such, I have denied Thee." Dismissed, then, on taking this oath, I returned to the upper world, and, to the surprise of all, I opened upon my eyes so drenched with tears that my distress served to convince even the credulous. And that this was no sleep nor idle dream, such as those by which we are often mocked, I call to witness the tribunal before which I lay, and the terrible judgement which I feared.... I profess that my shoulders were black and blue, that I felt the bruises long after I awoke from my sleep, and that thenceforth I read the books of God with a zeal greater than I had previously given to the books of men. (Kelsey 1974, 136–37)

2. Members of the True Church of God, an evangelistic, fundamentalist Christian church which originated in eastern Nigeria in 1953, regard dreams as a primary source of conversion. As reported by sociologist Richard Curley,

a typical convert is introduced to the church when he is faced with a critical problem which cannot be solved by conventional means.... Perhaps the clearest indication of a person's religious commitment is a vision which comes to him in the form of a dream. We can illustrate the conversion process with [this example:] Victoria is thirty years old with three young children, the oldest of whom is seven years of age. She is an Igbo and grew up in eastern Nigeria; she attended school up to the fifth grade. Both of her parents were Roman Catholics, and she attended the Catholic church and a Catholic missionary school.... Soon after the birth of a second child she began to be sickly and prone to nervous disorders.... [O]ne night her husband brought her to a prayer meeting of the True Church of God. The church is well known for its policy on medicines, and many people in [the region] believe that the church has effective healing powers. In any case church members prayed over Victoria on seven or eight separate occasions, and she soon found herself getting up to dance. On the night before she was to be baptized she dreamt that she had been driven from her father's house and sent to wander in the bush. She saw herself as a lame person walking through a dense forest in eastern Nigeria where she encountered numerous snakes but had nothing to eat except berries and water. Then one day a light appeared and guided her to a clearing which abounded with her favourite foods. Her lameness disappeared, and while she was drinking water from a clear pool she saw an image of God, who told her to renounce all of her medicines and follow the rules of the True Church as strictly as possible. She was baptized the following day, when she recounted the dream to the assembled congregation, which received it enthusiastically. (Curley 1983, 27–28)

3. A very interesting account of the ambiguous role of dreams in conversion comes from the Baptist missionary Kenneth Osborne, who worked among the people of the New Guinea Highlands. Osborne describes the founding of a "Christian Graveyard Cult" in 1967:

> Pyanjuwa, a local school teacher and prominent church leader, received a vision early one morning, when Christ appeared in bright clothing and told him to clear the undergrowth from the old graveyard not far from the church. In subsequent visions he was given directions to plant shrubs and lawns, and to begin dawn services in the cemetery. The services became very popular and were held twice weekly, drawing people from other churches for a radius of about five miles. . . . His strong belief in the reality of dreams and visions is one of the focal points of the movement. . . . [Pyanjuwa] had also decided to help analyze and interpret dreams for other people. He explained that as belief in direction through dreams and visions was very common among his people he had instituted this "advice service" to try and guard against wrong teaching and unwise action coming into the community through dreams. . . . There can be little doubt that Pyanjuwa is finding ways to make Christianity more meaningful to his people . . . [and] that the movement is responsible for a great deal of new enthusiasm in the churches. . . . A meeting of the Church District Executive was convened to discuss the new movement. Many of the pastors saw it as an exciting new possibility for renewal in the churches, but others saw the dangers of incorporating beliefs from the old religion, especially in regard to ancestor spirits. It was decided not to encourage the spread of the cult until the church leaders had time to observe its fruits. (Osborne 1970, 11–12, 14)

These three reports of dream-prompted spiritual conversions contain many of the key elements that religion scholars believe are integral to the conversion experience. In *Understanding Religious Conversion* Lewis Rambo describes two primary themes that run through virtually all conversion experiences. One is that the convert feels a new sense of relationship with the divine. Rambo says, "God is no longer an abstract concept but a living reality. Although the details given by converts may differ, there is a sense of intimacy and connection that was not there before" (Rambo 1993, 160). A second common consequence is that the convert gains a strong sense of mission, a belief that he or she has been called to carry out some special purpose in life.

We find both these themes running through the dream reports above. In each case the dreamer has a close, personal encounter with a powerful divine being; from that encounter a relationship develops that guides the dreamer into a new spiritual worldview. The relationship may be warm and caring, as when Victoria sees an image of God in a clearing filled with her favorite foods. Or the relationship may be rather demanding and harsh, as when the Lord orders the indecisive Jerome to be scourged with repeated "strokes of the lash." No matter what the emotional valence, the underlying experience in all these cases is an intimate connection between the dreamer and the divine being.

The new sense of mission or purpose that Rambo and other religion scholars find in conversion experiences also comes through very clearly in these dream reports. Jerome says that after his dream he read the Bible with more zeal than he had ever given to reading the classics. Victoria proclaims her dream to the congregation, and becomes a devoted, full-fledged member of the True Church of God. And the new religious movement that Pyanjuwa initiates in his community is directly inspired by his spiritually transformative dream.

So in terms of the primary religious features that scholars such as Rambo have found characterize conversion experiences, these three accounts of conversion via dreams make sense—they fit very well with what we know of other reported conversion experiences.

We find even stronger support for the legitimacy of dreamed conversions when we look to modern psychological research on the role of dreams in overcoming experiences of trauma. As religion scholars have long noted, most people who convert to a new religious or spiritual worldview do so in the context of some kind of crisis, some kind of deeply troubling, highly stressful situation in which they feel trapped; the conversion marks a resolution of the crisis, an escape from a situation that had seemed inescapable (Rambo 1993, 44–55). Again, this is true of our three cases. Jerome is deeply divided between his Christian family upbringing and his classical education, and Victoria has been suffering from serious physical and emotional difficulties. We do not know much of Pyanjuwa's personal life, but it seems likely that his role as mediator between his native community and the Christian missionaries has been a source of some stress and tension for him.

These features of conversion experience correlate very closely with some of the major findings of twentieth-century dream psychology. Researchers and clinicians have determined that a primary function of dreams is to help people adapt to and overcome crises of various sorts. Dozens of studies have demonstrated that dreams respond, directly and creatively, to deaths, illnesses, accidents, natural disasters, divorces, job losses, school failures—to almost every kind of stressful, traumatizing experience of our lives (Levin 1990; Moffitt, Kramer, and Hoffmann 1993; Barrett 1996). Psychologist Rosalind Cartwright, a leading psychological researcher on dreams and sleep disorders, has said:

My work in crisis dreaming strengthens my belief that dreams offer far more than nighttime entertainment. Rather, they tell us about aspects of our daily lives that we unwittingly may overlook or even choose not to think about when awake, particularly in times of crisis. . . . [D]reams may be at the core of our ability to assimilate major changes in our lives, good and bad, successes and failures. At such times, dreams review the experiences that give rise to strong feelings and match them to related images from the past. They enable us to revise our pictures of our present selves and to rehearse our responses to future challenges. In times of trouble, when we suffer a loss of self-esteem or have our belief in our competence knocked out from under us, dreams help repair our damaged sense of self. (Cartwright and Lamberg 1992, 269)

Thus, dreams leading to a religious conversion can be understood as instances in which the crisis-resolving function of dreams reaches an unusual degree of intensity, power, and effectiveness: "conversion dreams" are crisis-resolving dreams *par excellence*.

Still, skepticism may linger. Dreams prompting a conversion may well be reported throughout history from cultures all over the world, as the phenomenology of religions indicates; these dreams may possess all the essential features of conversion experiences, as recent religious studies scholarship suggests; and they may display the same "crisis-resolving" effect that psychologists believe is a basic function of "real" dreams. But don't these dreams just sound a little too good to be true? Don't they sound too coherent, too structured, too well crafted to be believed? Jerome's dream, for example, has such an elaborate, polished narrative structure. It's hard for us not to suspect that he made it up, perhaps by slightly modifying the well-known biblical story of the prophet Isaiah's humbling experience before the throne of the Lord (Isa. 6:1–8).

At this point, the recent work of psychologically minded anthropologists can be of help. Barbara Tedlock (1987), Waud Kracke (1979), M. C. Jedrej and Rosalind Shaw (1992), and many other anthropologists have demonstrated very clearly that individual dream experiences and the dreamer's culture exert a mutual influence on one another. On the one hand, the customs, languages, social structures, and religious beliefs at work in a given culture directly and profoundly influence people's dreams. On the other hand, individual dreams frequently inspire cultural innovations in matters such as healing practices, ritual performances, works of art, and religious and mythological narratives. Gananath Obeyesekere, in his book *Medusa's Hair: An Essay on Personal Symbols and Religious Experience*, provides this account of the mutual influence between dreams and myths:

Knowledge and meaning can be derived from hypnomantic states: dream (vision), trance, ecstasy, concentration. I believe that this mode of knowledge, . . . is one of the most powerful and ancient forms of knowing. . . . Myth is often generated out of the hypnomantic consciousness. . . . Insofar as some myths (not all of them) are constructed during hypnomantic states, they must partake of the type of thought characteristic of these states. . . . Yet, more than ordinary dreams, certain hypnomantic states such as trance and dream vision are also influenced by the culture and by the personal quest of the seeker after truth. . . . [The myths] in turn feed back into the hypnomantic state, influencing the thought structure of these states and the nature of our unconscious, including our dream life. The chicken and egg are not isolatable things: they belong to a single interlocking, yet causally interdependent, mutually interacting system. In other words, it is possible for a person to dream a myth rather than a dream, though the latter is the model for the former. (Obeyesekere 1981, 180–82)

Seen in this light, Jerome's dream appears much less fantastic, and much more credible. In Obeyesekere's terms, Jerome seems to have *dreamed a myth*: his dream evidently draws on religious themes and images that were prominent in his culture, and uses those themes and images to conceptually frame, to make sense of, his personal struggle. The result is a deeply meaningful and powerfully transformative experience that converts Jerome to the Christian faith. Indeed, Jerome himself anticipates the skepticism that people might feel when hearing of such a strikingly unusual dream. While admitting that this was not an "ordinary" dream, he insists that he has accurately reported the experience. The research of anthropologists like Obeyesekere provides strong support for the legitimacy of his claim.

Dreams of profound spiritual transformation do not occur in a vacuum. Such dreams emerge in contexts that have religious, psychological, and cultural dimensions. Once we recognize this, we are able to appreciate what I believe is an especially important feature of these dreams: the highly creative integration of these diverse elements *within* the dream experience. The Christian Graveyard Cult founded by Pyanjuwa offers a good illustration of this. Like so many native cultures that have come into contact with Western colonial powers, the New Guinea Highlanders are painfully struggling to reconcile their traditional spiritual beliefs with the teachings of the Christian missionaries. The suffering experienced by people caught in these (benignly termed) "contact situations" can be severe. By means of their dreams, Pyanjuwa and his followers are able to integrate their traditional spirituality with Christianity—their dreams provide a bridge to connect and to synthesize beliefs that had been in conflict at both the personal and the cultural level. The result is that Pyanjuwa and his people convert to a new "cult" that stirs up tremendous energy and religious enthusiasm. As the missionary Osborne uneasily admits, Pyanjuwa has found a way "to make Christianity more meaningful to his people" by encouraging them to listen to their dreams (Osborne 1970, 14).

The other examples examined in this chapter also reveal this capacity of dreams to integrate the new and the traditional, the personal and the cultural, the material and the spiritual—dreams have the capacity to bring all these disparate elements together into a creative synthesis that speaks directly to the dreamer's present life. It is this integrative capacity of dreams that has made them so prominent in conversion experiences, revitalization movements, cargo cults, and new religions of various sorts. When people face a crisis that either challenges their spiritual beliefs or reveals those beliefs to be inadequate, powerful dreams often emerge: dreams that respond to the crisis, integrate the painfully conflicting elements in the dreamer's life, and give the dreamer a new, energetic sense of spiritual purpose that he or she carries back into the waking world. Such dream experiences bring the renewing powers of the sacred into the dreamer's present, conflict-ridden life. The sacred is no longer simply the abstract subject of sermons, teachings, and traditions. By means of dreaming, the sacred becomes a living, vital force in the person's world.

3

Where Do Dreams Come From?

Between the ages of two and five children develop the cognitive and linguistic abilities necessary to remember, describe, and discuss what they have dreamed at night. As children begin sharing their dreams with parents, siblings, friends, and teachers, they start wondering where dreams come from, and why we have them. Some children say dreams come from the clouds. Other children say dreams come from inside their heads, while still others say dreams come from their closets or under their beds. A twelve-year-old girl once told me she thought her dreams came from her twin sister, whose thoughts somehow traveled into her mind at night. A teenage boy described to me how he had always assumed that dreams came only during vacations and weekends, because he never remembered any dreams during the alarm-clock driven routine of his family's weekday life.

For thousands of years humans have been wondering where dreams come from. Some of the oldest written texts ever discovered are devoted to describing and interpreting people's dreams (see Van de Castle 1994). These speculations about dreams have usually been expressed in the language of religion. Virtually every religious tradition in history, from cultures all over the world, has offered an explanation of dreaming that refers in some way to God, the Divine, or to some other transpersonal power or spiritual realm. On this point there is a broad historical and cross-cultural consensus: dreaming has its ultimate roots in religious powers and realities.

Twentieth-century psychologists have also considered the question of where dreams come from. Many of the leading psychological theories about dreams (specifically the theories of Sigmund Freud [1965a]; Calvin Hall [1966]; David Foulkes [1985]; and J. Allan Hobson [1988]) begin with a stark contrast between ancient religious beliefs

23

about dreams and modern scientific knowledge about dreams. According to the terms of this contrast, ancient religious traditions assert that dreams are caused by external, supernatural agents (God, the gods, spirits, etc.) in order to convey messages to their human recipients. But modern scientific research has proven, so the argument goes, that dreams are in fact produced by the natural internal activities of the sleeping mind-brain system and do not communicate any intentional messages to the dreamer. The most these psychologists will allow is that dreams may, if desired, be read as diagnostic indicators of the individual's mental and emotional well-being.

This "ancient religion versus modern psychology" contrast, which has played such a crucial role in orienting dream research in this century, is problematic for several reasons. It misrepresents what religious traditions have taught about dreams, it overstates what modern psychology has "proven" about dreams, and it ignores the subtle but significant influence that cultural teachings, traditions, and values can have on the types of dreams people do, and do not, experience. By dissolving this false antithesis between religious and psychological perspectives on dreams I hope to open up new possibilities in answering the perennial question of where dreams come from.

To begin with, most of the world's religious traditions do *not* teach that *all* dreams have a divine or supernatural origin. On the contrary, these traditions generally recognize that the majority of our dreams are relatively trivial and mundane, the products of our ordinary, day-to-day worries and concerns. An ancient Hindu text classifies dreams into several different categories, only one of which, "dreams that foretell the future," involves any supernatural elements; the other categories include dreams that reflect what has been seen in waking life, dreams that reflect what has been heard in waking life, dreams that reflect the disturbance of a bodily humor, and dreams that gratify desires that have not been satisfied in waking life (O'Flaherty 1984, 24). The Mohave culture of North America distinguishes relatively insignificant, everyday sleep experiences (*sumach*, "dream") from the traditional power-bestowing dream (*sumach ahot*, "dream lucky") (Wallace 1947, 252, 257). Likewise, members of the Jamaa movement, a syncretistic merging of charismatic Christianity with traditional African spirituality, distinguish between dreams that come from humans alone and dreams that come from God. A leader of the Jamaa movement said, "One dream we receive as a holy dream, the one we regard as *mawazo* (spiritual teaching) coming from God. . . . Another dream is just a dream, senseless things that come from man alone" (Fabian 1966, 551–52). The Islamic theologian Nabulusi (1641–1731) wrote an encyclopedic work on dream interpretation in which he provides an elaborate classification system, with three basic categories: (1) glad tidings from God; (2) dreams of warning from the devil; and (3) dreams that originate from the dreamer's own self. Examples of dreams that originate in the self are dreams of being with a loved one, seeing something one is afraid of, or eating when one is hungry (Von Grunebaum and Callois 1966, 7–8).

Perhaps the most familiar instance in the Western tradition of this basic distinction between the more significant, divinely charged type of dream and the less significant, humanly grounded type of dream comes in Homer's epic *The Odyssey*. In book 19 Penelope describes a dream in which twenty fat geese are slaughtered by a mountain eagle. She tells her dream to a kind beggar, whom she does not recognize (or, perhaps, does not acknowledge) as her husband Odysseus; he has disguised himself, and is plotting revenge against the suitors who have invaded his palace. The beggar/Odysseus assures Penelope that her dream's meaning is clear: her husband will return and kill all the suitors. Penelope, however, is not so sure, and says,

> Friend, many and many a dream is mere confusion, a cobweb of no consequence at all. Two gates for ghostly dreams there are: one gateway of honest horn, and one of ivory. Issuing by the ivory gate are dreams of glimmering illusion, fantasies, but those that come through solid polished horn may be borne out, if only mortals know them. I doubt it came by horn, my fearful dream—too good to be true, that, for my son and me. (Homer 1961, 371)

Far from assuming that every dream is a god-sent revelation of prophetic truth, Penelope clearly recognizes that many dreams are but "glimmering illusions," and that our own desires and wishes may deceive us into mistaking a mere fantasy for a divine message.

Many, many more examples could be brought forth, but hopefully the point has been made: the world's religious traditions have always recognized that many, if not most, of our dreams are rooted in the ordinary concerns and experiences of daily human life and do not have special religious meaning or significance.

However, the world's religious traditions have also always recognized that some dreams are *different*—that some dreams come with a special clarity, energy, and vividness, distinguishing them sharply from the more ordinary, mundane types of dreams. These are the powerful, transformative dreams that in many indigenous cultures first signal that a person is destined to be a shaman, a witchdoctor, or a community healer. These are the types of dreams that for many people have sparked an experience of religious conversion, opening up to them new realms of spiritual insight and meaning. These are the divine dream revelations that have inspired the leaders of revitalization movements, cargo cults, and new spiritual communities all over the world.

While the distinction between "human" dreams and "divine" dreams is often sharp, there are times when the one may gradually lead into the other. A series of dreams reported in a Chinese Buddhist text from Yuan times (A.D. 1279–1368) illustrates this process. A lay believer named Wang Chiu-lien was meditating devotedly, seeking enlightenment in the Pure Land tradition of Buddhism. At night he dreamed of the Buddha, but always in the form of a sculpture, not as the living Buddha. He finally went to a monk and told him about these dreams:

> "This is easy to deal with," said the monk. "When you think of your late father, can you hold in your mind his usual comportment?"
>
> "Yes," Wang replied.
>
> "Can you see him in your dreams in such a way that he is no different from when he was living?"
>
> Wang said, "There is no difference."
>
> The monk went on, "The Buddha in himself has no appearance—his appearance is manifested only in conformity with the way of things. From now on you should think of your late father as the Buddha. Little by little, imagine that there are white streaks of light in between his brows, that his face is as of real gold, and that he sits on a lotus flower. You can even imagine that his body grows larger and larger. Then your late father *is* himself the living Buddha."

Wang applied this method according to the monk's instructions, so that whenever he dreamed of his father, he told himself, "This is the Buddha." In time, he dreamed that his father led him to sit on the lotus, where he explained to his son the essence of the teachings" (Ong 1985, 93–94).

These historical and cross-cultural perspectives enable us to make a critical reevaluation of the dream theories of modern psychologists. The leading psychological theories of this century tell us a great deal about "human" dreams, about the regular, ordinary types of dreams that most people have most of the time. The theories tell us, for example, that on average dreams are not especially bizarre, but rather portray generally realistic settings and activities from our daily lives (Hall 1966; Foulkes 1985). The theories tell us that there are significant gender differences in dream content—men's dreams have twice as many male as female characters, while women's dreams have an equal number of male and female characters (Domhoff 1996). Modern psychologists also tell us that the images and feelings in our dreams are strongly influenced by the neurophysiological processes of REM sleep, and that in times of stress or crisis dreaming seems to have the function of helping people regain a sense of emotional equilibrium (Hobson 1988; Cartwright and Lamberg 1992; Moffitt, Kramer, and Hoffmann 1993).

These are all valuable findings, and modern psychologists deserve great credit for enriching our understanding and knowledge of dreaming. But for all their research into the average qualities of "human" dreams, modern psychologists have done little to help us understand better what I have been calling "divine" dreams. The psychologists I mentioned at the beginning of this chapter—Freud, Hall, Foulkes, and Hobson—pay virtually no attention to dreams that have an extraordinary sense of *realness*, or to dreams that involve numinous encounters with divine beings and journeys to otherworldly realms, or to dreams that seem to accurately foretell an accident, illness, or death.

There may be a good reason for this lack of attention. The primary modes of psychological research, while excellent for studying the more ordinary, common types of dreams, seem to systematically inhibit the experience or reporting of relatively rare or unusual types of dreams. Researchers call this "the lab effect." It has been widely documented that subjects sleeping in a sleep laboratory (where the most rigorously scientific dream research occurs) experience a narrower range of dream types than they do when sleeping outside the laboratory. For example, subjects in the laboratory experience fewer sexual dreams, fewer aggressive dreams, and fewer nightmares (Hartmann 1984; Van de Castle 1994; Bulkeley 1997). The sleep laboratory evidently has the effect of *homogenizing* people's dreams. This of course yields an artificially constricted picture of the full range of human dream experience, with precisely those rare types of dreams so treasured by the world's religious traditions most likely to be excluded.

The ultimate difference between "ancient religious" and "modern psychological" views of dreams is *not* that the one is naively superstitious while the other is hard-headedly scientific. Rather, the real difference is that ancient religious traditions have acknowledged that there is an irreducible mystery about where dreams come from and what they mean for human life. Many modern psychologists, by contrast, ignore that mystery, resist it, or try to explain it away.

This difference need not prevent us from seeking new ways of integrating religious and psychological approaches to dreams. William James points to one such way that I find particularly persuasive. Toward the end of *The Varieties of Religious Experience* James summarizes his long, careful investigation by saying that religious experiences frequently connect themselves with the subconscious part of our existence.... Let me then propose, as an hypothesis, that whatever it may be on its *farther* side, the "more" with which in religious experience we feel ourselves connected is on its *hither* side the subconscious continuation of our conscious life. (James 1958, 362, 386)

James's hypothesis, when applied to the study of dreams, suggests that modern psychology helps us understand the "hither" side of our dreams, their roots in both the unconscious activities of the mind and the brain's neurophysiological workings during REM sleep. Religious traditions have for the most part speculated about the "farther" side of dreams, their ultimate sources in transpersonal powers and realities. (To say that such a "farther" side does not exist is simply a statement of what James calls an "over-belief," an expression of metaphysical faith that cannot be proven or disproven.) Properly understood, then, religious and psychological approaches to dreams are logically compatible: both agree that dreams connect us with realms that extend beyond—and in some cases, *far* beyond—the reach of ordinary waking consciousness. To their credit, many psychologists do acknowledge the limits of their theories, and recognize that at least some dreams escape naturalistic analysis and explanation. Freud, as he analyzes his own "Dream of Irma's Injection" in chapter 2 of *The Interpretation of Dreams*, comments in a footnote:

> I had a feeling that the interpretation of this part of the dream was not carried far enough to make it possible to follow the whole of its concealed meaning.... There is at least one spot in every dream at which it is unplumbable—a navel, as it were, that is its point of contact with the unknown. (Freud 1965, 143)

Let me close with a comment about the influence of culture on dreaming. What psychologists call the "lab effect" is powerful evidence of how various external conditions can inhibit the experience of the more extraordinary types of human dream experience. Similar evidence comes from anthropological reports of "contact situations" between indigenous cultures and modern Western civilization. After the Mohave people of North America lost their battle to fend off the destructive encroachment of Anglo settlers, their dream life changed dramatically. Says one anthropologist,

> As Mohave culture gradually deteriorated the power-giving dream (*sumach ahot*) tended to disappear. The pattern depended upon the normal functioning of the culture and, as this declined, the *sumach ahot* also diminished in importance. Many of the older Mohave have had a great dream, but scarcely any of the young people. Some deny that revelations

occur any more. [A Mohave youth said,] "I don't think that they have dreams like that any more. There are no new songs. Sometimes a young fellow says he has had a *sumach ahot* and is a doctor, but I don't believe it." (Wallace 1947, 254)

Another example of this negative influence of culture on dreaming capacities comes from one of my students, a young woman I will call Lucille. When Lucille was a child she had several dreams that seemed to foretell future events in her waking life. Once she dreamed that her mother had a car accident the night of Lucille's eighth-grade prom. In the dream Lucille was not in the car, but her prom dress was, and so was her mother's collection of record albums. It turned out that the night of the prom her mother did indeed have a car accident: without telling Lucille, she had taken her prom dress to be hand-sewn, and was on her way home when the accident happened; the stereo and record albums her mother had brought in the car to loan to a friend were also damaged by the accident. Lucille had not told her mother about the dream beforehand, although she had described it to her best friend. When her mother heard about the dream and the friend's corroboration of it, and when she heard of other similar dreams Lucille had experienced, her mother (who was raising the family according to the traditions of a relatively strict Christian denomination) became frightened and angry: "I'm not going to be the mother of a *witch*," she declared to Lucille, effectively refusing to listen to any more such dreams. When this harshly negative interpretation was given to her prophetic dream experiences, Lucille suddenly stopped having them. "To this day," she says, "I believe I somehow chose to shun those abilities, but I do not know how I might turn them 'on' again if I wanted."

Knowing how strongly external, cultural forces can effect both the form and content of dreaming experience should, I believe, make us think very carefully about how best to respond to children when they ask us if dreams come from inside their heads, from under their beds, or from up in the clouds.

4

Sharing Dreams in Community Settings

The sharing of dreams in modern Western society has generally been confined to the clinician's office: a psychotherapy client describes a dream to a therapist, and the therapist helps the client understand what the dream reveals about his or her emotional and behavioral problems. However, an alternative to this client-to-therapist model of discussing dreams has arisen in recent years. Beginning approximately thirty years ago, a remarkably large number of dreamsharing *groups* began appearing in the United States (although my focus in this chapter is on the United States, there are also many dreamsharing groups active in Canada, Mexico, Australia, and Western Europe). Because these groups take so many different forms and appear in so many different contexts, there is virtually no academic research on the subject. However, the phenomenon of dreamsharing groups should be of interest to scholars of religion and psychology for a number of reasons. First, these groups often look to dreams specifically for spiritual insights; the groups thus represent a distinctive means of religious expression in contemporary American society. Second, the complex interplay of religious, psychological, and cultural elements in these groups can tell us something about where the historical process of secularization stands as we approach the close of the twentieth century. And third, dreamsharing groups frequently generate a powerful sense of community, a sense of deep, intimate bonding among the members of the group. Scholars who are concerned about how to create a sense of mutual understanding across differences of race, gender, ethnicity, and class should take note of the community-revitalizing potential of these groups.

Dreamsharing groups began appearing in this country in the late 1960s and early 1970s, most prominently in the San Francisco Bay Area. The first groups arose in response to the writings and public

31

workshops of Ann Faraday (*Dream Power* [1972] and *The Dream Game* [1974]), Patricia Garfield (*Creative Dreaming* [1974]), Montague Ullman and Nan Zimmerman (*Working with Dreams* [1979]), Gayle Delaney (*Living Your Dreams* [1979]), and Jeremy Taylor (*Dream Work* [1983]). Each of these authors argued that the disciplined, self-reflective practice of exploring dreams should be expanded beyond the confines of professional psychotherapy and made more accessible to the general population. Another important early stimulus was Kilton Stewart's essay on "Dream Theory in Malaya," reprinted in Charles Tart's best-selling anthology *Altered States of Consciousness* (1969). Stewart's description of the Senoi, a native people of the Malaysian rain forests whose practice of publically sharing and discussing dreams helped them create an idyllic, nearly conflict-free community life, inspired countless Americans to explore their own dreams and to begin sharing their dreams in group settings (for a highly skeptical evaluation of Stewart, see Domhoff 1985).

Contemporary dreamsharing groups take many different forms. But they also share many basic elements of structure and process. Let me offer the following "ideal type" of a dreamsharing group:

- Three to twelve people gather in a quiet, comfortable place.
- One of the people serves as leader or facilitator for the group.
- Each person in the group describes one of his or her dreams, speaking in the present tense to try and recreate as vividly as possible the immediacy of the given dream experience.
- The group chooses one person's dream to discuss in detail and proceeds to offer comments, ask questions, and suggest meanings regarding that dream.
- This discussion can take from fifteen minutes to two hours; usually, an effort is made to discuss more than one dream at a given meeting.
- Over the course of a few meetings, everyone in the group participates: everyone gets to share his or her own dreams, everyone gets to comment on other people's dreams, and everyone gets to have one of his or her dreams discussed by the group.

There are many variations on this ideal-typical pattern. For instance, the group's size may vary tremendously. I have seen dreamsharing groups function with as few as three, and as many as two hundred people. The group's leader or facilitator may play a very active role in steering the group process, or may do nothing more than keep an eye on the clock and remind people when it's time to stop. Many dreamsharing groups function effectively with no formal leaders or facilitators at all.

The greatest variations among different groups occur during the discussion process. The dreamer may actively participate in this process, or may sit quietly and observe the group's discussion of his or her dream. The group may use a relatively structured series of questions to ask of each dream, or may engage in an interpretive free-for-all. Some groups, in addition to verbal discussion of the dreams, will draw pictures of them, act them out in "dream theater," or engage in guided imagery exercises. The group's activities may be oriented by particular psychological theories (e.g., looking for Jungian archetypes), by particular theological perspectives (e.g., looking for the presence of the Holy Spirit), or by particular personal concerns (e.g., looking for help with troubled marriages or substance addictions). But no matter what their specific theoretical or ideological cast, the discussions of almost all dreamsharing groups are grounded in a core set of assumptions: that dreams are relevant to our important waking life concerns, that dreams can be understood without specialized knowledge, and that dreams have the potential to reveal profoundly transformational truths and insights.

The basic dreamsharing process described above has been used in a nearly limitless variety of settings and contexts: in churches and religious education programs (e.g., among Catholics, Unitarian Universalists, Presbyterians, Episcopalians, and Methodists); in schools, from grammar schools to high schools to colleges to seminaries to business schools to adult education programs; in psychology workshops, seminars, and retreats (e.g., conducted by members of Jungian, Gestalt, Humanistic, and Transpersonal schools of psychology); in twelve-step counseling programs of various sorts; in social service settings (e.g., in prisons, drug rehabilitation centers, and hospitals; for pregnant women and their partners, people with AIDS, and victims of physical and sexual abuse); in community centers, libraries, and neighbors' homes; and via the internet.

There are no precise demographic data on the participants in dreamsharing groups. Based on my research efforts to date, I have found that participants tend to be female, white, relatively educated and financially secure, and tend to live in one of the major metropolitan centers lining the East and West coasts. However, these must be taken as only the most preliminary of findings: there are numerous dreamsharing groups made up of all males, or of all blacks, and groups organized in the South, the Midwest, and the Plains states. Much more research needs to be done before the tentative generalizations I have offered can be more firmly established.

Overall, I would estimate that in the last thirty years there have been more than fifty thousand dreamsharing groups in the United States, meaning that approximately a half million people have participated in such groups. If the term "group" is expanded to include dreamsharing practices on radio and television talk shows, my estimate would be multiplied by at least a factor of ten.

As the preceding chapters of this book have suggested, dreams have historically been viewed in religious terms. In Western history, priests and church leaders held the position of ultimate authorities on what dreams meant, and their interpretations aimed primarily at determining whether a given dream was a revelation from God or a deceitful temptation from the Devil. In the twentieth century, however, the discipline of psychology has arisen and claimed authority over dreams. Psychologists are now the ones to whom we turn for interpretations, and we follow their lead in looking to dreams for reflections of the hidden dynamics of the individual's personality.

This transition from a religious to a psychological view of dreams is an ideal illustration of the historical process of secularization, the process by which modern scientific, economic, and cultural forces have combined to vanquish the authority of religion in Western society (see Homans 1979, 1989). Dreamsharing groups, in which a reliance on psychological dream theories is *combined* with an interest in the spiritual dimensions of dreams, would seem to mark an interesting new twist on the secularization process.

From one perspective, dreamsharing groups can be seen as resisting and even overcoming the spiritually destructive effects of modern secularized society. Dreams have always been regarded as a means of relating to the sacred, to those powers and realities that transcend ordinary human existence. Dreamsharing groups draw upon this universal source of religious experience and adapt it to the circumstances of people living in contemporary American society. The result is a form of spirituality that may not be formally religious and may not always take place within conventional religious contexts, but that genuinely satisfies people's spiritual needs. If secularization produces a spiritual disenchantment, as Max Weber argues in *The Protestant Ethic and the Spirit of Capitalism*, then dreamsharing groups offer the means to a *re*enchantment of the world, to a renewal and revival of authentic spiritual experience in contemporary society (Weber 1976).

But from a different perspective, dreamsharing groups can be seen as intensifying the destructive effects of secularization, making modern social life *more* fragmented, *more* alienated, and *more* spiritually confused. Paying so much attention to dreams can easily appear as socially irrelevant navel-gazing; by focusing so intently on one's personal psychological dynamics, people run the danger of losing touch with the public realm of community involvement. The outer world is so cold, busy, and impersonal, and the inner world is so warm, peaceful, and alluring, that modern Westerners feel a strong temptation to abandon the former and immerse themselves in the latter. By surrendering to this temptation, people become ever more detached, isolated, and alienated from society (see Rieff 1966; Berger 1967; Bellah et al. 1985).

The process of exploring one's dreams in a group setting would seem to minimize these potentially alienating effects. But as sociologist Robert Wuthnow argues in his recent work *Sharing the Journey* (Wuthnow 1994), participation in various kinds of small support groups (like dreamsharing groups) is often nothing more than a further defense against broader public engagement (Wuthnow 1994). Such groups are usually quite homogeneous, making it easier for participants to reinforce their established views and to avoid contact with different types of people. Wuthnow's concern is that small support groups provide a covert means of self-protection against the complications of a multicultural world, and thus a further erosion in people's broader sense of community belonging.

So taking these views together, it could appear that dreamsharing groups promote a kind of spirituality that is authentic, powerful, and personally fulfilling—but that is also helping to corrode the communal integrity of contemporary American society.

That harsh conclusion is not warranted, however, by a careful examination of the actual practices of various dreamsharing groups. Such an examination reveals that many dreamsharing groups enable participants to gain valuable insights into the relations between their personal lives and the broader social world in which they live. Furthermore, many dreamsharing groups give people a means of understanding *others*, of recognizing their connections with people who are different from themselves. In such cases, dreamsharing groups genuinely help to revitalize a sense of community and to renew people's active engagement with the world.

The following are two brief descriptions of actual dreamsharing group practices that have had this community-revitalizing effect.

1. Jane White Lewis, a Jungian analyst and educator, has for the past several years been teaching classes on dreams at a public high school in New Haven, Connecticut. New Haven suffers from many of the social problems that have increasingly plagued urban America: drug abuse, crime, poverty, the decay of infrastructure. Many of the teenagers in Lewis's classes are struggling simply to survive in their deeply troubled city. But Lewis has found that when the students begin exploring

and discussing their dreams they discover new resources of energy, creativity, and hope. In her class the students share their dreams, draw pictures of them, act them out in informal dramatic productions, and write essays and stories based on them. Many of the students who hate writing or think they just don't have the talent to write suddenly find their "voice" when writing about their dreams and about the memories, feelings, and thoughts that arise in connection with their dreams. For example, the students in one class often dreamed of the police, of fighting them, arguing with them, and trying to hide from them. Class discussions of these "police dreams" led the students to reflect on conflicts with authority, both in society and in their own personal lives. Similarly, the dreams of many of the girls about having babies raised the very immediate issue of teen pregnancy: the students discussed the social, psychological, and financial pressures girls felt in romantic relationships, and their dreams opened up new vistas of reflection on how to resist those pressures. In this case, encouraging the students to turn *inward* to their dreams became a valuable means of guiding them more wisely *outward* to the realm of public society.

2. Bette Ehlert is a New Mexico lawyer who for a number of years has been leading dreamsharing groups in jails, prisons, and other correctional facilities. As public opinion polls tell us, violent crime is widely regarded as one of the greatest threats to the American community. Politicians argue bitterly over what causes crime, how it can be stopped, and how to punish the criminals. In her prison groups Ehlert has found that dreamsharing can be an effective means of discovering symbolic links between the particular crimes committed by an offender and certain events, experiences, and conflicts in the offender's past. For example, a young African American man convicted of dealing crack cocaine had a dream of struggling to get away from a dark entity pushing down on him. In the group discussion the dreamer discovered the symbolic relations between his being sexually abused as a child and his crime as an adult of being a "pusher." Ehlert has also found that a more general value of dreamsharing groups was that they helped criminal offenders cultivate the vital cognitive abilities in which many of them are severely deficient: the abilities to reason critically, to empathetically take the perspective of others, and to envision alternatives, possibilities, and potentials. All of this strengthens their capacity to avoid becoming trapped in a lifelong cycle of crime and incarceration. (For fuller accounts of Lewis's and Ehlert's work see their chapters in Bulkeley 1995).

These two cases show that dreamsharing groups can actually give their participants valuable, focused insights into problems that involve an intersection of personal and social forces. Rather than promoting navel-gazing escapism, or further isolating people in homogeneous, defensive little social enclaves, dreamsharing groups enable participants to perceive, to understand, and to respect the lives of other people, of *different* people. Dreamsharing groups are not only a powerful means of personal spiritual discovery: they are also a powerful means of renewing a vivid, dynamic sense of community in contemporary American society.

This is not to say, of course, that dreamsharing groups can cure all of society's ills. Any attempt to address the plight of communities in the United States must acknowledge that there are no simple remedies, no magic wands that can make poverty and racism and crime and all our other social problems disappear. What I would like to suggest, however, is that dreamsharing groups offer a resource that may, in a great variety of situations, prove effective in revitalizing and deepening people's fundamental sense of community. Among their many practical virtues, dreamsharing groups are widely accessible (since almost everybody remembers at least an occasional dream), extremely low-cost (all you need is a quiet, comfortable space for people to sit in a circle), and capable of adapting to an endless variety of settings and circumstances.

Dreamsharing groups have an especially great potential, I believe, to enrich educational programs. Lewis's work in a public high school is one good example of this. In my own current research, I'm working with preschool children in various socioeconomic settings, trying to develop programs that integrate dreams, play, and storytelling (see Siegel and Bulkeley 1998).

When shared in a group setting, dreams can stimulate a deep and powerful sense of relatedness to others, enabling people to recognize a shared humanity in the midst of social and cultural differences. I would like to close with one of the more poetic statements of this point, by Synesius of Cyrene, an early fifth-century Neoplatonist philosopher who converted to Christianity and became the bishop of Ptolemais. In a treatise he wrote on dreams, Synesius says this:

> [T]he dream is visible to the man who is worth five hundred medimni, and equally to the possessor of three hundred, to the teamster no less than to the peasant who tills the boundary land for a livelihood, to the galley slave and the common labourer alike. . . . [To this oracle] then we must go, woman and man of us, young and old, poor and rich alike, the private citizen and the ruler, the town dweller and the rustic, the artisan and the orator. She repudiates neither race, nor age, nor condition, nor calling. She is present to everyone, everywhere, this zealous prophetess, this wise counsellor, who holdeth her peace. (Kelsey 1974, 247–48)

5

Dreams and Environmental Ethics

In a far-ranging article titled "Quantum Theory, Intrinsic Value, and Panentheism," philosopher Michael Zimmerman argues persuasively that an ethical attitude of respect for the natural environment will come "only as we move from atomistic, dualistic ego consciousness toward relational, nondualistic consciousness" (Zimmerman 1988, 4–5). In Zimmerman's view the Western world's exploitation of the environment is a product of our fundamentally dualistic metaphysical outlook: we think we are independent, autonomous, self-determined beings, and we thus regard the rest of the world as having little or no intrinsic value apart from its usefulness to us. Accordingly, we may plunder, pollute, and ravage the environment as we wish since we believe it is separate from us and so unworthy of the same regard we grant to ourselves.

Zimmerman discusses how recent discoveries in quantum physics may herald the emergence of a new *meta*physics, one that overcomes Cartesian dualism by positing the essential interrelationship of all being. Just as previous generations of moral philosophers grounded their theories in classical Newtonian physics, so Zimmerman believes that quantum physics may serve as a new conceptual paradigm for a nondualistic ethics—an ethics that, among other things, would radically change our treatment of the environment. Additionally, Zimmerman points to the religious doctrine of panentheism as having the same essentially nondualistic metaphysical vision as that expressed by quantum physics. Taking both Eastern and Western forms, panentheism holds that "the ego's isolation is illusory and that the ego is not a substantial entity at all, but instead merely a temporary, constricted mode of divine experience" (Zimmerman 1988, 26).

Despite finding such significant and even inspiring expressions of nondualistic consciousness, Zimmerman still admits that they are not enough to solve the practical problem of changing people's basic attitudes toward the environment. In his article Zimmerman repeatedly builds up a strong, rousing affirmation of the crucial importance of developing nondualistic consciousness, only to reach the despairing conclusion that ideas, theories, and arguments cannot by themselves bring about this development. For example: "The major drawback is that this model [quantum physics] remains operative only at the cognitive or rational level; the model does not transform dualistic rationality" (14); "The emergence of this new sense of self cannot occur solely on the basis of cognitive insight into the 'interrelatedness' of all things" (16); "As a theory, panentheism cannot in and of itself bring about nondualistic consciousness any more than quantum theory can" (25).

Zimmerman deserves credit for honestly facing the distressing fact that theories are not enough, and that there must be an *experiential* moment for the transformation of human consciousness that he describes to become a reality. In what follows I suggest that dreams and dreaming may provide precisely the kind of experience of nondualistic consciousness that Zimmerman asserts is the key to a new environmental ethic—not just the *knowledge* of nondualism, not just the theoretical appreciation of it as an idea, but an immediate, transformative *experience* of our membership in the web of all being.

On its face, this proposition would seem to invite skepticism and incredulity. After all, dreams are so strange, so hard to grasp, so foolish. When we can remember them (and that's not always very often), they seem to be nothing more than absurd little fragments having no particularly profound meaning or significance. My wife once dreamed that she and the nuns who taught at her Catholic grammar school all did a flying "high five" celebration in a football end zone. How could anything be sillier, or more nonsensical?

I could defend the meaningfulness of dreams by referring to the theories of various clinical and experimental psychologists, but that would probably not convince those who are skeptical about the contemporary relevance of psychology in general. In a world plagued by problems like the arms race, the destruction of rainforests, and the sufferings of Third World nations, critics may well argue that it is insignificant at best and morally irresponsible at worst to bother ourselves with psychological speculations about the whimsical images of our dreams.

But this argument raises a crucial philosophical issue in environmental ethics, namely, what exactly is involved in the *practical* solution to the problems afflicting the natural world. My response is that an important component of any genuine solution (i.e., a solution that is neither superficial, partial, nor temporary) is a transformation of consciousness.

Without a fundamental change in the dualistic mode by which people in our society perceive reality, it will be extremely difficult to convince people to adopt the laws and implement the technologies that would restore the world's environmental health. Without such a change in consciousness it is certain that even *with* those laws and technologies new environmental crises will arise again and again, like Hydra's heads, because the basic patterns of consciousness creating our environmental problems will remain unchanged.

One means of establishing the legitimacy and relevance of dream experience for environmental ethics is to consider briefly some parallels between modern Western society's attitudes toward the environment on the one hand and toward dreaming on the other. Are there ways in which our society takes the same view of the environment and of dreaming? Are there common assumptions, values, and perceptions underlying the ways that our society depreciates both? If there are, it might make more plausible the notion that discoveries regarding the nature and value of dreams might help in developing a new ethical attitude toward the environment.

Both the natural environment and the world of dreaming appear to us as wild, untamed, and filled with energy. We ignore both for the most part, despite the facts that the environment is literally all around us and that we experience several periods of dreaming (or at least several periods of REM sleep) every night. We usually notice them only when their beauty is too wonderful to miss (e.g., a stunning mountaintop vista, or a lovely dream whose memory lingers for days), or when their terrible power threatens to overwhelm us (e.g., a devastating earthquake, or a terrifying nightmare). Both strike us as "other," as belonging to a different order of being from our own. The laws governing the natural world and dreaming are equally difficult for us to understand, and similar types of arguments are used to deny any purpose to them. Many scientists insist that both evolution and REM sleep are in the final analysis blind, random processes (e.g., see Dawkins 1995; Hobson 1988).

The same strangely paradoxical beliefs underlie our society's views toward both. Although we condescendingly regard the environment and its resources as inferior to us, as raw, primitive, and thus ours to control and use, we also fear the environment's mighty and unpredictable forces, which often overwhelm us in the form of natural disasters like floods, tornadoes, volcanic eruptions, hurricanes, and earthquakes. Likewise, we see our dreams both as pointless bits of nonsense so far removed from rational thought as to be worthless *and* as sometimes so terrifying and troubling that we will often try extremely hard to forget them or to prevent them from coming in the first place.

The end result is that we work very hard to *control* both the environment and dreaming according to our conscious, rationalistic goals. We exploit both by means of our technological powers: with the environment we apply ever more sophisticated tools toward extracting the planet's various resources; with dreaming we use the techniques of psychotherapy to ferret out and tame our irrational desires, and we use the electronic instruments of the sleep laboratory to "capture" dreams while they are happening.

Freud himself makes a revealing observation about the connection between the modern world's attitude toward nature and dreaming. In one of his *New Introductory Lectures on Psychoanalysis* (1965b) he says:

> The therapeutic efforts of psychoanalysis . . . [are intended] to strengthen the ego, to make it more independent of the super-ego, to widen its field of perception and enlarge its organization, so that it can appropriate fresh portions of the id. Where id was, there ego shall be. It is a work of culture—not unlike the draining of the Zuider Zee [a prominent European lake]. (71)

A more explicit and self-confident expression of the modern West's passion for exploiting both "inner" and "outer" nature would be hard to find.

Such parallels between our society's views of the environment and dreams should not surprise us, for these views all derive from the same complex of attitudes—what Zimmerman refers to as dualistic, atomistic consciousness. In his article Zimmerman shows how these attitudes underlie many of our worst social problems, including gender inequalities, militarism, and economic injustice, in addition to our mistreatment of the environment. To this list of subjects that have suffered under the control of dualistic consciousness I would add the human experience of dreaming.

There is not such a wide gulf, then, separating the status of the environment and dreaming in modern Western society. I would suggest that the two are complementary aspects of the same process of dualistic perception—the natural environment is what lies outside the boundaries of our physical self, while dreams are what lie outside the boundaries of our psychical self.

From the perspective of dualistic consciousness both the environment and dreams are fundamentally *other* than ourselves. This being the case, it should seem less bizarre to look for resources in one realm to help resolve problems in the other.

My basic claim is that a greater appreciation for dreams and dreaming could help to promote the kinds of transformational experience of nondualistic consciousness that Zimmerman and others believe will lead to changes in our society's treatment of the environment. While dreams themselves have suffered under the reign of dualistic metaphysics, they have also been increasingly recognized in modern times as potent challengers to that reign. Beginning in the work of depth psychologists like C. G. Jung and continuing in the efforts of anthropologists, psychophysiologists, historians of religion, and modern artists, dreams have emerged as experiences that can yield new insights into realms *beyond* the limits of dualistic consciousness (Jung 1974; Tedlock 1987; Hunt 1989; LaBerge 1985; Gackenbach 1987; Moffitt and Hoffmann 1987; O'Flaherty 1984; Russo 1987). In dreams we experience the breakdown of ordinary, waking-life dualistic divisions. Sometimes this breakdown is terrifying, sometimes it is pleasant or funny, sometimes it is simply strange—but whatever our emotional reaction to it, a basic feature of almost all our dreams is the blurring or complete disappearance of our customary, day-to-day perceptual categories. For example, the relations of time and space become very confused in dreams, as people, places, and events from all throughout our lives may appear together in a single dream. Emotions, desires, wishes, and concerns of which we have little awareness in waking life have a distressing habit of emerging in our dreams. The lines separating our physical selves from the natural world often become unclear, for example when animals, trees, mountains, and so forth interact with us in our dreams as if they are humans, or when we ourselves take the form of animals, trees, or mountains in a dream. Our sexual identities frequently shift about in dreams—we may appear in the form of the opposite sex, or have sexual relations with any variety of different types of people or even animals. Many dreams present us with challenges to our waking consciousness' estimation of what we can and can't do in life. In a dream we may be surprised to find that we can fly, or sing, or play a sport we have never played before, or we may be frustrated at not being able to run at more than a snail's pace, or utter a sound despite trying to scream out. Occasionally dreams contain symbols, motifs, and themes that recur in mythologies throughout the world, suggesting that each individual to some extent shares a common psychological structure with all of humankind. In some dreams people encounter especially powerful, numinous figures like gods, demons, spirits, and angels, figures that lead many dreamers to believe that animate forces greater than humans do exist in the universe.

This list could go on and on. The point is that our dreams do genuinely challenge the patterns, beliefs, presuppositions, and categories by which our waking consciousness guides us in our daily lives. Even more importantly, dreams challenge these patterns *meaningfully*: as many psychologists have demonstrated, if we carefully reflect on our dreams we often find that their strangest elements refer directly to troubling issues in our waking lives (Barrett 1996; Delaney 1993; Koulack 1991; Moffitt, Kramer, and Hoffmann 1993). An important function of dreams seems to be that of directing our attention to just those conscious attitudes that most distort our perceptions of reality.

As recent sleep laboratory evidence indicates, these challenges coming through our dreams have a special force to them that makes them particularly influential on our attitudes and behavior. To dream that we are playing in a baseball game is not at all like simply imagining, in a waking state, that we are playing in a baseball game. In terms of the brain's activity, that is, in terms of the way our brain processes our experience, dreaming about playing in a baseball game is much more like actually playing in a baseball game. Stephen LaBerge, a sleep laboratory researcher and the leading figure in the study of lucid dreaming, has said,

> Taken together, our work at Stanford has amassed strong laboratory evidence indicating that what happens in the inner world of dreams—and lucid dreams especially—can produce physical effects on the dreamer's brain no less real than those produced by corresponding events happening in the external world. . . . [T]he impact of certain brain behaviors on brain and body can be fully equivalent to the impact produced by corresponding actual behaviors. This fits hand in glove with the fact that dreams are normally *experienced* by the dreamer as fully real, and indeed it is not unusual for dreams (especially when lucid) to seem more real than physical reality itself. This is far from the view prevalent in Western societies, seeing dreams as 'airy nothings' devoid of meaning and reality. On the contrary, what we do in dreams (or leave undone) can at times affect us as profoundly as what we do (or do not do) in our waking lives. (LaBerge 1985, 97–98; see also Dement 1972)

Putting this in the context of Zimmerman's discussion, to *dream* about our fundamentally nondualistic relations to the rest of life has a much deeper, more powerful, and more transformative effect on consciousness than merely *thinking* about these relations.

I often find that interdisciplinary discussions like this, which cover such a diverse range of subjects and fields, can easily become overwhelming. In an effort to bring some degree of conceptual clarity to this discussion (and to relate it to aspects of the previous chapters), I would like to close with a brief description of the work of cultural anthropologist Victor Turner. His thoughts on the experience of *communitas* will, I hope, offer a helpful framework in which to understand the central arguments of this chapter.

In his book *The Ritual Process* (1969) Turner addresses the question of how rituals *change* people. He says the key moment in any ritual is the "liminal" stage, when the participants are "betwixt and between" the structures imposed by social convention that govern ordinary life. The liminal stage is the point that ritually produces the change from one condition to another—the transformation of a child into an adult, a lay person into a church member, a citizen into a king. The universal phenomenon of such "rites of passage" testify, Turner says, to the fact that there are two different yet intimately connected modes for human interrelatedness. The first is that of society as a structured system of hierarchical relationships; this is the system that underlies our ordinary, day-to-day interactions with other people. The second mode of interrelatedness, which emerges in the realm of liminality and which rituals actively strive to recreate, is that of society as an *un*structured, *un*differentiated community of equals bound together by an essential unity. This second mode of human existence Turner calls *communitas*, wherein we discover and experience our fundamental relatedness to all people and to all being. Turner believes that rituals from cultures all over the world use symbols of liminality to produce in their participants a powerful sense of *communitas*, because it is only by means of such revitalization of the essential relatedness humans share with one another that people are able to participate most fully and most creatively in the hierarchical structures inevitable in any social group. Having ritually experienced *communitas*, we reenter our social world more aware of the necessity of openness and flexibility, more sensitive to the needs of others, and more intent on the creation and maintenance of a humane, constructive, life-enhancing society.

Turner's notion of the transformative power of experiences of *communitas* gets right to the heart of what Zimmerman is trying to say about quantum physics and religious panentheism and what I am trying to say about dreaming: all of these share the key characteristic of pointing us toward the dimensions of reality that lie beyond the structures and categories of our ordinary social world. The distinctive virtue of dreaming, in my view, is that it offers a regular and widely accessible experience of *communitas*, a nightly challenge to the conventional structures governing our waking identities. Our dreams carry us beyond the limits of our ordinary distinctions and categorizations to reveal that we are indeed part of a web of being that expands in many different directions—into the unconscious, into the natural world, into the collective psychic experiences of humankind, into the realm of transpersonal powers and realities.

As the Mehinaku people of the Amazonian forest (Gregor 1981a) say whenever they begin to describe one of their dreaming experiences, "Far, far away my soul wandered."

6

Dreaming in a Totalitarian Society: A Winnicottian Reading of Charlotte Beradt's The Third Reich of Dreams

Charlotte Beradt's *The Third Reich of Dreams*, published in 1966, adds a new dimension to our understanding of Nazism's brutal power: the Nazis succeeded in terrorizing people even in their dreams. Beradt's work is a poignant and disturbing record of hundreds of dreams she gathered from people living in Nazi Germany in the years 1933 to 1939. Many people were afraid to speak openly of their dreams, and Beradt had to copy the dreams in code, hide them in the bindings of books scattered through her home, and send them as letters to various people in countries abroad. Despite these obstacles, she managed to compile a fascinating collection of firsthand dream reports. These are a few examples:

1. A middle-aged male factory owner dreamed: "Goebbals was visiting my factory. He had all the workers line up in two rows facing each other. I had to stand in the middle and raise my arm in the Nazi salute. It took me half an hour to get my arm up, inch by inch. Goebbals showed neither approval nor disapproval as he watched my struggle, as if it were a play. When I finally managed to get my arm up, he said just five words—'I don't want your salute'—then turned and went to the door. There I stood in my own factory, arm raised, pilloried right in the midst of my own people. I was only able to keep from collapsing by staring at his clubfoot as he limped out. And so I stood until I woke up." (5)

2. A middle-aged housewife dreamed: "A Storm Trooper was standing by the large, old-fashioned, blue-tiled Dutch oven that stands in the corner of our living room, where we always sit and talk in the

evening. He opened the oven door and it began to talk in a harsh and penetrating voice. . . . It repeated every joke we had told and every word we had said against the government. I thought, 'Good Lord, what's it going to tell next—all my little snide remarks about Goebbals?' But at that moment I realized that one sentence more or less would make no difference—simply everything we have ever thought or said among ourselves is known." (45–46)

3. A German woman dreamed: "I was talking in my sleep and to be on the safe side was speaking Russian (which I don't know, and anyway I never talk in my sleep) so I'd not even understand myself and so no one else could understand me in case I said anything about the government, for that, of course, is not permitted and must be reported." (52)

4. A Jewish woman dreamed: "While out for a walk we heard a rumor in the streets that people should keep away from their apartments because something terrible was going to happen. We stood across the street and looked longingly up at our apartment where the blinds were drawn as if no one live there. . . . We went up the stairs in the building next door, but it, too, was the wrong one—a hotel. We came out by another door and tried to find our way back, but now we couldn't even find the street any more. . . . The woman who owned the hotel told us, 'It won't do you any good even if you do find that apartment. This is what's going to happen.' And in the manner of Christ's curse on Ahasuerus [the legendary Wandering Jew] she pronounced: 'There comes a law: They shall dwell nowhere. Their lot shall be to wander ever through the streets.' Then she changed her tone and, as if she were reading out some proclamation, droned: 'In conjunction with said law, everything previously permitted is now forbidden, to wit: entering shops and stores, employing craftsmen . . . We left the hotel and went out forever into the dismal rain." (56)

5. A young woman with a large, curved nose dreamed: "I went to the Bureau of Verification of Aryan Descent and presented a certificate attesting to my grandmother's descent, which I had obtained after months of running around. The official looked just like a marble statue and was sitting behind a low stone wall. He reached over the wall, took my paper, tore it to bits, and threw the pieces into an oven that was built into the wall. And he remarked [condescendingly, using the familiar form of address, "Du"], 'Think you're still pure Aryan now?'" (79–80)

6. A teenaged girl with dark hair and a dark complexion had the following dreams: "At a gathering made up exclusively of blond, blue-eyed people, a two-year-old child who couldn't talk yet opened its mouth and told me, 'The likes of you don't belong here at all.'"

"On a table were lying two passports which I dearly wanted so that I could get out and away from it all. I took them but after an inner struggle put them back again, thinking that I mustn't do anything that might reflect on my group, since all dark people are punished if one of them does anything forbidden."

"I dreamt I was no longer able to speak except in chorus with my group." (85–87)

It must be admitted that Beradt's collection of dreams does not have the scholarly precision that we find in scientific dream studies. The dream reports she provides are accompanied by only the barest of details about the dreamers, and there are no personal associations to the dreams themselves. We have no way of knowing how representative these dreamers are of the general population, nor do we know how much the dream reports were edited, altered, or otherwise influenced by the dreamers or by Beradt. All we have are the bare manifest dreams, as Beradt presents them to us.

Nevertheless, these dream reports are remarkably moving. They still manage, despite their fragmentary form, to articulate with haunting eloquence the experiences, the anxieties, and the sufferings of those people living in the early years of Nazi Germany.

The Third Reich of Dreams has been available to dream researchers for almost thirty years now. However, the book is cited only occasionally, and it is rarely discussed in any detail. This chapter will thus strive first and foremost to promote greater interest in this fascinating text. I will also, in the course of exploring Beradt's work, offer a theoretical model that I believe can be especially helpful in exploring the social and cultural dimensions of dreams. That theoretical model is based on the object-relations theory of D. W. Winnicott, and his brief but suggestive reflections on dreaming.

Winnicott is one of the foremost successors to Freud and a pioneer in the British Object-Relations school of psychoanalysis (see Greenberg and Mitchell 1983). He has had great success in pushing the Freudian orthodoxy toward a recognition that culture is more than something from which individuals must heroically detach themselves. In his many case studies and theoretical writings Winnicott describes the ways in which psychological development always occurs *within* a cultural environment, beginning with the first "culture" of the mother-infant relationship. Winnicott recognizes that "Freud did not have a place in his topography of the mind for the experience of things cultural," and he provides an understanding of the interrelationship between psyche and culture that is rooted in psychoanalytic theory but branches out far beyond it (1971, 95). What follows is a brief outline of Winnicott's

thinking on the role of culture, and of what he calls "transitional phenomena," in individual development.

Winnicott claims that, in addition to our conceptions of inner
psychic reality and outer public reality, there is a third area of experience, an area that partakes of both the other two but that has its own
special characteristics:

> The third part of the life of a human being, a part we cannot ignore, is
> an intermediate area of experiencing, to which inner reality and external
> life both contribute. It is an area that is not challenged, because no claim
> is made on its behalf except that it shall exist as a resting-place for the in-
> dividual engaged in the perpetual human task of keeping inner and outer
> reality separate yet interrelated. (1971, 2)

Within this third area we make use of what Winnicott terms
"transitional objects," or "transitional phenomena." Infants use such objects as the mother's breast, pacifiers, blankets, and teddy bears as transitional objects. Winnicott believes that these objects are experienced as
part of the infant: there is the illusion that they are subject to the infant's
omnipotent control (1971, 5)

The transitional phenomena of infancy represent our first use of
symbols. Winnicott says, "the object is a symbol of the union of the
baby and the mother. . . . The use of an object symbolizes the union of
two now-separate things, baby and mother, at the point in time and
space of the initiation of their state of separateness" (1971, 10–11).
When this intermediate space is relatively safe and when no severe
threats impinge on the illusion of omnipotent control (the condition established by what Winnicott calls "good-enough mothering"), the infant can explore the "otherness" of the pacifier, blanket, or teddy bear,
and can begin developing the capacity to relate to outer reality. This involves a process of "disillusioning," in which the infant gradually *loses*
the sense of omnipotence and comes to recognize the outer world and
its objects as separate and distinct from his or her own self.

In this way, Winnicott makes a case for the adaptive value of illusion. Rather than a barrier to successful reality-testing (as Freud would
have us believe), illusion appears in his theory as the crucial means by
which we learn to distinguish the self from the outer world. Without
any illusions, or with illusions that are ended too early or too abruptly,
the infant is unable to develop the capacity to relate creatively to other
objects.

The adaptive value of illusion continues into the growing child's
play. At this point Winnicott gives this intermediate area the name
"transitional space," wherein the child explores the further potentials of

the inner and the outer worlds. He or she pretends to run a grocery store, or builds a town with blocks, or parents a toy doll; in such playing Winnicott sees children choosing fragments of external reality and investing them with internal feeling and meaning. This illusory setting allows the child to create, to discover, to be surprised at new features of life, to learn about his or her inner world, and to understand the nature of the outer world.

From here Winnicott sees the child developing the ability to allow for an overlap of playing spaces, and to enjoy this overlap. In this way playing leads to group relations: "we can share a respect for illusory experience, and if we wish we may collect together and form a group on the basis of the similarity of our illusory experiences. This is a natural root of grouping among human beings" (1971, 3). This in turn leads us ultimately into cultural activities. Winnicott says,

> Cultural experience begins with creative living first manifested in play. . . . This intermediate area of experience . . . constitutes the greater part of the infant's experience, and throughout life is retained in the intense experiencing that belongs to the arts and to religion and to imaginative living, and to creative scientific work. . . . There is a direct development from transitional phenomena to playing, and from playing to shared playing, and from this to cultural experiences. (1971, 100, 14, 51)

Winnicott claims that the same basic dynamics found in infant-mother relations also characterize the relations between the individual and society. *Culture* is the transitional space that brings the individual and society together.

Winnicott's developmental theory suggests the following points about dreams. Dreams, dreaming, and the remembering and sharing of dreams are all members of this developmental line beginning with the earliest transitional objects and culminating in cultural activities. Dreams are one of the ways that humans, from childhood through adulthood, develop the relationship between their inner psychic reality and external social reality. In short, dreaming is a transitional phenomenon.

Although Winnicott devotes scant attention to dreams per se, the comments he does make clearly support this view of the significance of dreaming. For example, in *Playing and Reality* Winnicott concludes his discussion at one point by saying, "at this point my subject widens out into that of play, and of artistic creativity and appreciation, and of religious feeling, and of dreaming" (1971, 5). He comments in the chapter on "Why Children Play" in *The Child, the Family, and the Outside World* that

> when one meets with a child in whom the relation to inner reality is unjoined to the relation to external reality, . . . we see most clearly how

normal playing (like the remembering and telling of dreams) is one of the things that tends towards integration of personality. . . . The repressed unconscious must be kept hidden, but the rest of the unconscious is something that each individual wants to get to know, and play, like dreams, serves the function of self-revelation. (1987, 145–146)

Later in the same book Winnicott notes that "the child who can manage dreams is becoming ready for all kinds of playing, either alone or with other children" (1987, 235). A number of times in his case study *Holding and Interpretation* Winicott uses the metaphor of a *bridge* to describe the function of dreams to his client: "Yes, a dream is an ordinary bridge between inner reality and external reality"; "So part of the function of the dreaming was achieved, the formation of a bridge between the inner world and waking life" (1986b, 78, 128).

So from a Winnicottian view, dreaming is a transitional space in which we express ourselves symbolically, creatively, and spontaneously, a space in which we literally play with the relations between inner and outer reality. In dreams we discover new possibilities, try out new ideas, and explore the nature of our inner self and the outer world. When a dream is shared with someone else, for example, with a family member, friend, or therapist, it provides an opportunity for two or more people to enter and creatively explore a transitional space together.

Using this basic outline of a Winnicottian approach to dreams as a guide, I would like to return to Beradt's *The Third Reich of Dreams* and study some of the more striking features of the dreams that she gathered for her book, focusing in particular on how the dreams reveal with haunting power the ways in which the forces of a particular social environment (in this case, Nazi Germany) can deeply influence and disrupt people's experiences within their transitional spaces.

Insecurity, Fear, Loss of Privacy

A number of the dreams Beradt collected reveal a profound sense of insecurity, confusion, and guilt. The middle-aged housewife's dream of her oven betraying her to the Nazi Storm Trooper (dream no. 2 above) involves a common household object, and indeed an object symbolizing the warmth and well-being of the home, that has been turned into a tool of systematic terrorization. Beradt describes many such dreams in which objects like bedside lamps, desks, and clocks "turn traitor" and denounce the people who own them, reporting to the state the details of every secret transgression and crime. These people feel they can no longer trust anyone or anything; they can no longer relax even in the privacy of their living rooms or bedrooms.

In this way their dreams reveal the loss of just those qualities Winnicott believes are crucial to a viable transitional space and thus to a healthy, creative life. Without trust and relaxation a person is "not able to achieve the resting state out of which a creative reaching-out can take place" (1971, 55); without privacy and the ability to "keep secrets," people do not have the freedom to engage the forces of their own personal worlds in their social and political activities, and so can express only anxious "reactions" rather than genuinely personal *actions* (1986a, 157).

The most striking dream of this type, showing how state-produced fear and insecurity can destroy transitional spaces, is the third dream quoted above, in which the dreamer speaks in her sleep in Russian, guaranteeing that the government would not understand her but also that she would not understand herself anymore. The fears of this woman have led her to adopt such extreme defensive measures that her own creative play no longer makes sense even to herself.

Compromise, Compliance

The first dream Beradt discusses in her book is that of a middle-aged factory owner, whose wrenching struggle to salute Goebbals is scorned (dream no. 1). This dream illustrates remarkably well the process by which individuals slowly came to compromise with the Nazi regime. The dream also shows the same pathological extreme of what Winnicott calls "False Self" dominance that is exhibited by the woman sleep-talking in Russian. This man had owned his factory for more than twenty years and was very proud of how well he treated his workers. The dream came to him repeatedly, each time with new, torturous, humiliating details: in one of the dreams his struggling caused him to sweat so much that it appeared he was crying in front of Goebbals; another time the workers stared at him with an absolute emptiness, devoid of any comfort; and in yet another dream the great effort to lift his arm actually broke his backbone.

Beradt focuses on how these dreams reveal the ways in which the factory owner's will is crushed by Nazism's use of public humiliation, destruction of identity, and alienation from his environment. From a Winnicottian perspective we can also recognize how the factory owner has been forced into a fatal compliance with the Nazi state. In the transitional space of his dream the factory owner expresses his deep fear of not being able to continue living a meaningful, creative life under the pressures of the new regime (the first of these dreams came in 1933, soon after Hitler's rise to power). He tries to protect himself by conforming to the demands of Nazism, by "saluting" to it, but the effort required is too much—it "breaks his back." Winnicott is very clear on the dangers of such pressured conformity. He argues that the caregiver who fails to meet the infant's gesture and instead substitutes his or her own produces an attitude of compliance in the infant, an attitude Winnicott sees as the earliest stage of the False Self. If we substitute the Nazi regime for the caregiver and the factory owner for the infant, we can recognize this exact process occurring in the unfortunate man's recurrent dreams. His own gestures no longer seem to be of any worth, so he tries to preserve the relationship with his society by imitating the Nazi salute—by trying to conform with *its* gesture instead of creating his own. All the negative consequences of extreme False Self organization, that is, the disorientation, the helplessness, the alienation from both self and others, are clearly evident in his dreams.

Beradt presents many other dreams like this one that portray people struggling feebly against the powerful seductions of Nazism. A number of people found themselves in their dreams enjoying praise from a Nazi figure like Hitler or Goerring, and yet experiencing deep humiliation as well. Others were pulled to join the Nazis by their feelings of loneliness, isolation, and wanting to be a "part of things." In their dreams they appeared in beautiful uniforms, or at the sides of important leaders, or singing patriotic songs—their happy participation experienced in the dreams as both pleasurable and shameful (Beradt 1966, 111–19). In all of these dreams the people satisfy important needs (e.g., needs for praise, for community, for relief from tension), but only at the greater cost of losing the ability to fight the growing menace of Nazism. One man reported, "I dreamt I was saying, 'I don't have to always say *no* anymore'" (Beradt 1966, 119). We can say with Winnicott that these people have been seduced into compromising their True Selves, into surrendering the difficult but critical task of saying "no" to what is not authentic to themselves.

Traumatic Disillusionment

Beradt describes the dreams of a group of assimilated Jews living in Nazi Germany that illustrate what Winnicott sees as the danger of sudden, violent disillusionment. These were people who had deep family roots in Germany, who had lived and worked prosperously there, who had even fought for Germany in World War I. Suddenly, they found themselves the objects of scorn and contempt, violently cast out from their own society. Their dreams reflect the profoundly traumatic effect of this abrupt transformation of their country—the shock, the disorientiation, the despair. The Jewish woman's dream of wandering about the streets, trying vainly to find her apartment (dream no. 4) is a good example of this. Beradt discusses many such dreams which end in a similar fashion, with the expelled Jews wandering aimlessly, unable to find any place new that will tolerate them, any place where their language is spoken, any place where they can find simple comfort and peace. She says "these dreams describe in astonishing detail the type of person who was forced to emigrate when no longer young, forever possessed by a homesickness which is expressed in an inability to grasp the new and a rejection of all that is unfamiliar" (Beradt 1966, 141).

Beradt is portraying here the exact reactions Winnicott says an individual experiences in the face of an excessively abrupt disillusionment. With their cultural relations to their society suddenly and violently shattered, these Jews expressed through their dreams how deeply crippling this experience was for them. Their dreams reveal how the experience has destroyed their ability to respond creatively to new situations. Unable to face the future, they are left looking forever backwards, paralyzed by a painful nostalgia for the cultural world they have lost.

Propaganda and Persecution

In almost all the dreams recorded in *The Third Reich of Dreams* we find that the doctrines, slogans, and ideals of Nazism forced their way into people's dreams and distorted their experiences there, just in the way Winnicott says a caregiver may force persecutory material into the infant's transitional space. One man dreamed repeatedly that his radio was blaring over and over, "In the name of the Fuhrer, in the name of the Fuhrer . . .", while a girl dreamed that she saw the slogan "Public Interest Comes before Self-Interest" printed in endless repetition on a banner (Beradt 1966, 40). The Nazi doctrine of the superiority of the blond race had a particularly strong effect on the dreams of people who possessed some physical trait that deviated from this social norm. One young woman who had a large, curved nose dreamed continuously of noses and identity papers (dream no. 5). The incessant Nazi propaganda regarding the supreme virtues of Aryans and the inferiority of Jews filled this woman's dreams and forced her into the anxious position of having to justify herself according to the Nazi standards.

This deep effect of Nazi propaganda is further illustrated by the dreams of a teenaged girl with dark hair and a dark complexion (dream no. 6). What is striking in her dreams is that the social persecution goes so far as to threaten this girl's very identity. Winnicott says the violent imposition of the caregiver's gesture leads the infant to "build up a false set of relationships, and by means of introjections even [to] attain a show of being real, so that the child may grow up to be just like the mother, nurse, aunt, brother, or whomever at the time dominates the scene" (Winnicott 1960, 146). In the dreams of this dark-haired girl we see this process taken to still further extremes: she accepts being the *opposite* of the dominant figures, that which the dominant figures hate and despise. She has become what Nazism has told her she is, an anonymous member of the inferior non-Aryan races.

Being Forbidden to Dream at All

Finally, we see in this collection of dreams how the atmosphere of Nazism disrupts the very *form* of dreaming, the ability to have, remember, and share dreams. The fear that prevented many people from confiding their dreams to Beradt and that led her to record in a secret code the dreams she did gather is itself symptomatic of a severely disturbed social environment, one where people feel that the spontaneous creations of their sleeping minds may bring the violence of the state down upon them. The extreme depths at which people were gripped by this fear is indicated by the experiences many had of dreaming that "it was forbidden to dream, but I did anyway" (Beradt 1966, 10). One young man reported to Beradt that "I dreamt that I no longer dream about anything but rectangles, triangles, and octagons, all of which somehow look like Christmas cookies—you see, it was forbidden to dream" (Beradt 1966, 53). Beradt comments that "here is a person who decides to avoid risk altogether by dreaming nothing but abstract forms" (Beradt 1966, 53); in Winnicott's terms, this young man was so anxious about persecution by the Nazi state that he could no longer experience virtually *any* creative living in the transitional space of his dreams.

The fear simply to dream represents a devastating threat to the capacity for play within perhaps the most personal and most guarded transitional space we possess. That the state's persecution could penetrate so deeply into these people's souls as actually to disrupt their very capacity to dream is a testament to the profound violence of Nazism.

As a final note, it should be mentioned that psychologists Peretz

Lavie and Hanna Kaminer have recently studied the dreams of Holocaust survivors now living in Israel (Lavie and Kaminer 1991). They found that well-adjusted Holocaust survivors reported fewer dreams, with simpler contents and fewer references to the past, than did the less-adjusted survivors. Lavie and Kaminer argue that the suppression of dream recall in the well-adjusted survivors has served an adaptive protective function, preventing anxieties from surfacing and thus enabling these people to lead full and healthy lives (1991, 19). While not disputing Lavie and Kaminer's basic data about the incidence of dream recall among Holocaust survivors, I would question their interpretation of that data, and would suggest that their term "well-adjusted" means something quite different from Winnicott's "creative living."

7

Dreaming Is Play: A Response to Freud

The psychological understanding of dreams has, since the pioneering research of Freud, been oriented primarily by the metaphor of *work*. In the language of his theory we speak of the "work" of dream formation, the "work" of interpreting dreams, the role of dreams in the "work" of analysis. This "dreaming is work" metaphor has had subtle but very important effects on psychological theory, research, and clinical practice with dreams. Most constructively, it has made us aware of instances of repression, psychic conflict, and symbolic expression in dreams. It has helped us understand better the resistances, the painfully drawn-out struggles, and the sudden breakthroughs we encounter in the clinical analysis of dreams.

However, Freud's psychoanalytic theory has also, paradoxically, had the effect of drastically limiting our understanding of dreams. In their book *Metaphors We Live By* (1980) linguistic philosophers George Lakoff and Mark Johnson describe how every metaphor highlights some characteristics of a given phenomenon, and obscures others; every metaphor steers us toward certain theoretical and practical pursuits, and leads us away from others. I will argue in this chapter that the limitations of metaphorically viewing dreams as a kind of work have become severe—so severe that the further development of our understanding of dreams is in jeopardy. We need different metaphors, metaphors that can help us recognize and appreciate aspects of dreaming that have been obscured by Freud's primary metaphor. I would like to offer a metaphor for understanding dreams that draws upon our experiences with and knowledge of *play*, taking inspiration from the highly suggestive research of Jean Piaget (1962), Erik Erikson (1963), and D. W. Winnicott (1971). Instead of "dreaming as work," I suggest we try thinking in the metaphorical terms of "dreaming as play."

All human understanding, Lakoff and Johnson claim, is grounded in metaphorical thinking. Metaphors are the primary conceptual means we use to make sense of the world. When we encounter something strange or unusual, we use categories from more familiar, better-known realms of experience to understand the new phenomena. As examples, Lakoff and Johnson offer the many metaphors we Westerners use to describe the strange phenomenon of love: "love is madness" (e.g., "I'm crazy about him," "she drives me out of my mind"); "love is a patient" (e.g., "this is a sick relationship," "their marriage is on the mend"); "love is a physical force" (e.g., "sparks flew between us," "my life revolves around him"). In each case, experiences from a relatively well-known realm in our culture are used metaphorically to structure and thus make sense of a relatively *un*known realm. According to Lakoff and Johnson,

> In all aspects of life, not just in politics or in love, we define our reality in terms of metaphors and then proceed to act on the basis of the metaphors. We draw inferences, set goals, make commitments, and execute plans, all on the basis of how we in part structure our experience, consciously and unconsciously, by means of metaphor. (158)

Like love, dreaming has appeared to people throughout history as a strange and baffling phenomenon. One widespread metaphor used to understand dreaming refers to religion, and particularly to practices of divination—hence, "dreaming is prophetic utterance." In many cultures, prophetic utterances are relatively well understood, clearly defined phenomena. Accordingly, they are used as metaphors to make sense of dreams: dreams are seen as being sent by supernatural powers, as containing religiously symbolic content, and as having the function of foretelling the future. Another common dream metaphor, particularly in Western history, draws upon experiences with physical disorders—"dreaming is illness." From the viewpoint of this metaphor, dreaming is understood by means of concepts and experiences drawn from the realm of medicine. Dreaming is thus seen as being generated by certain somatic processes, as displaying the unhealthy or degraded functioning of these processes, and as having no real "meaning," religious or otherwise.

When Freud began his efforts to understand dreams, he discovered phenomena that were not adequately expressed by means of either metaphor, "dreaming is prophetic utterance" or "dreaming is illness." Indeed, Freud quickly found that these metaphors were obscuring what he believed were very important psychological aspects of dream experience. So he developed a new metaphor that enabled him to highlight these hitherto ignored qualities of dreams. He relied upon the imagery of an experiential realm that had become very familiar to people in early twentieth-century Western society: the physical sciences. Freud used concepts, images, and experiences from this realm as metaphors to help him understand and express what he was learning about dreams. The chief concept he used was *work*—work in the sense of forces, energies, and powers interacting in lawful and publically observable ways.

In chapter 6 of *The Interpretation of Dreams* (1965a) Freud introduced the concept of the "dreamwork" in order to describe his view of how dreams are formed. The dreamwork uses four different "mechanisms" to transform unconscious thoughts and wishes into the dream's manifest content. Each of these four mechanisms is explained in terms of the manipulation and control of psychic forces:

1. *Condensation* involves a forcible compression of different images, thoughts, and meanings into a smaller, more compact form (297–304).

2. *Displacement* "strips" some elements of their psychic intensity and transfers that energy to other dream elements (307).

3. The *considerations of representability* serve to "recast" abstract thoughts into visual forms (344).

4. *Secondary revision* seeks to "mold" the dream into a relatively more coherent mental expression (492).

Each mechanism, in short, accomplishes a kind of work.

Freud claimed that the dreamwork serves two essential functions. One is to protect sleep, to guard it from stimuli that might disturb our night's rest. As with dreaming, Freud described sleeping in energistic language: "When we decide to go to sleep, we may succeed in temporarily bringing to an end the cathexes of energy attaching to our waking thoughts" (554–55). When powerful unconscious thoughts and wishes threaten the mind's rest, the dreamwork transforms the thoughts and wishes in such a way that the mind is not disturbed and can go on sleeping. The second essential function of the dreamwork is simply the flip side of the first function, namely, the "venting" of those unconscious thoughts and wishes. The dreamwork provides them with a hallucinatory form of expression, and thereby disperses some of their energy.

Freud's psychoanalytic studies have highlighted many important qualities of dream experience, and have certainly promoted our knowledge of dreams. But we are now facing a situation almost identical to the one that Freud faced a century ago: our primary metaphor for understanding dreams has become more of an obstacle than an aid in furthering our knowledge. This is the origin of my interest in setting aside the language of work, and considering what comes from looking at dreaming as a kind of play.

So what do we know of play, and how might our knowledge of it help us to understand dreaming? There has been a tremendous amount of high-quality research in recent years on the phenomenon of play. Psychologists, educators, anthropologists, linguists, sociobiologists, neurologists, and scholars from many other fields have studied the nature and functions of play in different animal species and in various human cultures (see Berlyne 1960; Bruner, Jolly, and Sylva 1976; Erikson 1963; Gorlitz and Wohlwill 1987; Huizinga 1955; Piaget 1962; Rubin, Fein, and Vandenberg 1983; Scales, Almy, Nicolopoulou, and Ervin-Tripp 1991; and Yawkey and Pellegrini 1984). The findings of these researchers are, in some cases, still tentative, and debate continues on several important questions. Nevertheless, a general picture of the nature and functions of play has emerged from this research, and I would like to summarize the primary features of this picture.

The nature of play is commonly described in the following terms:

1. Play is "autotelic"—it is carried out for its own sake, without being directed toward any exterior goals. It is intrinsically motivated behavior that obeys the concerns, interests, and wishes of the player(s), instead of being oriented by aims or restraints external to the play.

2. It involves the creation of an "unreal" or "quasi-real" space, a special environmental context clearly set apart from nonplay reality by special gestures, signals, or rules. As a result, play is relatively "safe," in that play acts do not have the same consequences that similar acts would have outside of play.

3. Strong emotions usually emerge in play, both positive ones (affection, happiness, pleasure) and negative ones (aggression, frustration, anger).

4. The forms that play takes tend toward extravagance, exaggeration, and rich variation—this is what makes play often seem so foolish and nonsensical.

5. The forms of play are always governed by some structure, by a certain set of rules. Rather than being entirely random and structure-free, play is activity guided by structures that are *different* from those that order "serious" life.

Play behavior is found in all mammals and all bird species. Interestingly, play becomes more and more central in the lives of the young as primates have evolved from Old World monkeys to Great Apes to humans (Bruner, Jolly, and Sylva 1976). Humans seem to engage in a greater amount of play, and more varied kinds of play, than any other species.

In terms of functions, these are some of the ones that are most widely acknowledged by play researchers:

1. Play enables us to experiment with different possibilities in our experience. The imaginary, as-if atmosphere of play allows for the safe practice of the various skills (physical, cognitive, social, and emotional) that we will use in adult life. It thus promotes our general flexibility, adaptability, and creativity, and enhances our abilities to react well to novel experiences.

2. Play gives us the opportunity to learn about the forms, boundaries, and structures that govern our life—to see what we can *do* with those structures, what we can *make* out of them.

3. It cultivates our empathy, our ability to identify with others, and our capacity to adopt different social roles.

4. Play has a vital role in cultural education, as it leads to greater fluency with a culture's rules, norms, values, and beliefs.

Right off, I think it is clear that dreaming and play are strikingly similar in their manifest characteristics. Like play, dreaming is autotelic in the sense that it is a self-contained, noninstrumental activity. Dreaming certainly creates a special kind of reality different from ordinary waking reality. Dreaming is a "safe" environment, where we can do many experimental, dangerous, or even immoral things without putting ourselves in real jeopardy (hence our relieved exclamation when we awaken from a nightmare, "Thank God it was only a dream!"). Dreaming frequently brings forth a whole host of strong positive and negative emotions. It often presents us with bizarre, extravagant imagery. But despite the seeming nonsense of dreaming, careful analysis usually reveals a deeper-lying structure to our dreams. As is the case with play, dreaming does involve rules and structures—just ones that differ in various ways from those that govern waking life. And like play, dreaming seems to be an experience common to all mammals, although humans appear to develop relatively more sophisticated reactions to their dream experiences.

It must be admitted, however, that such manifest similarities do not necessarily mean much in themselves. A tennis ball and a lemon share many manifest similarities, and yet they are very different things. But the numerous surface-level parallels between play and dreaming should encourage us to explore the deeper relations that may exist between them.

Dream Formation

Almost from the moment that Freud published *The Interpretation of Dreams*, his theory has been criticized for offering a faulty view of how dreams are formed. Neuroscientists have shown that the brain plays a much larger role in the creation of dreaming experience than Freud and his "dreaming is work" metaphor allowed (the leading exponent of neurological dream research, J. Allan Hobson, will be discussed in detail in the next chapter). A "dreaming is play" metaphor, however, accommodates contemporary neurological research very smoothly, and puts it in easily comprehensible terms. According to this metaphor we can say that the mind "plays" with the neurological signals flooding the brain during REM sleep. Like a young child who encounters a set of novel objects and starts playing a game with them, the mind imaginatively transforms the sudden upsurge of "random" neurological signals generated by REM sleep into creative stories, experimenting with new possibilities, trying out different combinations, and symbolically expressing important fears, wishes, and concerns.

Note that the play metaphor does *not* ignore or obscure the vital role of unconscious wishes in dream formation (the core truth of Freud's psychoanalytic dream theory); for as I have already mentioned, it is widely acknowledged that play behavior is motivated largely by the child's desires and concerns. What the play metaphor clearly highlights is the genuine creativity that is involved in dream formation. Whereas Freud repeatedly depreciated the creativity of dreaming, the vast majority of contemporary dream researchers insist that creativity is an essential, integral part of the dream formation process (see Hobson 1988; Hunt 1989; Levin 1990; Van de Castle 1994).

The Functions of Dreams

Moving to contemporary research on the functions of dreams, we find many new findings that fit poorly within the framework of Freud's dream theory. Rosalind Cartwright's studies of the dreams of divorced women indicate that dreams promote the integration of troubling or stressful emotional experiences (Cartwright et al. 1984) Louis Breger offers an information-processing model of dreaming, arguing that dreams help us master and assimilate new experiences within the structure of preexisting cognitive systems; he says that we awake "refreshed" after a good night's sleep because our dreams have succeeded in this process of affective and cognitive integration (Breger 1967). Thomas French and Erika Fromm have studied dreams from the perspective of ego psychology, and found that dreams are active, deliberate attempts to solve problems, particularly problems of an emotionally charged nature. In this way, French and Fromm see dreams as promoting future adaptability: "Most dreams are groping to understand problems that cannot yet be adequately grasped" (French and Fromm 1964, 178). Richard Jones has taken a similar approach, and has shown that dreams contribute to the synthesizing and integrating functions of the ego. He has suggested that "dreaming may serve to reorganize patterns of ego defense or ego synthesis in response to the disorganizing effects of waking life" (Jones 1978, 168). James Fosshage, working within the Kohutian Self Psychology tradition, finds that dreams help to consolidate new internal representations of self and other, and to overcome internal and external threats to the self. In his view, "the supraordinate function of dreams is the development, maintenance (regulation), and, when necessary, restoration of psychic processes, structure, and organization" (Fosshage 1983, 657). And Ross Levin, in a remarkably thorough review of psychoanalytic research on dreams, concludes by emphasizing the powerful creativity of dreaming: "The ability to process information simultaneously in a form psychologically, neurochemically, and anatomically different from conventional waking life may often lead to highly creative and novel solutions to old conflicts" (Levin 1990, 38). What is especially noteworthy here is that many of these researchers are either psychoanalysts or people deeply indebted to psychoanalytic thought. Their findings, which strain Freud's original dream theory well beyond the breaking point, are not motivated by any animosity toward psychoanalysis; on the contrary, these researchers are in general quite friendly toward Freud. This, I believe, renders all the more persuasive the argument that Freud's "dreaming is work" metaphor needs to be supplemented by new metaphors.

Finally, the many exciting investigations of contemporary anthropologists have further enriched our understanding of the nature and functions of dreams. Barbara Tedlock and her colleagues have found that in many cultures dreaming plays a vital role in the integration of individuals into their culture (Tedlock 1987). This enculturing function of dreams, Tedlock shows, is rooted in the dream formation process itself: in addition to its intrapsychic sources, dreaming is always directly formed out of the linguistic, sociological, epistemological, and metaphysical structures of the dreamer's culture. Consequently, dreaming can legitimately be seen as having the function of promoting cultural adaptation. Indeed, other anthropologists have shown that dreaming often serves to promote cultural reform, in that dreams can suggest innovative changes to a culture's conventional structures (see Fabian 1966; Lanternari 1975; Stephen 1979; Sundkuler 1961).

So how are we to make sense of all of these new findings on the functions of dreaming? Again, I believe the realm of play offers us far richer metaphorical resources than does the realm of work. Let me say it once more, to avoid any misunderstanding: I am not saying that Freud's "dreaming is work" metaphor is bad, wrong, or worthless. Rather, I am claiming that his approach is *limited* in its validity and usefulness, and that a "dreaming is play" metaphor can promote a broader understanding of the nature and functions of dreaming. I would invite dream researchers to explore the many new perspectives that are opened up by comparing their work with current research on play. Both dreaming and playing involve free, unpressured experimentation with possibilities and potentials; both enable us to explore the rules, structures, and boundaries that govern our ordinary lives; both promote our flexibility, creativity, and adaptability; both cultivate our understanding of our culture's central values, beliefs, and norms; and both orient us toward the future resolution of emotional, cognitive, social, and physical problems. It may truly be said that each night in our dreams we *play*: we tell ourselves make-believe stories, we create our own versions of other people's stories, we pretend to be people we admire and people we fear, we imagine what it would be like to get the things we desire most, we revisit (in a safe space) recent experiences that were strange, disturbing, or scary, we mischievously overturn the many rules that burden us in our "serious" lives, and we envision what life might hold for us as we grow into the future.

Let's play around with these metaphorical connections, and see what else may come of them.

8

Gods, REMS, and What Neurology Has to Say about the Religious Meanings of Dreams

Interdisciplinary approaches to dreams have been flourishing in recent years. Dream researchers are showing a greater interest in the work of fields outside of their own, are more willing to engage in active debates with members of other disciplines, and are increasingly sensitive to the limitations of studying dreams from only one scholarly perspective.

However, we are far from having reached any sort of interdisciplinary utopia. For one thing, a massive split still runs right through the heart of the dream studies community—a split between what may be called the "interpretive" and the "scientific" approaches to dreams. Stated in the simplest terms, the interpretive approach tries to understand dreams in their meaning for human life, while the scientific approach tries to explain dreaming according to material causes. The discord and even hostility between these two camps has a long history—we find the conflict as early as Aristotle's critique of Plato and as recently as the sleep laboratory researcher community's critique of Freud. One of our greatest challenges in further developing the interdisciplinary potentials of the contemporary study of dreams is to find a way to integrate the best findings of both interpretive and scientific approaches to dreaming.

But even if we grant the theoretical importance of such an integration, we still face the key question: How, as a practical matter, do we go about creating this integration? How do we *do* interdisciplinary dream research?

Given the growing importance of this question, the appearance of neuroscientist J. Allan Hobson's book *The Dreaming Brain* (1988) is a

67

welcome event. Not only is it one of the most comprehensive books on dream science written in decades, *The Dreaming Brain* also aims at overcoming the split between scientific and interpretive approaches to dreams. Hobson tries to integrate neuroscientific findings with the views of Freud, Jung, and other dream psychologists: in other words, he works to develop a truly interdisciplinary understanding of dreams. Because his work has had such a large and widespread impact on current thought about dreams, it deserves careful study and evaluation.

My aims in this chapter are twofold. First, I will examine the many valuable contributions that Hobson makes toward an integrative understanding of dreams. And second, I will challenge his stridently negative attitude toward the religious dimensions of dreaming, and try to draw from his work insights that may enhance, rather than demean, our efforts to appreciate those dimensions.

The primary thrust of *The Dreaming Brain* is to vigorously affirm the adaptive and progressive aspects of dreaming. Hobson claims that neuroscientific research validates the time-honored belief that dreams reflect special processes of human creativity. He says "the new science of dreaming shows us that the creative process is an independent given. It [creativity] is an integral part of healthy brain-mind activity, whether one is asleep or awake" (Hobson 1988, 18; see also 15, 49, 297). *The Dreaming Brain* is to a large extent a broadside against Freud and the excesses of his psychoanalytic dream theories. Hobson is quite successful in challenging us to take a new, more sophisticated look at the different roles of neuroscience and psychoanalysis in the study of dreams. His painstakingly thorough comparison of the "new science of dreaming" with the theories of Freud marks the strongest and most valuable part of *The Dreaming Brain*. While I feel Hobson is wrong in his view that Freud made a fatal mistake by turning away from neurology early in his career (Paul Ricoeur gives a much better account of Freud's intellectual history in his book *Freud and Philosophy* [1970]), I fully agree with Hobson that Freud's theories have historically had the effect of depreciating the work of those who performed scientific research on the nature and functions of dreaming.

To his further credit, Hobson explicitly addresses the significance of neurological research on dreams for broader issues in contemporary society. The philosophical debate between materialism and idealism has plagued Western culture for centuries, influencing important questions in law, education, and morality. Hobson, in his findings about the strong correlations between the neurology of REM sleep and the mental activity of dreaming, sees glimmers of "a unified theory of brain and mind," and thus of a resolution to that often bitter debate (16, 299).

This reflection on the potential relevance of his research to broader social discussions shows how fully Hobson has developed the interdisciplinary potentials of the study of dreams.

These valuable contributions to the interdisciplinary inquiry of dreams are not, however, the whole story of *The Dreaming Brain*. Hobson says neurological research demonstrates that the "nonsense" of dreams really is nonsense; the contents of our dreams are primarily the product of random neuronal activity, and only secondarily the result of higher mental processes. Based on this view of current research on the neurological basis of dream formation, Hobson makes two claims regarding the interpretation of dreams. First, not everything in our dreams is meaningful (as Freud said), so endlessly pondering over the puzzles of our dreams is a foolish waste of time (214, 258, 274). Second, whatever meaning *is* present in the dream is "transparent"—that is Hobson's word, and it is the key one. Against Freud's ideas about disguise and censorship, Hobson claims that interpretation should be nothing more than reading the unedited, clear, transparent meaning that is right on the surface of the dream (7, 12, 65, 233–34, 258, 272–80).

I believe that Hobson badly misjudges the import of neuroscientific research. This research indicates that random neuronal activity underlies the dreaming process. That's fine and well—but does it mean that Freud is wrong to seek hidden meanings in the bizarre imagery of dreams? Not at all. Freud based his psychoanalytic approach not just on dreams but also on his interpretations of jokes, slips of the tongue, and various psychosomatic symptoms. Freud gives good reasons why we should often suspect a sense behind apparent nonsense, in our dreams as well as in other psychological phenomena, and why we should acknowledge the reality of disturbing feelings that we would like to deny, hide from ourselves, and hold down in the unconscious.

The research of neuroscientists like Hobson suggests that sometimes nonsense may be just nonsense. But the really crucial question in dream interpretation is, how do we ever *tell?* How do we know if a dream image is really nonsense, or if it is a deeply meaningful expression of the unconscious? There is only one way to know: ask some critical questions and see what comes of it. We might ask, does this dream image relate to a troubled or conflicted aspect of my life? We might ask, could this image *appear* nonsensical only because I do not understand it, or am afraid of its meaning? We might ask, could I be resisting some of the meanings of this dream because I do not want to face them?

This process of open-ended reflection and dialogue is, unfortunately, just the sort of thing that Hobson thunders against. He scorns such interpretive approaches toward dreams as offering mere "speculation" that may be "entertaining" but is ultimately pointless and unnecessary (57, 274). Hobson says whatever meaning a dream has is right there on the surface, plain as day, so there's no need for any elaborate questioning (Hobson asks at one point in his discussion of a dream, "with such a rich manifest content to work with, why delve deeper?" [234]. The answer, I would say, is because there might be *more* to the dream than what our first impression suggests). Elsewhere, Hobson ominously hints that looking beyond the transparent meaning and engaging in "symbolic" interpretation may be "unhealthy," and even "dangerous"—although he never says exactly how (11, 258).

A good way, I think, to get some insight into the philosophical problems with Hobson's ideas about dream interpretation is to compare them to biblical fundamentalism. Fundamentalists generally believe there is a "transparent" meaning to the Bible; the meaning of the Bible is right there, on the surface, and there is no need to ask a lot of fancy critical questions to get "behind" the plain, self-evident meaning of the Good Book's words. And, fundamentalists will warn you, God has special plans for those who ask lots of foolish questions.

Biblical fundamentalism is justly criticized for this simplistic belief about interpretation. Fundamentalists do not adequately recognize how their own social and historical position shapes what appears to them as the "transparent" meaning of the Bible. Their reluctance to engage in critical debates over the different possible interpretations of the Bible strikes non-fundamentalists as cowardly and irrational.

I am not claiming that J. Allan Hobson is a biblical fundamentalist. Rather, I am claiming that his scornful ideas about interpretation are equally as unjustified and problematic as those held by fundamentalists. Just like biblical fundamentalists, Hobson ignores the extent to which what appears "transparent" to *him* reflects more of his own unwitting assumptions than any fixed meaning there on the alleged surface of the dream. The basic problem is that Hobson's dream research leans too heavily on a natural scientific model of study. The natural sciences demand certainty, simplicity, and universality (Hobson, personal correspondence). While these criteria may be entirely valid in certain areas of research and experimentation, they are not appropriate in judging interpretations of the meaning of dreams. Hobson, however, insists that they are appropriate. He denounces all interpretations that are "speculative" and "unscientific," that do not yield simple, straightforward meanings, that can't be conclusively *proved* (9, 11, 52–68, 123, 158, 222, 274). This is the exact problem, though: Hobson extends the standards of the natural sciences beyond their sphere of legitimate and useful applicability.

Ironically, Hobson's interdisciplinary failure here exactly mirrors his earlier success. In the context of describing the latest findings of neuroscientific dream research, Hobson engaged in a careful comparison of his ideas with those of Freud and argued convincingly that Freud's theories have strayed beyond their proper bounds. But now, in Hobson's discussion of what his research implies for the practice of dream interpretation, he does just what he accused Freud of: now Hobson is the one straying outside his own field and making unwise and illegitimate pronouncements on the work of others. Instead of providing more critical comparisons between his views and Freud's, he now huffs that such comparisons are mere "literary games" that Freud would win only by virtue of superior rhetorical skills.

These clumsy attempts to discredit interpretive approaches to dreams do not help the cause of interdisciplinary dream research. However, I would like to close this chapter with a discussion of what I believe is an extremely valuable contribution that Hobson makes to the interdisciplinary study of dreams—although it is a contribution he probably did not intend to make. I believe *The Dreaming Brain* helps us understand better the religious significance of dreams.

Hobson's book opens with a forceful attack on what he calls the "religious" approach to dreams. He accuses this approach of assuming that external, supernatural beings cause dreams, that dream symbols are secretly coded messages from those divine beings, and that dreamers must have the aid of religous authorities to interpret these messages (9–11). In characterizing religion as authoritarian, antirational, and mystifying, Hobson sets up a contrast with his own approach to dreams, which he claims is humanistic, rational, and commonsensical (81, 222, 298). He devotes many pages of his book to denouncing the religious approach to dreams, particularly in what he regards as its modern form of Freudian psychoanalysis, and asserting the superiority of his own approach.

Hobson's portrait of religion is extremely unfavorable. I would propose a quite different view of religion, a view that leads to a different evaluation of the religious significance of dreams. Religion, as I have discussed in earlier chapters of this book, may be seen as expressing a fundamental human need to answer questions about the ultimate nature of our lives. We humans need to find or create meanings, images, and values that can provide us with existential orientation. Religion is not, in this view, a matter of churches, priests, or dogmas; rather, religion is essentially concerned with seeking vital, trustworthy meanings that express our responses to these ultimate questions and concerns (see Tillich 1952; Tracy 1975; McFague 1982; Browning 1987).

When religion is characterized in this way, as a matter of ultimate existential concerns, I do not believe that Hobson's neuroscientific research takes away from our appreciation of the religious qualities of dreams. On the contrary, Hobson actually offers some ideas that have intriguing implications for our understanding of the relationship between religion and dreaming. Hobson's theory states that dreaming is activated by essentially random neuronal activity; once this neuronal activity begins, higher mental functions seek to form some sort of narrative coherence out of the random signals being generated. What Hobson describes as the "synthetic" process of dream formation bears striking similarities to the process of creating religious meaning. This attempt in the dream state to form *narrative* coherence seems to correspond very closely to what I have been suggesting is the fundamentally religious need for ultimate meaning and value, for *existential* coherence.

This point may become clearer by looking at one of the dreams of the Engine Man, the person whose dream diary Hobson uses to illustrate his theories. Hobson says we can see in the Engine Man's "Custom's Building" dream how the brain's random activity has created an utterly chaotic scene, which the mind tries to make some sense of.

> Walking South on 14th St., just south of Pennsylvania Ave. Street was very muddy. A few blocks (about 3) south of the avenue (Pa. Ave.) I turned east, passing behind various buildings none of which seemed large. No one in sight except my companion, a child of perhaps 6 to 8 years, who later turned into Jason [his nephew] but who, at first, seemed like a stranger. I asked him if he knew the location of the Customs Building; he said "no," and I remember thinking that it very probably was in some other part of town. It was at the Customs Bldg. where all the animals (except small ones such as cats) must be registered or declared, weighed, and the proper tax paid. . . . Some person we were looking for had brought an animal from the train to the Customs Bldg. (272)

In this long dream (I have quoted only about a third of the full text), the Engine Man wanders about city streets and building corridors, unsure of his location or his purpose. He is forced, Hobson says, to ask himself "Where am I? What am I doing here? Who is with me? What is my relationship to that person?" (273) Hobson's analysis of the dream focuses on how the Engine Man tries to fix his "orientational bearings" in the dream by synthetically creating answers to these questions.

Now listen to those questions again—"*Where* am I? *What* am I doing here? *Who* is with me? *What* is my relationship to that person?" At another level these questions have profoundly spiritual connotations, connotations that relate to the sorts of ultimate, existential questions I believe lie at the heart of religion. Hobson's Activation-

Synthesis model suggests that the emergence of such questions is a central feature of human dreaming experience. This model thus legitimates looking to our dreams for potentially religious meanings—asking if the orienting questions raised in our dreams may not *also* have deeper spiritual significance.

Another example might help further illuminate my admittedly "non-Hobsonian" reading of *The Dreaming Brain*. In Freud's case study *Dora: Fragment of an Analysis of a Case of Hysteria* (Freud 1963a) he describes the troubled life of Dora, an eighteen-year-old girl from a well-to-do Viennese family (for an excellent account of the Dora case see Decker 1991). Dora had been sent to Freud by her father to be treated for a variety of hysterical ailments, which Freud discovered had grown out of the complex web of extramarital sexual relations that pervaded the life of Dora's parents and their friends. This is the second of the two dreams Dora shares with Freud:

> I was walking about in a town which I did not know. I saw streets and squares which were strange to me. Then I came into a house where I lived, went to my room, and found a letter from Mother lying there. She wrote saying that as I had left home without my parents' knowledge she had not wished to write to me to say that Father was ill. "Now he is dead, and if you like you can come." I then went to the station and asked about a hundred times: "Where is the station?" I always got the answer: "Five minutes." I then saw a thick wood before me which I went into, and there I asked a man whom I met. He said to me: "Two and a half hours more." He offered to accompany me. But I refused and went alone. I saw the station in front of me and could not reach it. At the same time I had the usual feeling of anxiety that one has in dreams when one cannot move forward. Then I was at home . . . I walked into the porter's lodge, and enquired for our flat. The maidservant opened the door to me and replied that Mother and the others were already at the cemetery. . . . After she had answered I went to my room, but not the least sadly, and began reading a big book that lay on my writing table. (94)

We can imagine that Hobson would look at Dora's dream as he does the dream of the Engine Man. He would see Dora's sleeping mind, beset by a surge of random, disorienting neural activity, as struggling to shape all that activity into some sort of narrative coherence. Like the Engine Man, Dora tries within her dream to answer such basic orientational questions as "where am I?", "who am I with?," and "where am I going?"

But these questions have also been posed to Dora in her waking life—indeed, these are the *exact* questions that Dora's profoundly troubled life has raised for her. In the language I'm using, these questions emerge out of an essentially existential or religious disorientation. Dora's body is afflicted with sufferings that have no apparent cause or cure; every person she has been close to has betrayed her; she is fighting to clarify the truth about her past and the possibilities for her future; she is trying to understand how the qualities of love, trust, identity, and femininity can become realities in her life. For Dora, the questions "Where am I? Who am I with? Where am I going?" arise directly out of the most fundamental, immediate concerns of her life.

Her dream addresses these concerns. As a number of critics and scholars have noted, the theme of personal independence is prominent in this dream (McCaffrey 1984; Marcus 1985; Ramas 1985). Dora refuses the assistance of the man, who seems to represent a young engineer who had been courting Dora, and goes into the thick forest alone. Most importantly, the dream portrays her father, the dominant figure in her life (and in her illness), as dead; and rather than going to his funeral, Dora goes up to a room of her own and calmly reads from a big book. The dream thus concludes with an image of Dora as independent, mature, and oriented toward the development of an identity grounded in her own needs. Dora's life has been a chaos of violent forces, of supposedly caring people ignoring her needs and manipulating her both sexually and emotionally. Her dream contributes something to the development of an existential orientation that could enable Dora to live a more fulfilling life.

This example illustrates how those questions that Hobson identifies as central in the formation of any ordinary dream may also have existential or religious overtones. Dora's dream indicates how the story that the sleeping mind creates in response to those questions may provide the dreamer with an essentially religious kind of orientation toward life's ultimate concerns—even when that dream story does not appear conventionally "religious."

There are a couple of brief moments in *The Dreaming Brain* when Hobson seems to recognize these broader implications of neuroscientific research for our understanding of the religious dimensions of dreams. Early in the book he states that his Activation-Synthesis hypothesis illuminates an "essentially human" capacity to imagine and create. He says, "Activation-Synthesis thus includes creativity among its assumptions. This theory sees the brain as so inexorably bent upon the quest for meaning that it attributes and even creates meaning when there is little or none to be found in the data it is asked to process" (15). Later he comments that the brain labors, in sleeping as in waking, to create a meaningful integration of its experience, "even if it must resort to creative storytelling" (219). Indeed, the utterly chaotic and random data that bombard us during REM sleep often confound all ordinary means of organizing our perceptions, leading to extraordinary attempts at synthesis: "it may be that the symbolic, prophetic character [of dreams] arises from the integrative strain of this synthetic effort. The brain-mind may need to call upon its deepest myths to find a narrative frame that can contain the data" (214).

Essentially, Hobson is saying that the neurological activity during REM sleep can become *so* frenzied, *so* chaotic that the mind must reach down for its most durable meaning patterns in order to make sense of the mental input; and sometimes, even those patterns of meaning don't work, and the mind must create entirely *new* structures of comprehension and understanding.

This neurological explanation of dream formation offers a new way of looking at two central characteristics of religiously meaningful dreams. First is the way that dreams frequently involve traditional religious symbols, figures, and symbols. This occurs, following Hobson's theory, because the mind is sometimes compelled to call forth its "deepest myths" in the process of creating a dream. Second is the way that dreams often involve religious images that are strikingly original and creative, occasionally even heretical. The Activation-Synthesis hypothesis suggests that such novel, unorthodox religious imagery is the product of the mind's inherent powers of creativity, which are called into play each night to meet the challenge posed by the sudden influx of random neural data during REM sleep.

The conclusion cannot be avoided that, despite his own faulty view of religion, Hobson's neuroscientific research and theorizing gives us some intriguing new ways of thinking about the religious dimensions of dreaming.

9

The Evil Dreams of Gilgamesh: *Interpreting Dreams in Mythological Texts*

If the interpretation of a person's dreams is a daunting pursuit, filled with ambiguity and uncertainty, then trying to interpret dreams in mythological texts would seem to be a nearly impossible endeavor. Dreams in mythological texts are generally thousands of years old, from cultures that have largely disappeared. We have no way of knowing if the dreams in such texts were ever really dreamed by an actual person, or if the dreams are merely fabrications created by the author to serve as literary devices. And what we now have of the myth has passed through the various hands of oral tellers, scribes, editors, and translators, with an unknown degree of corruption to the earlier versions.

Yet despite such difficulties, we still find that myths often narrate dream experiences that move us deeply. Across the long ages and through the fragmented texts, something about certain dreams in mythological texts resonates within us. Jacob's revelatory dream vision of the divine ladder spanning heaven and earth, and Penelope's haunting dreams of the return of her long-absent husband Odysseus are two of the most prominent Western examples of dreams in mythological texts that speak to us even now, many centuries later.

What sense, then, can we make of dreams in mythological texts? On the one hand it is tempting to view myths as "psychology writ large," and accordingly to interpret dreams in these texts as we would one of our own dreams. On the other hand, it seems clear that dreams in mythological texts are so thoroughly shaped by literary, cultural, and historical forces that a headlong rush into psychological interpretation would be naïve in the extreme.

There need not, however, be an irreconcilable opposition between the literary analysis of a mythological dream text, focusing on its linguistic, narrative, and aesthetic aspects, and a psychological analysis, using one or more modern psychological theories to interpret the motivation of characters, the development of the plot, and the experiential qualities of the dream. My aim in this chapter will be to show that a careful and reflective integration of literary and psychological approaches may in fact lead to a much fuller, more interesting, and more solidly grounded understanding of the meanings of dreams in mythological texts.

The ancient Sumerian epic *Gilgamesh* provides a good opportunity to demonstrate the potentials of such an interdisciplinary approach. *Gilgamesh* is filled with remarkably strange, vivid dreams that play crucial roles in the unfolding of the plot. While both literary critics and psychological interpreters have devoted much attention to the epic, their efforts have generally been ignorant of the other field of scholarship (see Oppenheim 1956; Heidel 1963; Tigay 1987; Jung 1967). If we work to bring the findings of the two approaches together we may find that we enrich our overall understanding of these mythological dreams.

In his *The Interpretation of Dreams in the Ancient Near East* (1956) A. Leo Oppenheim argues that most dream accounts in the ancient Near East conform to certain well-established literary conventions. Oppenheim's work, which after half a century remains the most authoritative analysis of dreams in ancient Near Eastern culture, examines a wide variety of reports of dreams in mythological, religious, and historical texts. He finds that the basic pattern involves the following standard elements:

- The dreamer, almost always a king;
- The description of the setting of the dream, usually a temple or some sacred place;
- The dream itself;
- An interpretation.

Oppenheim claims that almost all ancient Near Eastern dream accounts have a primarily literary function, serving as plot devices used with deliberate narrative intention by the authors of the given texts. Consequently, Oppenheim asserts that psychological inquiry into these dreams is vain, for it is highly unlikely, and impossible to prove, that these reports are based on genuine dream experiences (Oppenheim 1956, 185). Nevertheless, Oppenheim's work is the best place to start a study of *Gilgamesh*, for his analysis is detailed, comprehensive, and clearly stated. Oppenheim finds many signs in this epic of conformity to the standard ancient Near Eastern patterns, and he concludes that the meaning and function of the dreams in *Gilgamesh* are basically the same as in any other ancient Near Eastern text—in short, the dreams are literary devices used to further the epic's plot.

But a close reading of *Gilgamesh* reveals that Oppenheim neglects to explore an important literary-critical question: in what ways do the dreams in the epic *deviate* from the standard forms of the ancient Near Eastern dream accounts? If we look for the unique rather than the conventional in these dreams, we find a tremendous number of features that differ dramatically from the basic narrative patterns that Oppenheim says govern ancient Near Eastern dream reports. Most strikingly, all the dreams in *Gilgamesh* are *evil* dreams—frightening, confusing nightmares of struggle, violence, and death. Accounts of evil dreams are extremely rare in these texts, Oppenheim notes, and no other ancient Near Eastern work he cites reports as large a number of nightmare experiences.

> Gilgamesh rises, speaks to Ninsun his mother to untie his dream.
> "Last night, Mother, I saw a dream.
> There was a star in the heavens.
> Like a shooting star of Anu it fell on me.
> I tried to lift it; too much for me.
> I tried to move it; I could not move it."
>   (Gardner and Maier 1984, 81)

The first dream experienced by Gilgamesh, the hero of the epic, contains many elements common to the basic pattern that structures ancient Near Eastern dream reports: The dream comes to a king, it contains a message regarding the future, and its content is repeated in a slightly differing second dream. But this dream is more notable for the many unusual features it has. Rather than passively receiving a divine message, Gilgamesh actively struggles against the fallen star; instead of joy or satisfaction, the predominant emotions he seems to feel are distress and frustration; and, most importantly, Gilgamesh does not know what the dream means. Instead of the clear, almost stately dreams that most ancient Near Eastern kings receive, Gilgamesh experiences a strange, confusing nightmare.

Since the majority of ancient Near Eastern dream reports serve to establish the power and divine favor a king enjoys, the striking deviation of Gilgamesh's dream from the standard patterns can only call into question the legitimacy of his rule. If a king is having nightmares, the immediate suspicion is that the gods must be angry with him. The closest parallel in the ancient Near Eastern texts to Gilgamesh's first dream are the dreams of Pharaoh in Genesis 41. Pharaoh's dreams also have strange symbols that he cannot readily understand. Joseph's success in interpreting these dreams demonstrates how Joseph, and not Pharaoh, has God's support and favor. Elsewhere in the Hebrew Bible the distinction is made between the clear dreams of the Jews and the "dark speech" of the Gentiles' dreams as a way of illustrating the special relationship of the Jews with God (see also Gen. 15, 40, 41; Dan. 2, 4; Judg. 7; 1 Sam. 3; 1 Kings 3). This is a very consistent theme in the Hebrew Bible: people not favored by God have opaque, symbolic dreams that require interpretation, while people favored by God have clear, direct dreams in which God's message requires no interpretation to be understood.

Gilgamesh's dreams, however, take this theme of divine disfavor being expressed through opaque dreams even further. While Pharaoh simply fails to receive a direct message dream, he does not personally experience any fear or suffering in his dreams; Gilgamesh's terrifying nightmare, however, shows that he has somehow earned the gods' active antagonism.

The opening scenes of the epic reveal just what it is that Gilgamesh has been doing wrong. In Tablet I.ii we read "Gilgamesh does not allow the son to go with his father; day and night he oppresses the weak. . . . Is this our shepherd, strong, shining, full of thought? Gilgamesh does not let the young woman go to her mother, the girl to the warrior, the bride to the young groom" (Gardner and Maier 1984, 67). The people of Gilgamesh's city of Uruk cry out in distress to the gods, and the gods agree that Gilgamesh has been abusing his power as king. Their response is to create Enkidu, "a second image of Gilgamesh," to counteract Gilgamesh's excesses and return peace to Uruk. Gilgamesh's dreams, then, reflect the fact that he has transgressed the gods' laws; dreams, which customarily establish a king's legitimacy, here reveal instead a king's criminality.

As symbolic dreams these require interpretation, and Gilgamesh's mother Ninsun helps him discover the meaning of his nightmares. Gilgamesh's anxiety that his mother quickly "untie" the dreams stems from the ancient Near Eastern belief that a symbolic dream without an interpretation will have evil consequences (Oppenheim 1956, 206). Oppenheim describes how the original Sumerian word here, "*bur,*" actually means much more than is denoted by our word "interpret." Included in this term's meanings are the notions of (1) reporting the dream to someone, (2) translating the symbols, and (3) dispelling the potentially evil consequences (219). The rendering of this term in the Gardner and Maier translation of *Gilgamesh* as "untie" accurately conveys the cathartic effect that is essential to any ancient Near Eastern dream interpretation. Here, the interpretation/untying is successful: Ninsun discerns the meaning of the symbols, explains their significance for Gilgamesh's future, and tells him what he should do now that he understands the message of the dream.

The next dreams come when Gilgamesh and Enkidu go up to Cedar Mountain, and Enkidu prays to the mountain to bring the king a dream of encouragement before their journey to battle the monster Humbaba. But Gilgamesh does not get what he expected:

> Friend, I saw a dream—bad luck troublesome . . .
> I took hold of a wild bull of the wilderness.
> He bellowed and [kicked up] earth; dust made the sky [dark].
> I ran from him.
> [With terrible strength] he seized my flank.
> He tore out. . . .
> Besides my first dream, I saw a second dream.
> In my dream, friend, a mountain toppled.
> It laid me low and took hold of my feet.
> The glare was overpowering. A man appeared, the handsomest in the
>   land, his grace. . . .
> From under the mountain he pulled me out, gave me water to drink. . . .
> Friend, I saw a third dream, and the dream I saw was in every way
>   frightening.
> The heavens cried out; earth roared.
> Daylight vanished and darkness issued forth.
> Lightning flashed, fire broke out, clouds swelled; it rained death.
> The glow disappeared, the fire went out, [and all that] had fallen turned
>   to ashes.
> Let us go down to the plain and consider this.
>   (Gardner and Maier 1984, 134, 139, 140)

As with his first dream, the three dreams Gilgamesh has up on Cedar Mountain are also grounded in common ancient Near Eastern patterns. In particular, these dreams make explicit use of the theme of incubated dreams, that is, dreams invoked by means of rituals, prayers, or sleeping at sacred localities. Oppenheim says that incubated dreams provide the basic formula for most ancient Near Eastern dream reports. Gilgamesh's dreams at Cedar Mountain include many of the conventional elements found in all incubated dreams. A king sleeps at some holy place on the eve of a great undertaking; certain rituals are performed and prayers recited (the two heroes ceremonially dig a pit, pour food into it, and Enkidu prays, "Mountain, bring him a dream, do it for him" (Gardner and Maier 1984, 138)); and the king is awakened in surprise with the dream and immediately reports its contents for interpretation.

But again, the few ordinary features of Gilgamesh's dreams only serve to highlight how strikingly unusual the dreams are in other ways. Once more Gilgamesh receives not clear, direct-message dreams but baffling symbolic dreams, an extremely rare result of a dream incubation. Rather than expressing divine confirmation of the undertaking, these dreams are nightmares even more terrifying than the previous two. First Gilgamesh flees from a violent, wild bull, then barely escapes the fearsome collapse of the mountain, and finally has an apocalyptic vision of the heavens crying and the earth roaring. Instead of passively receiving a dream theophany (such as that received by King Solomon in 1 Kings 3), Gilgamesh dreams of struggling desperately to fight and escape strange, unidentified antagonists.

All three of these dreams fill Gilgamesh with dread and a sense of impending doom. He had just been boasting that he is going to kill the monster Humbaba, that he has no fear of death, and that making a name for oneself is a hero's supreme achievement; now, however, Gilgamesh cannot avoid seeing that the nightmares bode ill for his and Enkidu's venture. Although the text becomes very fragmentary at this point, we do have records of Enkidu's attempts to "untie" the first two of the dreams. Enkidu dismisses Gilgamesh's fear, arguing that the wild bull actually represents the god Shamash, who will help them in their battle. Of the second dream Enkidu exclaims, "Friend, your dream is good luck, the dream is valuable. . . . Friend, the mountain you saw . . . we'll seize Humbaba and throw down his shape, and his height will lie prone on the plain" (Gardner and Maier 1984, 138).

But Enkidu's interpretations are wrong. The validity of his interpretation of the falling mountain is shattered by the simple fact that there is a third dream. It is extremely rare in ancient Near Eastern dream reports, Oppenheim says, for anyone to have more than two dreams (208). Having a third dream, then, is a good indication that the message of the first two has not been understood (see 1 Sam. 3). And not only does Gilgamesh have a third dream, but the contents of this third dream are by far the most intense and terrifying of all.

The rare occurrence of three dreams and the increasing intensity of the dreams, culminating in an overwhelming vision of cosmic destruction, confirm the conclusion that Enkidu has misinterpreted them. While Enkidu is right about the victory over Humbaba, he appears to miss the far more important meaning of these dreams, a meaning that only later events reveal: by defeating Humbaba the two heroes rouse the displeasure of the gods, and the gods' response is to doom one to death and the other to a long, sorrowful journey.

Up to the point where Gilgamesh and Enkidu have valiantly killed the Bull of Heaven, however, the heroic quest appears to be a success. The ever-dissatisfied Gilgamesh, on whom the gods have laid "a restless heart that will not sleep" and who has suffered from a series of evil dreams, is finally able to lie down and sleep peacefully. But it is at precisely this moment, when Gilgamesh appears at long last to have achieved all he has wanted, that Enkidu experiences his own terrible nightmares announcing his impending death. When morning comes, Enkidu tearfully says to Gilgamesh,

> Hear the dream I had last night:
> Anu, Enlil, Ea, and heavenly Shamash [were in council], and Anu said
>   to Enlil:
> "Because they have slain the Bull of Heaven, and
> Humbaba they have slain, for that reason"—said Anu—"the one of
>   them who stripped the mountain of its cedar [must die]."
> But Enlil said: "Enkidu must die.
> Gilgamesh shall not die."
>
> (Gardner and Maier 1984, 167)

A little later Enkidu reports having another visionary dream experience:

> [Friend,] I saw a dream in the night.
> The heavens groaned; earth resounded.
> Between them alone I stood.
> [There was a man], his face was dark. . . .
> He seized me and led me down to the house of darkness, house of
>   Irkalla,
> The house where one who goes in never comes out again. . . .
> In the house of ashes, where I entered,
> I saw [the mighty], their crowns fallen to the dirt. . . .
> There sits the queen of below-earth, Ereshkigal. . . .
> Lifting her head, [Erishkigal] looked directly at me—*me*:
> "[Who] has brought this one here. . . ?"
>
> (Gardner and Maier 1984, 177–78)

This is a wonderfully effective use of dreams as a literary device, for Enkidu's nightmares not only make for a dramatic contrast with Gilgamesh's first restful sleep, but they also signal a fundamental shift in the plot of the story: now that Enkidu is to die, Gilgamesh's quest changes from making a name for himself to trying to understand the meaning of death.

Enkidu's dreams are quite different from Gilgamesh's, both in form and content. Rather than the "kingly" type dreams of Gilgamesh, Enkidu has what Oppenheim calls "subjective" dreams, which refer more to the specific conditions of the dreamer's mind, body, and religious status than to royal or national affairs (227). Oppenheim notes that most ancient Near Eastern reports of subjective dreams reveal the dreamer's sins; the people have such dreams because they are guilty of some religious transgression. The fact that Enkidu has evil dreams of this type, then, suggests that he is guilty of a "sin" of some sort. And indeed, Enkidu's misinterpretation of Gilgamesh's dreams *is* a genuine sin: the accurate interpretation of dreams is an important religious practice, and Enkidu has failed to discharge it. Not only did Enkidu miss the true message, but the meaning he falsely drew from the dreams was the exact opposite of what the gods intended. In this light, Enkidu's misinterpretation appears as a direct insult to the gods.

As with Gilgamesh's dreams, these two dreams of Enkidu also deviate from many dream report patterns in the ancient Near East. First, Enkidu travels outside his body in his dream to visit other places and realms, rather than passively receiving a more conventional visit from a god. Second, the particular places to which Enkidu makes his dream travels are extremely unusual: to the council of the gods, and to the underworld. Other than Jacob's dream of the ladder spanning heaven and earth (Gen. 28:10–17) and Isaiah's vision of God's throne (Isa. 6:1–13), there are practically no other dream or visionary experiences of such mythical wonder recorded in the ancient Near Eastern texts Oppenheim considers. Third, Enkidu's reaction to his dreams is unique: rather than passively accepting what he has seen and what has been decided for him, he bitterly curses his fate.

Now it is Gilgamesh's turn to interpret one of Enkidu's dreams, but he can only go so far in untying it. Gilgamesh understands what the dream means, he knows that "the dream is sound. For the living man it brings sorrow: the dream causes the living to mourn" (Gardner and Maier 1984, 169). But with this dream, understanding its message cannot make the evil go away; Enkidu will die, and there is nothing Gilgamesh can do to stop it.

Given the close conceptual relationship between sleep, dreams, and death in the mythologies of Babylonia and of many other cultures, we may justly describe the rest of the story as Gilgamesh's attempt to interpret death, to untie its effects. When Enkidu finally dies, Gilgamesh cries out, "What is this sleep that has taken hold of you?" (Gardner and Maier 1984, 187). The king's long journey that culminates in his meeting with the mysterious and immortal Utnapishtim is a quest to interpret this most impenetrable and most terrifying of nightmares. This quest ends in the realization that there is no interpretation of death, there is no way to untie its effects. While Enkidu made a wrong interpretation, Gilgamesh has come up against something that cannot be interpreted at all.

Once Enkidu has died, Gilgamesh sets out on his journey to find Utnapishtim, hoping that the immortal man may be able to tell Gilgamesh something about death. As he begins his journey, Gilgamesh again asks for divine guidance and sanction by means of an incubated dream: "I lift my head to pray to the moon god Sin: For . . . a dream I go to the gods in prayer: . . . preserve me!" (Gardner and Maier 1984, 196). As he did at Cedar Mountain, Gilgamesh is here invoking an acknowledged prerogative of ancient Near Eastern kings, namely, to use an incubated dream to initiate a major undertaking and establish its legitimacy. Here, however, Gilgamesh is not even warned by terrifying nightmares; here he receives no dream at all. "Though he lay down [to sleep], the dream did not come" (Gardner and Maier 1984, 196). If the nightmares signified that the gods were angry with Gilgamesh, at least that meant that the gods still cared enough about what he was doing to warn him against it. Now it seems that the gods do not even consider Gilgamesh and his quest worthy of a nightmare. The silence from the gods is clearly far more upsetting to Gilgamesh than were the evil dreams, as his violent reaction upon awakening shows: "Gilgamesh takes up the axe in his hand; he drew [the weapon] from his belt [and] like an arrow . . . he fell among them. He struck . . . smashing them" (Gardner and Maier 1984, 196; the fragmented nature of this part of the text means that we do not know the identity of the "them" whom Gilgamesh attacks).

This failed dream incubation marks another powerful literary use of the standard ancient Near Eastern dream-report patterns to highlight a key theme of the story at this point, namely, Gilgamesh's detachment from the world of civilization, order, and status. Gilgamesh is leaving his city, leaving his kingdom, leaving the whole world as he knows it to seek out Utnapishtim and learn the meaning of death. The failure of his dream incubation attempt indicates as clearly as possible how Gilgamesh has entirely lost his status as a king and how his journey is leading him beyond all bounds of religiously and socially ordered life.

Gilgamesh has one final visionary experience that bears intriguing relations to his earlier dreams and nightmares. In the last tablet of the epic, Gilgamesh, after prayers to many different gods, finally succeeds in receiving a visit from the spirit of Enkidu. The great hero Nergal "opened up a hole now to the underworld. The ghost of Enkidu issued from the darkness like a dream. They [Enkidu and Gilgamesh] tried to embrace, to kiss one another. They traded words, groaning at one another" (Gardner and Maier 1984, 263). While this incident is not presented as a dream, it contains many strong similarities to other dreams reported in the ancient Near East. Oppenheim points out that the wording of this scene is identical to that used in other texts to describe the appearance of spirits in dreams (234). Throughout the ancient Near East there is an intimate relationship between ghosts, spirits, and the figures appearing in dreams.

Even though the text indicates this is *not* a dream, the episode turns out, surprisingly, to be the closest thing to a "typical" dream report in the whole story. The experience has the distinct form of a dream incubation, what Oppenheim calls the paradigmatic frame for nearly all ancient Near Eastern dream reports. It is not an easy incubation that Gilgamesh attempts, as he must ask three different gods for help, but at least he does finally receive the experience he seeks rather than enigmatic nightmares or frightening silence. In this last "dream" experience a figure comes to Gilgamesh and presents him with a direct message. Gilgamesh receives the message quietly and passively, and no special interpretation is needed to help him understand what it means. With all of these characteristics, the experience is unique in the epic, and yet entirely typical in the context of the ancient Near East's dream report conventions. This is exactly the sort of dream one would commonly expect a king of this era to report. As such, it would seem to suggest that Gilgamesh has now returned to the world of order, status, and responsibility he had left at the outset of the story. It is a qualified return, however, for the vision is still somewhat unusual (e.g., the repeated requests, the figure being a recently deceased person rather than a god), and the message is certainly a gloomy one, but at least it is clear and direct. The vision thus serves the important literary function of complementing Gilgamesh's return to Uruk in the epic's last tablet. The king returns to the city not with a triumphant flourish but with a genuine, sobering wisdom about life and death won at the cost of much suffering. Gilgamesh is not the same king now as he was at the beginning of the story—but he is still king, and he does return to the city, to his people, and to civilized life. After so many deviations from the standard dream-report patterns, this final vision with its great conformity to those cultural patterns makes it clear that Gilgamesh is once again king and that his rule is more legitimately grounded than it ever was before.

The foregoing literary analysis of the dreams and nightmares in *Gilgamesh* establishes that they do serve as important narrative devices. The dreams attributed to Gilgamesh and Enkidu show many signs of being shaped by the literary conventions of the ancient Near East, and they clearly play a significant role in the development of the epic's plot.

But if the dreams in *Gilgamesh* are indeed literary devices, does that necessarily mean that they are *only* literary devices? In other words, does that automatically rule out any psychological analysis of these dreams?

In my view the answer to both questions is no. Literary and psychological analyses can be integrated so as to greatly enhance our understanding of the epic as a whole. A literary approach can take us a long way, but it leaves many important questions unanswered. Why, for example, does Gilgamesh have such a "restless heart," and why does he oppress the people of Uruk so? What is the nature of the deep friend-ship between Gilgamesh and Enkidu? How has Gilgamesh changed by the end of the story? Questions such as these involve fundamentally psychological issues. To ignore or deny this, I believe, is merely to sub-stitute a covert kind of psychological interpretation for one that is more open, honest, and self-reflective.

Likewise, a psychological approach that lacks a sufficient under-standing of literary qualities cannot do full justice to the epic either. Without a thorough appreciation of the literary, cultural, and historical factors that have shaped the story, any psychological interpretation of *Gilgamesh* risks being an arbitrary, distorting projection (to use a psychological term) of our own expectations onto the epic. However, if we first take the time to make a detailed study of the literary dimen-sions of the story of Gilgamesh, we may then legitimately draw on var-ious psychological perspectives to see what additional light they shed on the text.

For example, we may find much of interest in the studies of sleep researcher Ernest Hartmann. In his book *The Nightmare* (1984) Hart-mann describes the biological and psychological factors involved in nightmares. His fundamental conclusion is that nightmare sufferers have "thin boundaries" in terms of their general personality characteristics:

> The formation of boundaries is part of a child's development of mental structures. Partly as a simple matter of neurological maturation and partly as a result of interaction with the environment, a child learns to distinguish between himself and others, between fantasy and reality, between dreaming and waking, between men and women, and so on. Each of these distinctions implies mental boundaries around them. Boundaries of many kinds are built up and all of them can vary from very "thin," "fluid," or "permeable," to "thick," "solid," or "rigid." In every sense . . . people with frequent nightmares appear to me to have "thin" or "permeable" boundaries. (Hartmann 1984, 137)

Hartmann describes how nightmare sufferers typically have weaker ego structures, less ability to distinguish fantasy from reality, less resistance to intimate interpersonal relationships, a stronger sense of bisexuality, and a greater tendency to think of themselves as childlike or even as animal-like (138–46). He states that "clinical summaries, done on a blind basis, describe most of the nightmare subjects as more pathological, more primitive, more vulnerable than the controls. . . . These descriptions characterize the nightmare sufferers as an unusual group with unusual openness and considerable psychopathology" (94, 88).

All of these discoveries of Hartmann's laboratory and clinical research give striking confirmations of what we learned through a literary analysis to be distinctive qualities of the personalities of Gilgamesh and Enkidu. Both of them do indeed have "thin boundaries" in many ways. Gilgamesh cannot maintain an orderly rule of his kingdom, as he oppresses the people of Uruk with his rampant aggressive and sexual urges; put psychologically, he cannot maintain the boundaries between his office as king and his desires as an instinctually driven human. He forms an intense personal bond with Enkidu almost as soon as he meets him, a relationship verging on a total merger of identities. While being a very masculine and fearless warrior, Gilgamesh is also likened to a wife and a wailing woman, he sleeps in the fetal position, and upon beginning his journey to Utnapishtim he covers himself with a dog's skin (Gardner and Maier 1984, 82, 187, 140, 190). This journey itself takes him far beyond the ken, beyond the boundaries, of the civilized world.

Enkidu, of course, begins his life in a state devoid of any boundaries whatsoever. He is raised out in the wilderness by animals and never entirely adapts to civilization. He addresses one of his most moving speeches not to a person, but to a door (Gardner and Maier 1984, 170). In addition to his fluid relations with the wilderness, civilization, and the world of inanimate objects, Enkidu also makes fabulous journeys to the council gods and to the underworld realm of the dead. From one end of the universe to the other, there are no boundaries for Enkidu.

These are only a few of the many examples in the epic indicating that the notion of thin, fluid, or permeable boundaries accurately characterizes the personalities of both Gilgamesh and Enkidu. Hartmann's sleep laboratory and clinical research provides strong evidence for the contention that it makes good psychological sense that Gilgamesh and Enkidu suffer harrowing nightmares. We have already noted the literary basis for their nightmares, the way their "evil dreams" clash with the standard dream-report conventions in ways that add important meaning to the story. Here we see that there is also a psychological basis for the nightmares: given the many signs that the two heroes have thin psychological boundaries, we would expect that this quality of their personalities would also manifest itself in their dreams, in the form of nightmares.

Other psychological theories can add still more to our understanding of the epic. C. G. Jung's theory of dreams as compensations for the excesses of consciousness can illuminate some important aspects of the nightmares in *Gilgamesh*. The portrait of Gilgamesh's rule in the first few episodes of the story indicate that he is abusing his powers, that his behavior as a king is excessive and out of control. His proud boasting in anticipation of the battle with Humbaba gives us the impression of an overbearing arrogance and self-confidence. He exhorts Enkidu to "stand, friend. . . . Let your heart grow light in battle. Forget death, fear nothing" (Gardner and Maier 1984, 130). But Gilgamesh's nightmares show him in an entirely different light—as impotent, frustrated, fearful, in need of help. In his first nightmare he is unable to lift the fallen star off himself, no matter how hard he struggles, and in the three Cedar Mountain nightmares he is helpless in the face of the wild bull, the falling mountain, and the roaring of the earth.

These nightmares present mirror images of his waking behavior and attitudes. In Jung's terms, they may be seen as the attempts of Gilgamesh's unconscious to balance the unstable, destructive forces dominating his consciousness. Jung claims that the unconscious tries

> to restore our psychological balance by producing dream material that re-establishes, in a subtle way, the total psychic equilibrium. . . . Dream symbols are the essential message carriers from the instinctive to the rational parts of the human mind, and their interpretation enriches the poverty of consciousness so that it learns to understand again the forgotten language of the instincts. (Jung 1979, 34, 37)

Seen in the light of the compensation theory, Gilgamesh's nightmares do indeed make sense as efforts to balance his conscious excesses. His first nightmare startles Gilgamesh, as he experiences within the dream difficulties he cannot overcome. Since his behavior in the city of Uruk has been entirely without control or limitation, this is deeply troubling to him. With the help of Ninsun's interpretation, Gilgamesh understands that he will soon meet with a figure, a "companion," who will help check his excessive activities and achieve a more balanced rule. But the mere appearance of Enkidu does not end the restlessness of Gilgamesh's heart or the one-sidedness of his attitudes. Indeed, Gilgamesh appears to corrupt Enkidu to the point where Enkidu shares his inflated ambitions. Thus when Gilgamesh has the three nightmares at Cedar Mountain that clearly warn him against his reckless pursuit of heroic glory, Enkidu is unable to help him with the interpretation. Seen from this perspective, it is the failure of the heroes to heed the compensating imagery of their nightmares that results in the tragedy of Enkidu's death and Gilgamesh's sorrowful journey.

In addition to the studies of Hartmann and Jung, we may also find that some of the insights of Freud's psychological theory can be helpful in discerning the significance of the final visionary "dream" experience Gilgamesh has of meeting Enkidu's spirit.

Freud believed that one of the most important forces in human development was the psychological process of mourning. His clinical experiences led him to argue that when we lose something, be it a person, an ideal, or a time of life, we react by trying to take that object into ourselves, by introjecting it. The result of this introjection is the creation of psychic structure, and a general strengthening of the personality (Freud 1961; see also Homans 1989).

If we consider the experiences of Gilgamesh in this Freudian context, we can see how Gilgamesh's reaction to the loss of his intimate friend leads to the development of the greater maturity, psychic structure, and impulse control he has gained by the end of the epic. In this sense the latter half of *Gilgamesh* could be seen as a symbolic portrayal of the mourning process, with the "dream" of Enkidu's spirit marking the successful internalization of Enkidu into Gilgamesh's psyche.

This Freudian reading finds strong support in the literary evidence we have considered above. The dream of Enkidu, because it conforms to the more conventional type of the incubated dream, indicates that Gilgamesh has now returned to the traditional world of an ancient Near Eastern king. He has gone back to his city, sadder but with a deeper understanding of life. The loss of Enkidu has tempered his grandiose ambitions, has made him admit his own mortality, and yet has not entirely crushed his vigor or vitality. When Gilgamesh returns to Uruk he still proudly describes the city to his companion Urshanabi: "Go up, Urshanabi, onto the walls of Uruk. Inspect the base, view the brickwork. Is not the very core made of oven-fired brick? Did not the seven sages lay down its foundations?" (Gardner and Maier 1984, 250). All of this behavior corresponds remarkably well with Freud's belief that true psychological maturity consists of the honest acceptance of our limitations, a humble resignation to the laws of nature, and a modest faith in human will and industry (Freud 1961, 1963d).

A study of the evil dreams of *Gilgamesh* in its literary context reveals that these nightmares make a very subtle and sophisticated use of the narrative patterns of conventional ancient Near Eastern dream reports. Many of the most important details and nuances of Gilgamesh's and Enkidu's nightmares can emerge only when set within this literary context. At the same time, psychological reflections show that besides being masterful literary devices these dreams are also highly accurate representations of genuine psychological experience. These are not the clumsy, stylized sorts of psuedodreams that Oppenheim finds in such abundance in the ancient Near Eastern literature, where an author seems first to decide that a character will have a divine experience and then, almost as an afterthought, decides to frame the experience as a dream. On the contrary, contemporary psychological thought on dreams suggests that the evil dreams in *Gilgamesh* are utterly true-to-life, and cohere in every way with the personalities of Gilgamesh and Enkidu as presented in the story.

As comparative literature scholar Carol Schreier Rupprecht noted while helping me with early drafts of this chapter, the evolution of Gilgamesh's dreams suggest that a person's dream life may correspond most closely to traditional dream forms when that person is in "sync" with his or her culture and community. The integrated literary-psychological approach I use in this chapter thus contributes to a discussion begun in the earlier chapters about the social and political dimensions of dreaming, and about the broader relevance of dream studies for the critical investigation of power, authority, and rebellion.

10

Wisdom's Refuge in the Night: Dreams in The Mahabharata, The Ramayana, *and* Richard III

At the center of the two great Indian epics *The Ramayana* and *The Mahabharata* lies the mythological theme of a kingship gone wrong. The line of royal succession in these stories expresses a just and lawful worldly order that is patterned upon and sanctioned by the divine order of the cosmos. A threat to the throne, then, threatens the structures that govern the social world and the universe itself. Such a danger provokes the strongest possible response by humans and gods alike, who strive to restore the fundamental laws of reality embodied in the monarchical line of succession.

Many other cultures have stories very similar to these ancient Indian epics, for the mythological motif of temporal and cosmic order being violently disrupted expresses a basic human concern about the fragility of life. A Western story with particularly intriguing similarities to *The Ramayana* and *The Mahabharata* is Shakespeare's early history play *Richard III*. The plot in the two epics and *Richard III* is roughly the same: the normal succession to the throne is interrupted, and a younger prince becomes or seeks to become king, while his brothers and the older generation of the royal family resist. Schemes are plotted, queens are abused, friends are betrayed, powerful curses are hurled, and crimes are committed that come back to haunt their perpetrators. In the end a great and dramatic battle is fought. The villains lose, and the throne is restored to its rightful heir.

In addition to sharing these general narrative themes, the three stories also share a special interest in dream experiences. Dreams have great significance in all three tales, serving to relate memories of the past to crises in the present and to hopes for the future. A variety of unusual types of dream experiences occur in these stories, including shared dreams, ignored or misinterpreted dreams, terrifying nightmares, dreams dreamt for other people, and prophetic dreams that ultimately come true. In this chapter I will look at how the different types of dreams described in *The Mahabharata*, *The Ramayana*, and *Richard III* contribute to the development of that nearly universal mythological motif of the royal consecration gone wrong. Beyond that, I will consider the broader question of how the "fictional" dreams in these stories can deepen our understanding of "real" existential questions regarding the nature of dreaming. The dreams experienced by the characters in these three stories express powerful truths that extend beyond the narratives to challenge the audience's own ultimate beliefs. Are dreams *real*? Should we heed their messages, or ignore them as phantoms of our imaginations without any authority over our waking lives? How does the past, and our memories of the past, affect our present and guide our future? Can the will of the individual ever overcome the mysterious powers of Destiny?

The most strikingly parallel dreams in these three stories are those experienced by the warriors on the eve of the climactic battles in *The Mahabharata* and *Richard III*. In *The Mahabharata* the Kuru leader Karna tells his friend Krishna about the dreams that he and the other Kuru warriors are dreaming about their enemies the Pandavas:

> Many horrible dreams are being seen by the Kurus, and many terrible signs and gruesome omens, predicting victory for the Pandavas. Meteors are falling from the sky, and there are hurricanes and earthquakes. The elephants are trumpeting, and horses are shedding tears and refusing food and water. Horses, elephants, and men are eating little, yet they are shitting prodigiously. . . . And I had a dream in which I saw all the Pandavas climb to a palace with a thousand pillars. All of them wore white turbans and white robes. And in my dream I saw you, Krishna, drape entrails around the earth, which was awash with blood, and I saw the Pandava [leader] Yudhisthira climb a pile of bones and joyously eat rice and butter from a golden bowl. And I saw him swallow the earth that you had given to him; clearly he will take over the earth. The Pandavas were mounted on men, and they were wearing white robes and turbans and carrying white umbrellas, while we Kurus were wearing red turbans and were riding in a cart drawn by a camel, travelling to the South. (O'Flaherty 1984, 31–32)

In *Richard III* several ghosts of people who were murdered by Richard during his lawless seizure of the throne visit him and Richmond, the leader of the opposing army, during the night before their final combat. Here are the dream declarations of two of the ghosts:

> *Ghost* [of Prince Edward] (to Richard III): Let me sit heavy on
>   thy soul tomorrow!
> Think how thou stab'st me in my prime of youth
> At Tewkesbury. Despair therefor and die!
> (To Richmond): Be cheerful, Richmond; for the wronged souls
> Of butchered princes fight in thy behalf.
> King Henry's issue, Richmond, comforts thee. (*Exit.*)
>
> *Ghost* [of Henry the Sixth] (to Richard III): When I was mortal,
>   my annointed body
> By thee was punched full of deadly holes.
> Think on the Tower and me. Despair and die!
> (To Richmond): Virtuous and holy, be thou conqueror!
> Harry, that prophesied thou shouldst be king,
> Doth comfort thee in thy sleep. Live and flourish!
>   (Shakespeare V.iii.119–31)

In both *The Mahabharata* and *Richard III* ominous, nightmarish dreams portend suffering and destruction for the armies who will be defeated in the next day's battle, while auspicious dreams foreshadow the good fortune and divine blessing of those who will go on to victory. In *The Mahabharata* the Kuru soldiers and Karna experience *complementary* dreams, with the soldiers having dreams filled with traditional symbols of woe and suffering and Karna having dreams presenting the Pandavas amidst the corresponding traditional symbols of success and prosperity. In *Richard III* Richard and his opponent Richmond have a *shared* dream, with complementary messages: the same ghosts come to them, the souls of all those murdered by Richard, first to curse Richard to "despair and die!" and then to bless Richmond to "live and flourish!"

The prebattle dreams in these stories both have the important effect of setting the combatants and the war as a whole firmly within a broader framework of cosmic justice and divine authority. The dreams indicate that the challenges made to that framework by the Kurus and by Richard will be defeated, and the disrupted order of reality will be reestablished. The curses will be fulfilled, the misdeeds of the usurpers will be punished, and the virtuous acts of the rightful heirs to the throne will be rewarded. By means of these dreams the characters, and the audience, understand that the morning's battle will bring final, inevitable defeat to the wicked rebels and will herald the restoration of the legitimate monarch's reign.

Two remarkably similar dreams also link *Richard III* and *The Ramayana*. Clarence, the brother of Richard, and Bharata, the brother of Rama, both have troubling dreams early in their stories. Clarence wakes up and ponders the strange nightmare he's just had:

> *Clarence*: Methoughts that I had broken from the Tower
> And was embarked to cross to Burgundy,
> And in my company my brother Gloucester [Richard],
> Who from my cabin tempted me to walk
> Upon the hatches. Thence we looked toward England
> And cited up a thousand heavy times,
> During the wars of York and Lancaster,
> That had befall'n us. As we paced along
> Upon the giddy footing of the hatches,
> Methought that Gloucester stumbled, and in falling
> Struck me (that thought to stay him) overboard
> Into the tumbling billows of the main.
> O Lord, methought what pain it was to drown!
> What dreadful noise of water in mine ears!
> What sights of ugly death within my eyes!
> Methoughts I saw a thousand fearful wracks;
> A thousand men that fishes gnawed upon;
> Wedges of gold, great anchors, heaps of pearl,
> Inestimable stones, unvalued jewels,
> All scattered in the bottom of the sea.
> Some lay in dead men's skulls, and in the holes
> Where eyes did once inhabit there were crept,
> As 'twere in scorn of eyes, reflecting gems
> That wooed the slimy bottom of the deep
> And mocked the dead bones that lay scatt'red by.
>
>   (I.iv.9–33)

And Prince Bharata, the next in line for the throne after his elder brother Rama, wonders at this strangely distressing dream:

> Hear the reason for my present sadness! In a dream, my father appeared to me in faded apparel, his hair dishevelled, falling from a mountain peak into a pit of dung! It seemed to me he was wallowing in that sea of dung, drinking oil from the hollow of his hands, bursting into laughter again and again.... And in my dream I saw the ocean dry up and the moon fall on the earth, the world being plunged into darkness.... Finally I beheld a woman dressed in red, a female demon of hideous aspect, who, as if in play, was bearing the king away. This is what I beheld during this terrible night! Assuredly, either I or Rama or the king or Lakshmana [another one of Bharata's brothers] are about to die.... My throat is dry; and my mind is uneasy. I see no reason for my apprehension and yet I am full of

fear; my voice shakes, my features are wan, I am ashamed of myself and yet I do not know the reason. (Shastri 1953, 331–32)

These two dreams are not nearly as clear and readily understandable as the prebattle dreams. Clarence and Bharata have difficulty interpreting their dreams, and in important ways actually *fail* to interpret them, that is, neglect to make even the most basic attempt at discovering the deeper meanings of their dreams. Both dreams present visions of impending death: Clarence has a vivid, seemingly endless nightmare of his own drowning, and Bharata also has a nightmare foretelling death, although he says he is not sure exactly whose death the dream portends—his own, Rama's, his other brother Lakshmana's, or his father King Dasaratha's. While they are deeply troubled by their experiences, neither Clarence nor Bharata sees the *true* meaning of his dream, in sharp contrast to what the audience has learned in earlier scenes of the story. Clarence naively interprets his dream's image of Richard knocking him overboard into the sea as a mere accident, but the audience knows that in fact Richard has just hired two assassins to murder his brother. Likewise, though Bharata says his dream does not make it clear who will die, the audience has just heard that messengers are on their way to tell Bharata that the aged King Dasaratha is stepping down from the throne and that Bharata, not Rama, has been chosen to take their father's place as King.

These failed interpretations yield quite different outcomes. Clarence's foolish trust of his brother's loyalty blinds him to any suspicion that this dream might suggest that Richard in fact intends to kill him. His failed dream interpretation mirrors his waking failure to see Richard for what he is, and as a result Clarence dies just as his dream predicts. Bharata says he cannot tell what his dream means despite the feelings of sadness, agitation, and shame it has stirred up within him. His failure of interpretation consists in not considering what role he might have in the impending tragedy following his father's abdication; Bharata makes no effort to look within himself for the reasons why he might be feeling so upset and ashamed. As a result of his passive attitude toward his dream, Bharata's illegitimate rise to the throne is allowed to proceed unimpeded.

Clarence's and Bharata's failed dream interpretations underscore their roles as shadows of their brothers and, more broadly, reveal key details about the disruptions to the royal line of succession.

Clarence is trusting and naïve, his brother Richard ruthless and deceitful. Clarence's nightmare reveals Richard's true nature and intentions, but Clarence's own nature is so opposite to Richard's that he is unable to grasp the real meaning of his dream. This mirrors the general failure of the English people to see through Richard's sweet and noble declarations of benevolence. Like Clarence, the people cannot bring themselves to see that someone might so brazenly subvert the social order by violently seizing the throne. To a large extent Richard's success in his criminal scheme depends on this foolish trustfulness of Clarence and the people of England.

Bharata's brother Rama is the rightful heir to the throne of the holy city of Ayodhya. When King Dasaratha is compelled by one of his wives to decree that her son Bharata shall assume the throne and that Rama (the king's oldest son, borne by another wife) must be exiled from the land, Rama nobly sacrifices his own rights and ambitions and accepts his father's command. Although Bharata knows nothing of his mother's plot, Dasaratha's decree opens the way for the fulfillment of Bharata's own ambitions to become king. Looking at his failed dream interpretation in this light, Bharata has good reason to resist conscious recognition of any moral considerations that might interfere with his opportunity to leap over Rama in the line of succession and become king himself. If Bharata were to become aware of his dream's true meaning, the divine law of Dharma would oblige him to act to avert the impending crisis of succession. But by regarding the dream as so confusing and vague as to be uninterpretable, Bharata is relieved of any such moral obligations. Events may continue on their "natural" course, Bharata rather than Rama becomes king, and the city of Ayodhya is plunged into chaos.

This theme of ignoring the truths revealed at night by dreams runs through all three of these stories, although there are different causes of this ignorance. With Clarence it is naïveté and gullibility, and with Bharata it appears to be the power of hidden ambition. Yet other characters resist what their dreams reveal to them for a different reason: for them dreams just are not *real* enough to take seriously. As the stories unfold, however, it becomes clear that dreams are actually much more real than the characters at first will admit.

Two particular characters have almost the identical difficulty believing in dreams: Lord Hastings, an ally of Richard's, and Princess Sita, Rama's wife. Through the course of their stories both these characters experience drastic changes of fate. Although Hastings originally helps Richard in many of his treacherous plots, Hastings will in the end be betrayed by the usurper king. Princess Sita has been taken captive by the ten-headed, twenty-armed demon Ravana, but Rama will eventually break into Ravana's palace and rescue her. Both Hastings and Sita are alerted to these impending changes by dreams—not their *own* dreams, significantly, but the dreams of others. Hastings is awakened in the middle of the night by a messenger from his friend Lord Stanley, another ally of the wicked Richard:

> *Hastings*: Cannot my Lord Stanley sleep these tedious nights?

> *Messenger*: So it appears by that I have to say:
> First, he commends him to your noble self.

> *Hastings*: What then?

> *Messenger*: Then he certifies your lordship that this night
> He dreamt the boar [a heraldic symbol of Richard] had rased off his
>   helm.
> Besides, he says there are two councils kept,
> And that may be determined at the one
> Which may make you and him to rue at th' other.
> Therefore he sends to know your lordship's pleasure,
> If you will presently take horse with him
> And with all speed post with him toward the north
> To shun the danger that his soul divines.
>
> (3.2.6–18)

The captive Sita, while she languishes in Ravana's palace, overhears Trijata, one of her demoness guards, tell the other demonesses of her dream:

> Last night, I had a terrible dream causing my hair to stand on end, foretelling the overthrow of the titans and the triumph of this woman's [Sita's] husband. . . . I saw Rama, clothed in brilliant attire, wearing garlands, accompanied by Lakshmana, in a chariot drawn by eight white bullocks and I beheld that foremost of men, Rama, whose essence is valour with his brother Lakshmana and Sita ascending in a celestial flowery car, bright as the sun, driving towards the northern regions. Then I saw Ravana, lying on the earth covered in oil, shaven, attired in red, garlanded with oleander flowers, intoxicated and still drinking. . . . Then, proceeding towards the south, he [Ravana] entered a lake where even the mud had dried up and a dark woman clad in red, besmeared with mud, placed a rope around [his] neck dragging him to the region of death. (Shastri 1953, 398–400)

It seems the stunning changes of fate looming ahead for these two characters are so incredible that Hastings and Sita will not believe just any dream prophesizing their unexpected futures. Consequently, the prophetic truths of these dreams must be "hardened" by being sent to *other* people. In this way Hastings and Sita cannot dismiss the dreams and their messages as merely the products of their own emotion-clouded imaginations. But even the additional authority of another person dreaming the dream is not enough to convince either Hastings or Sita of the truth of these startling messages of future change. Hastings dismisses Stanley's messenger with the scornful words, "Tell him his fears are shallow, without instance;/ And for his dreams, I wonder he's so simple/ To trust the mock'ry of unquiet slumbers" (3.2.25–27). Sita, overcome by sorrow and despair, pays no heed to Trijata's dream and begins to untie her hair cord in order to hang herself. Sita is finally convinced, however, when the physical portents Trijata described in addition to her dream come to pass. The auspicious signs of the demoness's twitching eye, arm, and thigh overcome Sita's skepticism and reassure her that Rama will indeed rescue her. Even the harder proof of physical omens cannot persuade Hastings of the truth of Stanley's dream, however, and he sadly regrets this as he is led to his execution: "Stanley did dream the boar did rase our helms, / And I did scorn it and disdain to fly./ Three times today my footcloth horse did stumble, / And started when he looked upon the Tower, / As loath to bear me to the slaughter-house" (3.4.81–85). Hastings does not understand until it is too late what the dream and the omens were trying to tell him, that he would ultimately be a victim of the social and religious disruption that he helped Richard create.

Many characters in these three stories gain access to important knowledge, truths, and warnings from dreams, and yet take no heed of them. Clarence and Bharata fail to grasp the deeper meanings of their dreams, while for Hastings and Sita even the dreams dreamt for them by other people do not have sufficient authority to be accepted as legitimate messages. King Richard himself rejects the truth of dreams for yet another reason—because he realizes his dreams are *too* real, *too* threatening, *too* frightening to be tolerated. Richard's wife, Anne, complains that the recurrent plague of his "timorous dreams" have prevented her from ever having a peaceful night's sleep (4.1.84). But Richard does not simply ignore the urgent warnings of his dreams; he goes so far as to commission an assassin to murder "Two deep enemies, / Foes to my rest and my sweet sleep's disturbers" (4.2.71–72). Richard thus takes a violently hardheaded approach to rejecting the wisdom of the night, by literally killing those who plague him in his nightmares.

This fearful attitude becomes more understandable, however, when we consider how each of the stories portrays the ever-present dangers of night and darkness. In the two Indian epics it is common knowledge among all the characters that the demons are more powerful at nighttime. The night before Rama's triumphant coronation at the end of *The Ramayana* Dasaratha (who has had a frightening dream about this) warns Rama that dangerous obstructions often arise on the nights before coronations. *The Mahabharata* depicts numerous treacheries committed at night, including the house fire that almost kills the five Pandava brothers and the slaughter by Duryodhana's soldiers of all the Pandava armies while they sleep. In *Richard III* Clarence meets his end at the hands of ruthless murderers while he sleeps at night in his Tower cell. There is obviously good reason in these stories to be extremely careful and wary at night. The night appears as a time of great danger, of traps, illusions, deceptions, and violence.

How then can we account for this ambivalent view of dreams—revered for their valuable wisdom, yet feared for their dangerous deceptiveness? I believe this ambivalence illustrates how the disruption of the lines of royal succession has upset all cosmic order and has completely reversed the ordinary patterns of life. In "normal" circumstances wisdom resides in the light of day, and ignorance in the dark of night. But now that the royal thrones have been wrested away from their rightful heirs, now that willful individuals have defied the laws of religion and morality and forcefully asserted their own ambitious desires, people can no longer turn to conventional sources of meaning and guidance. In this new world of chaos, disruption, and rebellion, only those will survive who know how to discern and heed the wisdom that emerges in the night.

11

Dreamily Deconstructing the Dream Factory: The Wizard of Oz and A Nightmare on Elm Street

The relationship between films and dreams has received a modest degree of scholarly attention over the past few decades. Some directors have described how they occasionally take images from their dreams and incorporate them into their films (Gabbard and Gabbard 1987). A handful of film critics have noted the dreamlike quality of the experience of viewing movies (Ebert 1997). Several psychological studies have examined the influences of films on the dream contents of subjects sleeping in a sleep laboratory (Koulack 1991). And a number of psychologically minded scholars have used the dream theories of Freud, Jung, and others to interpret the symbolism in various films.

In this chapter I want to examine each of these dimensions of the complex interplay between films and dreams, focusing on two films in particular: *The Wizard of Oz* (1939, directed by Victor Fleming) and *A Nightmare on Elm Street* (1984, directed by Wes Craven). Both of these movies portray the dream adventures of an adolescent girl struggling to survive in and make sense of a world filled with danger, evil, and injustice. However, the two films offer strikingly different portraits of adolescent experience, with *The Wizard of Oz* presenting a grandly staged and highly polished fairy tale, and the low-budget *A Nightmare on Elm Street* telling a crude, blood-drenched horror story. While both films have enjoyed tremendous and enduring popularity among adolescent audiences, adults have generally praised the former as a treasure of American cultural heritage, while villifying the latter for its corrosive effects on the moral development of the nation's youth.

Looking at these two dream-oriented movies from several different angles—considering their narrative plots, their cinematic artistry, their treatment of religion, their psychological impact on their audiences, and their relations to their social and historical contexts—gives us valuable insights into what may be called "the American unconscious." By that perhaps mysterious phrase I mean the distinctive cluster of instinctually rooted desires, fears, hopes, and conflicts that bond the American people together at a deep, though largely unconscious, psychological level. My goal in this chapter is to show that a careful exploration of *The Wizard of Oz* and *A Nightmare on Elm Street* reveals important features of a particular realm of the American unconscious: namely, the dreams and nightmares of American adolescents.

To begin with, I will look at the influence of dreaming on these two films and the ways in which the films make narrative use of common themes and patterns in people's dream experiences. I trust that most readers are familiar with the three-part narrative structure of *The Wizard of Oz*: The film opens with Dorothy's waking-life experiences in Kansas, then follows her through a long series of fantastic dreaming experiences in Oz, and then finishes with a second, much briefer set of Dorothy's waking experiences back in Kansas. The basic trajectory of the film's plot involves Dorothy's efforts to get out of Oz and return home, and it concludes with her succeeding in these efforts and passionately declaring, "Oh, Auntie Em, there's *no* place like home!" The moral of the story, then, is that the waking world of home and family is the best place, the place we should be, the place we should never wish to leave, the place toward which we should always strive to return.

But the film has a second plot trajectory that parallels the first and subtly *reverses* its overt moral message. According to this second trajectory, Dorothy temporarily escapes the dry, dusty tedium of waking-life Kansas and discovers Oz, a world of *dreams*, a wonderous, exciting, beautiful world filled with mystery and adventure. The sharp contrast between the utter dreariness of her waking world and the enchanting magic of her dreaming world is established with stunning power by the use of a cinematic technique that will never again be used to such breathtaking effect: the sudden transformation, as Dorothy steps out of her tornado-tossed house, from the black-and-white of Kansas to the lush, vibrant, almost gaudy Technicolor of Oz. Paralleling this visual contrast is a moral contrast, for in Oz Dorothy finds the justice she could not find in Kansas. In the first, "waking life" section of the movie nothing can stop the cruel and socially powerful Mrs. Gulch (who, we're told, "owns half the county") from seizing Dorothy's beloved pet dog, Toto. Dorothy discovers that the adult social order of the waking world cannot protect her most cherished interests, and cannot care for her deepest needs. But in the dreaming world of Oz, she learns that good *can* triumph over evil. Dorothy and her magical friends do finally succeed in defeating the Wicked Witch, thereby restoring the principles of right, fairness, and justice. So the second, more covert moral of Dorothy's story is that while there may be no place like home, there's no place like *Oz*, either. The dream world of Oz reveals to Dorothy visions of sublime beauty and moral justice far surpassing the imperfections of her waking world.

I don't know if Victor Fleming drew directly upon his own dreams in the making of *The Wizard of Oz*. But it is clear that the film deliberately, and very effectively, evokes common features of dreaming experience: for example, the magical animism of the dreamworld (e.g., talking trees, flying monkeys), the transformation of people from waking life into dream characters (Mrs. Gulch→the Wicked Witch, the three farm hands→the Scare Crow, Tin Man, and Cowardly Lion, the huckster fortune teller→the Wizard), and the exquisite sense of beauty and wonder that simply can't be communicated to others (as Dorothy discovers when she awakens at the end of the movie and tries unsuccessfully to describe to everyone what her dream was like). In all these ways, the movie's many references to common features of our dreams serve to intensify the audience's emotional immersion in Dorothy's story.

Very much like *The Wizard of Oz*, *A Nightmare on Elm Street* generates its narrative power by tapping into people's common dream experiences—in this case, the experience of recurrent nightmares. Wes Craven, the film's director, has acknowledged in interviews a fascination with dreams and nightmares, and has said that the basic nightmare theme of being relentlessly pursued by a malevolent antagonist is the backbone of his film's story (Cooper 1987, 10).

I imagine that few readers have ever seen *A Nightmare on Elm Street*, so let me recount the basic story. A nice, normal high school girl named Nancy Thompson lives with her parents in a pleasant suburban house on Elm Street (Nancy's mother is an alcoholic housewife, her father the stoic chief of police of their nameless middle-American town). Nancy and her teenage friends start having the exact same recurrent nightmares of a horribly disfigured man in a dirty red and green sweater who attacks them with his razor-blade fingers. When two of her friends are found brutally murdered, Nancy desperately tries to tell her father that it's the fiend from her nightmares who killed them, and that he's trying to kill her, too. Her police chief father, however, refuses to believe that any such thing could possibly happen. But when Nancy mentions to her mother that she's learned the nightmare man's name—

Freddy Krueger—her mother realizes what's been happening. Reluctantly, she tells Nancy that ten years ago their town was terrorized by a sadistic child murderer, who turned out to be a seemingly ordinary neighbor named Fred Krueger. Krueger was caught, but he escaped conviction on a legal technicality. So the outraged parents of their neighborhood (including Nancy's mother and father) secretly formed a vigilante group, trapped Krueger in the boiler room of an abandoned building, and burned him to death. The parents then made a vow to keep the truth of what they did to punish Krueger forever hidden. When Nancy hears this story, she decides she must go back into her nightmares. With no help from her father or her boyfriend (who is the fiend's next victim), she confronts Freddy and declares that she knows his secret now, and she isn't afraid of him anymore. This courageous assertion finally breaks the power Freddy has had over her, and with an agonized shriek he vanishes, as Nancy safely awakens to a bright, sunny morning.

A Nightmare on Elm Street does everything it can to recreate the sensation of being trapped within the terrifying world of a recurrent nightmare. Feelings of fear, helplessness, impotence, and vulnerability pervade the film. Nancy and her friends (and we in the audience) are repeatedly startled and disoriented by abrupt shifts from waking to dreaming and back again, and we are relentlessly assaulted by sudden, shocking bursts of violence and bloody physical mutilation. Like Dorothy, Nancy is unable to convince the adults out in the waking world of the reality of what she's experiencing in her dreams. And also like Dorothy, Nancy ultimately finds in her dreams the deep resources of personal strength to overcome an evil that the adult social world had failed to defeat.

In both films, Christianity plays a small but significant role as an emblem of the impotence of the adult world in helping adolescents fight off evil and injustice. In the first section of *The Wizard of Oz*, when it becomes clear that nothing will stop Mrs. Gulch from impounding Toto, Aunt Em emotionally declares that she's been waiting for many years to tell how she really feels about Mrs. Gulch—but "being a Christian woman, I can't." In *A Nightmare on Elm Street* Nancy has a crucifix hung over her bed, which conspiciously fails to protect her from Freddy Kruger's nightly attacks. Christianity in these two films thus represents both the adult world's highest ideals and the *failure* of those ideals to save adolescents from the dangers that threaten them.

In evoking so powerfully a variety of common dream and nightmare sensations, the two films build upon qualities shared by all movies. Film critics have long recognized the dreamlike nature of watching movies. We sit relaxed and motionless in a quiet, darkened space and become immersed in a flow of narrative, allowing vibrant waves of sound and visual imagery to wash over us. In this sense, *every* film works to simulate the experience of dreaming; every film draws its power from its capacity to recreate the formal experiential qualities of a dream.

This is one reason why films have been used so frequently in experimental dream research. From the earliest days of sleep laboratory examinations of REM sleep, researchers have been using films to examine the impact of waking stimuli on dream content. A number of experiments have involved subjects watching films with especially strong emotional content (e.g., pornographic films, movies showing the autopsy of a human corpse). The subjects are then awakened during their REM sleep the next night to see what impact the films had on their dreams. The basic result of these studies is that material from the films does frequently become incorporated directly or indirectly into the subjects's dreams, although it remains unclear why some subjects have more film references in their dreams and other subjects less, and why some film images are incorporated directly into a person's dreams while other images are referred to more indirectly (Koulack 1991).

I know of no studies focusing on the impact of these two particular films on people's dreams. However, I would offer the following two speculations. The first is that *The Wizard of Oz* has been the primary source of the American people's fascination with the question of whether we dream in color or black-and-white. This is a question that I do not believe could have meaningfully arisen in a society in which people were not exposed to the modern technologies of photography and cinema. The second is that *A Nightmare on Elm Street* has helped to stimulate the capacity of American teenagers to experience lucid dreams (i.e., becoming conscious within the dream state that one is dreaming), beyond what most adults seem to have experienced in their lives. In this way I believe the film has had a huge influence on this particular generation's understanding of what dreams are and what is possible within them.

One of the biggest differences between films and dreams is that while dreams are purely private experiences, films are collective experiences. We have our dreams in the privacy of our own personal imaginations (setting aside, for this chapter's purposes, the interesting question of whether dreams can be *shared*), but we usually watch movies with groups of other people. This brings up another interesting feature of the two films under discussion, namely that both films have become the objects of what I would call "ritual viewing practices." For many decades, in the pre-VCR era, the annual showing of the *The Wizard of Oz* on network television was an eagerly anticipated family event. I myself still have glowing memories of getting settled on the couch with my parents and my sister and watching, for the umpteenth time, the wonderful adventures of Dorothy and Toto in the land of Oz. There are also ritual viewing practices associated with *A Nightmare on Elm Street* (and its half-dozen sequels), but they take a quite different form. This movie is very much a product of the VCR revolution in the viewing (and the production) of contemporary films. Produced with little money and less technical sophistication, *A Nightmare on Elm Street* had only a brief original run in theaters and it has of course never been shown on network TV. The film's spectacular success has depended almost entirely on the VCR rental market, and more specifically on the phenomenon of teenagers renting the movie for repeated, or perhaps "recurrent," viewings. I first learned about this from my brother Alex, who's twelve years younger than I am. He knows of my interest in dreams, and several years ago, when he was in his early teens, he said, "Kelly, you've got to check out the *Nightmare on Elm Street* movies, dude, they're *all* about dreams!" As I talked with Alex about the movies, I discovered that he and his friends had all seen them at least six or seven times each. The usual routine was for everyone to gather at someone's house on a Saturday night, turn out all the lights, and (with no grown-ups anywhere around) watch yet again Nancy's terrifying nightmare battles with Freddy Krueger.

I find one especially significant difference between the ritual viewing practices associated with these two films. The audiences for *The Wizard of Oz* tend to be intergenerational, that is, parents and children all watching together as a family. The audiences for *A Nightmare on Elm Street*, however, are usually composed of adolescents only, and primarily adolescent *boys*. I believe this difference in ritual viewing practices gives us some insight into the ultimate meaning of the dreams in *The Wizard of Oz* and *A Nightmare on Elm Street*.

At the most basic level, the dreams in both films are about the struggles of adolescents in American society: struggles that in our society are conceptualized as a transformation from childhood to adulthood, from dependence to independence, from innocence to sexuality, from a life of play to a life of work. The dreams in both films work to stimulate profound empathy for and identification with the fears and sufferings of adolescents as they go through this transformation. And the dreams in both films sharply criticize the failure of parents, and of the whole adult social order generally, to protect adolescents from evils, injustices, and threats to their budding sense of emotional and physical integrity.

The Wizard of Oz concludes on a note of stirring hopefulness and optimism. Dorothy ultimately survives her frightening trials in the land of Oz, and at the end of the movie returns, with a newfound sense of devotion and trustfulness, to her home and her family. This is a moral message that naturally makes the film appealing to family audiences. It's true that this message is clouded somewhat by the fact that Mrs. Gulch is probably still around and is thus likely to continue her vendetta against Toto (unless the tornado managed to get her—an appealing possibility, but we never hear one way or the other). And it's true that what I have called the film's second or covert moral message points Dorothy, and those in the audience, toward the enchanting reality of a very different kind of world. But in the end, the two messages work together to propel Dorothy (and the audience) back into waking life with renewed commitments to her community. Recalling that *The Wizard of Oz* was released in 1939, I think the film can be seen on one level as a response to the challenges facing adolescents of that particular historical period: overcoming the despair engendered by growing up during the Great Depression, resisting the temptations of escapist fantasizing, and finding the inner strength to confront the mounting danger to the American community posed by facism overseas.

So I would say the meaning of Dorothy's dream is this: always remember the beauty, the friendship, and the strength of purpose you experienced in Oz—never forget that. But now it's time to go back, rejoin your family, and do what you can to help them through their hard times.

The conclusion of *A Nightmare on Elm Street* is quite different. If *The Wizard of Oz* ends on a note of hope, *A Nightmare on Elm Street* ends with a mixed message at best. Yes, Nancy has defeated Freddy Krueger, and yes, she's back with her mother and father, in their nice suburban house with the white picket fence on Elm Street. But Freddy's not really gone. Everybody in the audience knows that Freddy is going to come back; it's simply the nature of recurrent nightmares, and of the low-budget horror movies patterned after them, that the evil fiend will come back. Thus, the reassurance that Nancy and we in the audience receive at the end of the movie is only temporary, only provisional. We've gotten a bit of a breather, but that's about it.

This moral message—that evil may be defeated, but it's going to come back—has a special resonance, I believe, for the adolescent boys that tend to be the film's primary audience. This is because they identify not simply with Nancy and her teenage friends, but with Freddy Krueger himself. For adolescent boys, Freddy expresses all the terribly urgent sexual desires they feel rising up within themselves. The *Nightmare on Elm Street* movies are brutally honest about how frightening these desires can be, stimulating fears and fantasies of violent fragmentation, death, and destruction. By watching these horrible movies again and again, in small, furtive, emphatically *non*-family gatherings, adolescent boys seem to find a measure of comfort in sharing their inner experiences of trying to come to terms with the Freddy Krueger within each of them.

The importance of this comfort should be evaluated in the context of the movie's distinctive historical period. In 1984, the year the original *Nightmare on Elm Street* movie was released, the U.S. economy was booming, Wall Street was awash in merger-and-acquisition money, the Pentagon was busily amassing stockpiles of bombs and missles to defend against the "Evil Empire" of the Soviet Union, and Ronald Reagan was gliding to a second presidential term on the reelection theme that "It's Morning in America." Culturally speaking, it was a time of vigorous masculine assertiveness, when vulnerability was scorned and raw power glorified. The challenges facing an adolescent boy growing up in such a culture are portrayed quite starkly in *A Nightmare on Elm Street*. The adults think everything is great, and they don't want to hear anything about being scared, feeling helpless, or worrying that there's something very frightening and very dangerous lurking in the shadowy night.

So the meaning of the nightmares of Nancy and her friends, in my view, is this: there is a real and terribly powerful force of evil haunting our world, but the grown-ups can't, or won't, acknowledge it. So adolescents have to join together, use their wits, and be prepared to face that evil when it comes again—for it will come again.

12

Dreams within Films, Films within Dreams

Two recent movies, though separated widely by geography, language, and temperament, share an unusual narrative framework that makes them particularly interesting to a discussion of the relationship between dreams and films. In both *Dreams* (directed by Karen Shakhnazarov and Alexander Borodyansky, 1993 [Russia]) and *Wes Craven's New Nightmare* (directed by Wes Craven, 1994 [United States]) a young heroine is suddenly, and frighteningly, unable to distinguish her dreams from her waking life. Both films also share the quality of making the audience feel just as disoriented as the young woman, through the cinematic technique of abruptly shifting between scenes appearing to portray dreams and scenes appearing to portray the waking lives of the characters. By skillfully intertwining the epistemological confusion experienced by the characters *and* by the audiences, the two films force us to reconsider our own conventional perceptions of reality. *Dreams* lays bare the grubby, Westernized decadence of post-Communist Russia, while *Wes Craven's New Nightmare* unmasks the horrors always lurking behind the white fences and green lawns of suburban America. In effect, these two films strive to reach into the dreaming imaginations of each individual audience member and to confront us with disturbing but important truths about the world of our collective waking life.

Dreams begins with images of paintings from tsarist-era Russia, showing us a series of beautiful, idyllic country landscapes. We then see a young countess named Masha Stepanova telling an elderly doctor of her troubling erotic dreams. Masha tells the doctor that she's been dreaming of the future, of 1993, and of working in a seedy Moscow canteen where the owner has been making passes at her. The prim doctor, flustered by Masha's forthright references to sexuality, tells her to ignore the dreams and just get some rest.

Next we see Masha, dressed as a waitress, asleep in the grimy kitchen of that 1993 canteen (the jerky motion of the camera throughout this scene seems intended to suggest that this is a "dream," in relation to the "waking" scene of Masha in the doctor's office). The canteen owner wakes her up and awkwardly asks if she'd like to go and watch a pornographic video with him. Masha brushes him off and goes out to clear the tables. At one counter stands a tall man in an overcoat, who slyly asks if Masha would like to star in a movie he's making. Intrigued, she listens to him describe the plot: it's about the August 1991 revolution, when the old-guard Communists had the democratic resistance surrounded at the Russian Parliament building, commonly known as the White House. In this proposed film, the resistance fighters know that the army is planning an attack, and they need a young woman to go out and seduce the army's top general into revealing the time of the attack. As the tall man in the overcoat spins out the tale, Masha is suddenly *in that film*; suddenly she's inside the general's tent, dressed in an absurdly seductive military outfit, with a low-cut jacket and extremely short skirt, and as the general lustfully embraces her Masha realizes he's the canteen owner.

Masha the tsarist-era countess abruptly wakes up, and her husband the count (who, we now see, is the same character as the tall man in the overcoat from the canteen) asks with deep concern if she's all right. When Masha tells him she had another strange dream, the count says he's going to take her on a vacation to their dacha in the Crimea, so she can rest her nerves.

If all this sounds hard for an audience to follow, it's supposed to be. As the film goes on, Masha's bizarrely tangled experiences become more and more ludicrous. In the next scene of her 1993 life, Masha is literally sold, with precious American dollars changing hands, by her hustler husband (once again the same character as the count) to two Russian government officials. The officials make her the country's new Minister of the Economy, so she can meet and seduce an emissary from the International Monetary Fund, and thereby persuade him to give Russia desperately needed hard currency. The scene suddenly changes again, and Masha is now part of a Western-style glam rock band, shaking her barely clad body to a pulsing electric beat while the big-haired lead singer (the count again) grunts out dirty, moronic lyrics. And *then* the scene shifts once more, and Masha finds herself a contestant in a garish "Best Bust Contest," in which the show's host (once again, the count) compliments Masha's brightly spotlit breasts for their superb patriotic service in representing the Russian nation. He asks the audience to bid for the privilege of kissing her bust, with the proceeds going to a Pentecostal Christian charity.

Thrown back into her tsarist-era life once again, Masha begs the incredulous count to believe that what she's been seeing in her dreams is *true*. But he just can't accept the idea that such a chaotic, corrupt, debauchery-filled culture—which she says is now called "CIS," although nobody knows what that means—could possibly lie in Russia's future. However, after a famous hypnotist examines Masha and concludes that she's neither ill nor insane, the count finally accepts that his wife is telling the truth about her dreams. Feeling it his duty as a Russian patriot, he goes to the tsar and makes an earnest report that warns of what the future holds for Russia and details the social and economic reforms that must be taken to avert such a catastrophe. The tsar doesn't listen to him, of course, and the count leaves the meeting in deep despair.

But when Masha hears what he's done, she is overjoyed. What matters to her is that he *believed* her. She leads him by the arm to a carriage, which carries them to their beautiful Crimean dacha.

At this point Masha the canteen waitress is jostled awake by the owner, who gruffly tells her it's closing time and they have to clean up. As she clears the greasy tables, the film's audience realizes that this is Masha's *real* reality; this plain, drab 1993 existence in the canteen is her true waking life. Back in the kitchen, the canteen owner awkwardly asks Masha if she would like to come with him to visit an old dacha he has bought out in the country. After a long pause, Masha says yes. The two of them drive together through the gray city, past the row after row of decrepit factories and run-down apartment buildings, to the dacha. It's immense, stately, and almost totally ruined. Thick weeds and mounds of rubble surround the burned-out, crumbling structure. As Masha and the canteen owner walk through the building he shyly tells her of his dreams of rebuilding it; he wants to fix the roof, repaint the walls, clear the grounds, restore its original furnishings. . . . As she listens to him, Masha wanders into what used to be a grand living room, and she sees on the floor an old, faded painting. It's a portrait of a countess. The face Masha sees is her own.

Dreams develops a wonderful set of parallels, contrasts, and mediations between Russian cultures of the late nineteenth and the late twentieth centuries. In a question-and-answer session after the showing I attended, one of the directors said the film "is dealing with present difficulties by making fun comparisons between the past and the present." The late nineteenth century in Russia was an era of glory, of sophistication, of elegance; the late twentieth, by contrast, is a time of poverty, shame, and tawdriness. But the film pointedly reminds us that the tsarist era suffered from a moral prudishness that severely inhibited free expression, especially regarding sexuality. The Russia of 1993, if nothing else, is wide open to sponteneity, bawdiness, and ribald comedy.

The key to the film is the concluding scene in which Masha, standing in the decrepit dacha, discovers the old portrait. Masha finds a lovely image of herself—an image of her deepest hopes, ideals, and dreams—lying neglected in those shabby ruins. This is a moment of intense mourning for that which she has lost, and for that which she will never have. But as Masha looks into the beautiful eyes of her own reflected face, that very experience becomes a source of renewed vitality and hope. The dacha is in terrible shape, but it *could* be repaired with enough hard work. The canteen owner is not particularly attractive, but he *is* nice and respectful to her, and he *does* have noble aspirations for the future. At the end of her long ordeal Masha has gained a deeper appreciation for her dreams and a clear-eyed understanding of her social reality. The achievement of this mournful integration breaks the spell of passivity that binds her throughout the film, freeing her to become the creator of her own future.

Like Masha, Heather Langenkamp, the heroine of *Wes Craven's New Nightmare*, finds herself thrown into an Alice-in-Wonderland world where the boundaries between dreams, films, and the waking world have abruptly disappeared. The movie begins with a film crew shooting a scene in which a new set of claws is forged for Freddy Kruger, the demonic villain who haunts teenagers' dreams in the *Nightmare on Elm Street* movies. Heather is the actress who played the character of Nancy in those movies, and she watches uneasily as the shooting of this new scene proceeds. Heather's husband is the special effects technician in charge of creating the new claws, and for a moment the filming stops so he can work with the crew to adjust the claws' razor-sharp blades. Suddenly the claws start moving by themselves. A second later they've gone wild, brutally slashing and killing two crew members; and now they're coming straight for Heather's husband, slicing his hand, as bright red blood spurts in the air—and then Heather wakes up, and is seized by a new surge of panic as her whole bedroom violently heaves, shakes, and crashes. It's the 1994 Northridge earthquake, and she and her husband stagger out of bed and careen through their wildly bucking house to reach the room of their young son, Dylan. The earthquake finally ends, and calm returns, but suddenly Heather gasps in horror. Her husband's hand is covered with blood, slashed open just like it was in her dream. She anxiously describes the dream to him, but he tells Heather not to worry, and explains that she was probably just half-awake when he cut himself on some glass. Dreams are like that, he reassures her. But then a sharp aftershock hits the house, and Heather watches four long cracks rip across the living room wall, exactly as if a huge claw were tearing its way into their home.

As the movie proceeds, Heather discovers that Freddy Kruger is indeed back, and that he is somehow reaching into the "real" world. She doesn't want to believe it, but when her son Dylan tells her that he's scared of the "mean old man with the claws" who threatens him in his dreams, and when he shows his mother the four vicious slashes that suddenly appeared in his stuffed dinosaur Rex one night, Heather realizes she has to do something. So she drives out to the Malibu mansion of Wes Craven, the creator of the *Nightmare on Elm Street* series (playing himself in this film), and asks him if by chance he's been having nightmares of Freddy. Yes he has, Craven replies, and now he's actually in the process of writing a new script—he has a dream, he writes a scene, he has another dream, he writes another scene. But Freddy's not *real*, Heather insists. Craven sits Heather down and tells her what he thinks is going on. Freddy is the latest incarnation of an ancient, evil entity which lives for the sole pleasure, Craven says, of "murdering innocence." That entity has gotten used to the Freddy form, and now it wants out of the films and into the waking world.

When Heather asks how they can stop Freddy, Craven says the only way to capture the entity is through stories. Stories can bind the evil and hold it, for a time, like a genie in a bottle. Heather suddenly realizes what she has to do to defeat Freddy and save her family—she has to play Nancy again, and make another *Nightmare on Elm Street* movie. She glances over at Craven's computer, and sees on the screen the last scene he has written for his new script—it's the exact conversation he and Heather have just had.

So filming of the new movie begins, and Heather, as Nancy, goes to war with Freddy. When Dylan abruptly falls into a mysterious coma and is taken to the hospital, Heather takes a deep breath and descends straight into Freddy's hellish nightmare kingdom to fight for the life of her son. The climactic battle between Heather and Freddy is, of course, extremely gory. Just as Freddy has Dylan in his grasp, pulling the screaming boy's head into his horrible, impossibly widened mouth, Heather plunges a butcher's knife "deep between Freddy's legs—her body blocking sight of exactly where, but we all get the idea. She shoves it hard and twists—as the howls of Freddy fill the world" (quoted from the October 26, 1993 version of Craven's screenplay, p. 98).

Freddy finally dies in a fiery, shrieking explosion, and Heather and Dylan tumble out of the boy's bed and collapse onto the toy-strewn floor of his room. Realizing that Freddy is gone for good, Heather hugs her son tightly. Then she sees lying next to them a finished script—the script of Craven's new movie. Is it a story?, Dylan asks. Yes, Heather answers, it's a story. Will you read me some? he says. Dylan snuggles up next to his mother as she opens to the first page and reads the scene about the film crew working on the new claws.

The tremendous popularity of the *Nightmare on Elm Street* movies derives from Wes Craven's brilliant ability to create a deep psychological bond between his characters and the audience. Heather's experiences with the nightmares, the earthquake, the cracks in the wall, the strange phone calls she receives, the bizarre television malfunctions that plague their home, all have apparently rational, non-mysterious explanations. Everyone reassures Heather that there's really nothing to worry about. But Heather *knows*, and the audience knows *with* her, that no matter what other people say, Freddy is back, and he's threatening her family. From that increasingly wide chasm between what society *says* and what Heather and the audience *know*, the fear intensifies to almost unbearable degrees, because now we're totally isolated, and totally vulnerable—the evil is really out there, and we're facing it all by ourselves.

The most interesting aspect of *Wes Craven's New Nightmare* is the way it reflects on the horror movie genre itself. As Craven says to Heather during their scene at his Malibu estate, horror movies serve as a means of evoking, and then containing (for a time), the violent, aggressive impulses that are seething just below the surface of contemporary American society. Throughout *Wes Craven's New Nightmare* Craven draws parallels between horror movies and fairy tales, and the comparison does indeed have merit. Both horror movies and fairy tales portray the experiences and perspectives of children, both have very spare, essentially mythological narrative themes, both are filled with blood, brutality, and violence, and both have moments of crude sexual humor. Heather's reading "Hansel and Gretel" to Dylan earlier in the film, and then reading the script to him at the end, makes this equation as plain as possible.

Craven is suggesting that just as in earlier times fairy tales served to address the psychological and spiritual needs of children (despite the persistent disapproval of moralizing adults), so today horror movies speak to those same needs felt by children in our society (despite the persistent disapproval of moralizing adults). Fairy tales and horror movies appeal so deeply to children precisely because adult rationality is ultimately incapable of helping kids in their struggles against the evils surging both in and around them.

Dreams and *Wes Craven's New Nightmare* build up multiple nestings of dreams, films, and waking realities that are every bit as complex as the mind-bending dream-within-dream plots of certain Indian myths (of the sort that Wendy Doniger O'Flaherty analyzes in *Dreams, Illusion, and Other Realities* [1984]). To summarize the two films, if that's possible:

> *Dreams* is a film about a 1993 canteen waitress named Masha Stepanova, who is dreaming of being a nineteenth-century countess, who is dreaming of being a 1993 canteen waitress, who is suddenly thrust into a ridiculous movie set during the 1991 revolution.

> *Wes Craven's New Nightmare* is a film about Heather Langenkamp, the actress from the "Nightmare on Elm Street" movies, dreaming of Freddy Kruger, the arch-villain from those movies, and having to act in a new film, and then descend through a dream into his cinematically created nightmare world, so she can save her son and stop Freddy from escaping out of the movie and into her waking world.

What are we, as the audience watching these films from the "outside," to make of all this? My own thoughts immediately turn to Freud's comment in *The Interpretation of Dreams* about dreams within dreams: "If a particular event is inserted into a dream as a dream by the dreamwork itself, this implies the most decided confirmation of the reality of the event—the strongest *affirmation* of it" (Freud 1965a, 374, emphasis in original). Freud is suggesting that a dream within a dream may be a uniquely direct and uncensored expression of the dreamer's deepest *reality*. Thus, Masha's film-within-a-dream-within-a-dream-within-a-film could be seen to reveal in comic, exaggerated, but painfully honest terms something that's *really happening* in contemporary Russia: a crass commercial exploitation of the nation's natural and cultural treasures. Heather's film within-a-dream-within-a-film may be showing us, amid all the blood-spattered mayhem, something that's *really happening* in contemporary America: a failure by adults to recognize that children desperately need help in dealing with an increasingly violent society.

I must admit that my feelings about these films are colored by the ways they have influenced my own dreams. The night after seeing *Dreams*, I dreamed I was in a film—it was a bad science-fiction movie, just like the 1950s cult classic *The Amazing Colossal Man*, which was one of my favorite movies as a boy. And the night after seeing *Wes Craven's New Nightmare*, I dreamed that Freddy Kruger was chasing after me and Heather, threatening my young son (who happens to be named, in waking life, Dylan). All of which leads me to ask a modern American variant of the ancient Hindu question: Could it be that I am just a character in some director's film?

13

Dreaming in Russia, August 1991

One of the primary themes woven throughout the chapters of this book regards a paradoxical quality at the very heart of dreaming. Dreams carry us deep *within* ourselves, into a realm of memory, feeling, and desire, at the same time as they lead us far *outside* ourselves, into realms of human community, the natural environment, and the Divine. It is out of the mysterious interplay between these centripetal and centrifugal forces in dreaming that people experience the various kinds of creative inspiration, psychological transformation, and religious revelation discussed in the preceding chapters. I would like to close the book with a personal story about how I gained a particularly deep insight into this central paradox of human dreaming experience.

Like many people, I don't really like plane flights, especially long ones. So when our Lufthansa DC-10 from Chicago finally landed in Frankfurt some ten hours after we had taken off, I felt just terrible. When I'm feeling that bad I tend to become very antisocial, so the last thing I wanted to do during our four-hour layover in Frankfurt was chit-chat with the group members whose flights had already arrived at the airport from other points of origin. I wandered around the terminal until I found a quiet, unpopulated waiting area where I could lie down and be miserable all by myself.

Our group was gathering here to take a chartered flight into the Soviet Union for the first conference on dream studies ever convened between Euro-American and Soviet researchers. "Dreaming in Russia," as the conference was titled, was organized by Robert Bosnak, a Jungian analyst from the Netherlands who now practices in the Boston area. Presentations were scheduled to be made by psychologist Robert van de Castle and anthropologists Barbara and Dennis Tedlock on the Euro-American side and by psychologist Alexander Asmolov, anthropologist

Levon Abrahamian, and literary scholar Yuri Karyakin on the Soviet side. I already knew several of the conference attendees, and I was eagerly looking forward to meeting the others. The week-long gathering promised to be a uniquely interesting and educational event, opening up all sorts of new perspectives on the study of dreams. And beyond the scholarly appeal of the conference, I was very curious to visit the Soviet Union itself—America's great enemy and antagonist, the other superpower competing with us for dominance on the world's stage. What, I wondered, are the people really like who live in the "Evil Empire"?

But for this moment, after many, many hours on a plane and with many more still to go, I didn't want to think or talk about any of that. We'll have a whole week, I reassured myself, to do nothing but relax and peaceably converse with each other.

Because I was lying semiconscious in a secluded little waiting area, I missed hearing the first rumors. "Something's wrong with Gorbachev; he's sick, he's been taken somewhere, the vice president is supposedly in control, it sounds really serious." This was the disturbing fragment of news that suddenly swept through the Frankfurt airport during our layover. When I finally returned to our gate a few minutes before our flight's scheduled departure, I found our group anxiously discussing whether or not we should continue on our journey. The consensus feeling was that we had all traveled awfully far to be turning around and going back home now; and really, there weren't any hard facts about what might be going on in the Soviet government, just a lot of guesses and speculations. When the Lufthansa customer-service agents announced that our flight was ready to board, we decided we might as well just go ahead, and see what happened.

Our flight from Frankfurt was uneventful, and we landed in Moscow on the afternoon of Monday, August 19, 1991. As we got off the plane, retrieved our luggage, and wearily made our way through customs, we began hearing more rumors. Ours was evidently one of the last flights allowed to land. Less than an hour ago the army had appeared at the airport and was in the process of closing it to all incoming and outgoing flights. Nobody knew what had happened to Mikhail Gorbachev, but dark suspicions were growing.

Outside the airport we boarded the two large buses that had been arranged for us and began the last leg of our trip, a forty-five-minute drive through the city to the town of Golitsyno, on the western outskirts of Moscow. It was raining heavily as we drove, and everything we saw—buildings, fields, cars, people—was wet and gray. A large number of military vehicles, including several monstrous tanks, rumbled heavily down the road opposite us, heading into the center of Moscow. It was hard to judge whether or not this was unusual, since few of us had ever been in the Soviet Union before, but we were already starting to imagine the worst.

We reached Golitsyno around 5:30 p.m., and were surprised and relieved by the clean, comfortable, well-tended accomodations. Our home for the next week was a small conference center for trade unions and academic organizations, with dorm-style rooms and numerous meeting halls and amphitheaters. The complex was surrounded by a dozen thickly wooded acres, criss-crossed by small walking paths. Far out among the tall, dark fir trees was a recreation cabin, with a dance floor and small bar, which the center's staff had christened "the Magic House."

We all took our bags to our rooms, ate supper, and then nervously gathered around a TV set in one of the lounges. The government had announced that an official statement on the unfolding political situation would be made this evening. When it began our chief translator for the conference repeated in English the news as it was broadcast, and our shock and amazement grew with every word. The newscaster began by saying Gorbachev was ill, and was being cared for at his dacha along the Crimean shore. We heard no more about him after that. A group of military officials was now in charge of the country, the newscaster continued, and the army had been mobilized to maintain public order. A "Committee on Martial Law" had been formed to take responsibility for insuring order and stability and for putting an end to the dangerous "weakness" and "decline" the nation had been suffering in recent times. Tanks were stationing themselves in Moscow to protect the people from any civil unrest. The TV then showed a brief film clip of Boris Yeltsin complaining about the martial law (our translator commented that this was done to prove that Yeltsin was still alive, and hadn't been physically removed as had the "ill" Gorbachev). The Committee on Martial Law concluded its statement by warning the rest of the world not to interfere in these "internal" Soviet developments.

Once the news broadcast ended and the enormity of what was happening sank in, we quietly discussed the practical question of what these stunning political events would mean for our conference. Karen Melik-Simonian, a Moscow psychologist who was the main conference organizer on the Soviet side, stood up and told us not to worry. He said that what we had just seen on TV was, in a way, "very beautiful" (a mysterious comment that I still don't quite understand). He emphasized that we were completely safe in Golitsyno and that these events would undoubtedly work themselves out. He added, however, that it was unlikely we would be able to communicate with our families outside the U.S.S.R. anytime soon.

With that, we returned to our rooms, and for the first time in many, many hours, we slept.

❀

Tuesday was scheduled to be a rest day, with the conference program beginning Wednesday. So on Tuesday morning we ate a late breakfast, climbed aboard our buses, and drove through the cold, steady rain for a sight-seeing trip to the famous Russian Orthodox monastery at Zwinigorod. During the bus ride one of our translators filled us in on the latest news about the coup (which she and her friends had gleaned by listening to BBC radio broadcasts). She said hundreds of tanks and several batallions of armed troops had taken up positions on the streets of Moscow. The members of the Committee on Martial Law were, in most people's view, the worst, most brutal officials of the whole Soviet government. Gorbachev was certainly not ill but had simply been imprisoned, and perhaps murdered, by the military. Yeltsin was already the leading voice of resistance to the coup, and he had called a meeting of the Supreme Soviet of Russia for Wednesday to formulate a response to the situation.

The Zwinigorod monastery was beautiful, despite the dark clouds and the chilling rains beating down upon us. The copper-plated towers with their distinctive bulb shapes glowed luminously against the gray, gloomy skies. Inside the small, thickly walled chambers was displayed the monastery's supreme treasure: a collection of lovingly painted icons, many portraying the great saints of the Church's history, and others showing figures and scenes from the Bible. Gazing at a radiant image of Mary with the infant Jesus, I couldn't help but admire the tremendously deep roots of Russia's religious faith. The monastery was almost five hundred years old, and there was an atmosphere of stubborn determination to it, a proud defiance toward the Soviet government, toward the outside world, toward time itself.

Back at the conference center on Tuesday evening we watched the TV newsbroadcast again, and learned that an 11 p.m. to 5 a.m. curfew had been imposed on Moscow. A series of gray-clad military officials appeared on the screen, each of them instructing the people to be calm, to obey the martial law decrees, and to ignore the treacherous complaints of violence-minded resisters.

After the news was over, the conference organizers informed us that the U.S. Embassy had issued a travel advisory suggesting that visitors within the Soviet Union "consider changing their plans" for departure. Unfortunately, it appeared the earliest possible time we could get on a flight out of the country would be Friday, three days from now. And there was still no way to call our families, whom we could only imagine were terribly concerned about our safety. After some discussion we decided to go on with the conference and do as much work as we could before leaving on Friday. Karen Melik-Simonian concluded our meeting by saying that we should all stay put at the conference center in Golitsyno, and under no circumstances go into Moscow. The situation was quite unpredictable, he said, as the tensions between the military and the resistance were intensifying by the minute.

A common trait I've noticed among people who study dreams is a visceral discomfort with conventional authority. For many of us, being told *not* to do something often becomes an immediate and irresible motivation to go ahead and *do* it. At breakfast Wednesday morning a group of us discovered that we all shared an overwhelming urge to go to Moscow—none of us could bear the idea of sitting passively in a conference center while something truly amazing was unfolding only a few miles away. So we quietly went back to our rooms, grabbed our raincoats and umbrellas, counted our rubles, checked our maps and passports, and hurried out to the Golitsyno train station, making sure to leave without letting any of the conference organizers see us.

There were eight of us making the journey into the city: four Americans, three Lithuanians, and a Dutch woman. We got to the train station in Moscow with no problems, and we then took a series of subways to Red Square. At many of the subway stations small crowds of people clustered around handbills posted on the walls. The Lithuanians (who, fortunately for the rest of us, were fluent in Russian) told us that these were notices put up by the resistance movement to provide people with information on the coup. Since the TV and newspapers had been seized by the military, the people had no other source of reliable information. I was startled when, in the process of taking a picture of a crowd reading these handbills, my camera's flash sent everyone suddenly hustling away. I belatedly realized that no one wanted to be photographed reading "unpatriotic" material.

The city's streets seemed fairly empty, although because of the cold, never-ending rain or the heavily armed troops we couldn't tell. Only a few businesses and shops were open, but there weren't many customers. Several major avenues were blocked off by troops and defensively positioned lines of tanks and armored personnel carriers (APCs). Now we began to see some large crowds of people, quietly milling about the military vehicles, talking with the troops. I was struck by the intimacy of the interactions between the soldiers and the people. The people were sharing food and cigarettes with the troops, putting flowers on the tanks, and calmly discussing with the soldiers their feelings about the national crisis.

We kept walking, and at one point we met a tight line of APCs that was blocking off a large intersection near Red Square (this evidently would have been a likely spot for antimilitary demonstrations). At first we thought we would have to turn back and walk around the block, but one of our Lithuanian friends somehow convinced the leader of the troops to let us through the APC barrier and over to the other side. As a group of soldiers, Kalashnikov rifles in hand, escorted us in single file across the big, empty intersection, the bizarre feeling came over me that this was a kind of hallowed realm, with the eerie electrical charge of a ritual circle. The ring of dark green army vehicles surrounding us all had their gun barrels pointed outward; there was no sound within except for the soft splashing of our shoes walking across the wet pavement. For a few strange moments we were inside whatever space it was they were guarding the people *against*. I felt intensely uncomfortable there, although I'm still not sure exactly why. When we finally reached the other side of the intersection, squeezed between the APCs, walked through the line of troops, and reentered the "normal" space of the city's streets, I was deeply relieved to be back among the warm crowd of soggy Muscovites.

We walked as close to Red Square as we could, marvelling at the dramatic scene before us: the stunningly beautiful towers of St. Basil's in the background, the ominous blockade of tanks and APCs in the foreground. By this time it was after 2 p.m., and we were all quite hungry, so we found a little canteen and bought ourselves some lunch. As we ate we decided to try to reach the U.S. Embassy so the Euro-Americans among us could try to send messages to our families, and perhaps get some new information on the crisis. The Lithuanians knew it was useless to seek any reliable news about what was happening in their homeland, which had been a reluctant member of the Soviet Union since its violent annexation at the end of World War II. They were extremely worried, though, because just a few years earlier a group of Lithuanian political leaders had organized a move toward greater independence, and the Red Army had come to swiftly and brutally reimpose Soviet control over their resistant subjects.

We rode the subway again, and when we left the station and started walking toward the American Embassy we saw a big commotion ahead of us. A huge crowd of people had gathered around a cluster of mangled, burned-out city buses. From what our Lithuanian friends could gather, the resistance forces had been using the buses as a barricade against the military; but that night tanks had come and smashed through the buses, killing a number of people in the process. We could see the crowd circling around a couple of particular spots on the street. I went toward one of these spots, and found it to be a spontaneously created shrine, with icons, prayer candles, and a growing pile of fresh flowers. This, evidently, was the place where one of the people had been killed by the tanks. As we moved along, a Lithuanian friend pointed to other places along the street where the pavement was all chewed and broken up. You can see that the tanks have been here, she said.

We continued on toward the Embassy, very alarmed by what we had just seen. This was no longer just a rocky transfer of political power; the military had actually killed protestors, and now a strong resistance movement was clearly building up. More violence seemed inevitable. We reached the Embassy (itself protected by hastily erected walls of cement blocks), where the staff members informed us that the travel advisory had been upgraded: we were now urged to "seriously consider leaving the country" as soon as we could. The staff members took our messages for our families, gave us what information they had (most of it garnered from watching CNN broadcasts), and let us use the bathroom. Our business finished, we left, more worried than ever.

The Russian Parliament building, commonly known as the White House, was just down the hill from the embassy. We had heard that the resistance forces were gathering there to protect Boris Yeltsin and the other Russian national leaders inside the building. As we walked toward the White House we heard a rumor sweep through the crowds and up the hill toward and then past us—"Yanayev has been arrested!" people cried out happily. The arrest of Yanayev, the Soviet vice president whom the Committee on Martial Law had placed in Gorbachev's office, was apparently good news to the resistance. But we were baffled. *Who* had arrested him? How could he be "arrested?" What did it mean that he had been arrested? This strange rumor only made it more obvious to us how completely everything was in flux, how all ordinary authority structures had vanished.

The White House was surrounded by huge piles of steel pipes and wood planks, strategically placed clusters of overturned trucks, and more people than I've ever seen in one place in my life. The Russian national flag was everywhere, flying from flagpoles, pinned to lapels, and draping the podium where resistance leaders had come outside to give fiery, defiant speeches to the ever-growing crowd.

Suddenly, for the first time all day, our little group felt threatened. Throughout the day the eight of us had maintained a strong sense of group unity; each of us had continuously stayed aware of where the other seven were. But now, with torrents of people rushing in to help defend the White House barricades, we were having trouble staying together as a group. We also sensed that if there was going to be further violence, it would likely happen here—the resistance forces were making their stand at this place, and we had just seen evidence that the military was willing to kill to enforce its authority. We decided it was time for us to leave.

And then, in the brief time it took our train to carry us from Moscow back to Golitsyno, it was all over.

We reached the conference center and found everyone around the TV again. This time they were listening to reports of how the tanks and troops were *leaving* the city, and how people were literally dancing in the streets, celebrating the shocking victory of the resistance. It turned out that the Red Army soldiers had refused their orders to storm the White House, and some military units had actually turned around and defended the building against attack. The members of the Committee on Martial Law were reportedly fleeing to Siberia, pursued by anticoup air force jets. The same reporters who the previous two nights had spoken of Boris Yeltsin's "inflammatory" words against the Committee on Martial Law were now praising his heroism in defeating the attempted coup.

Despite the tremendously positive turn of events and the relieved jubilation of everyone at the conference, I somehow felt more disoriented than ever. We left Moscow at the darkest moment of the crisis, having seen the intimidating display of military force, the places where people had been killed, and the courageous but desperate people at the White House barricades; then, we arrived at Golitsyno and discovered that the crisis was over, the darkness had passed, and everything was back to normal. It had all happened *so fast* . . .

Not knowing what sense to make of these strange feelings, I tried to put them out of my mind, and I joined with our group in celebrating the resistance' victory. The conference program had begun at last, meaning that the coming days would be filled with fascinating lectures, workshops, and discussion groups. I turned my energies toward the exciting conversations about current dream research that, I reminded myself, were my primary business in Russia.

That night I had the following dream:

> I'm back at Stanford. . . . Dad drives me and some others. . . . He drives kind of spastically, over easy roads; he almost hits curbs. . . . I get out of the car, and look around to find a catalog, and time schedule. . . . I'm very excited to be back in school.

What first struck me about the dream when I woke up was my dad's almost hitting the curbs. It immediately reminded me of the tanks in Moscow having broken up the street curbs in the process of killing the protesters. The feeling of elation at being back at school reminded me of the excitement I felt as the conference started, and the excitement all the local people felt as the coup was defeated. The dream was clearly relating the current political transformations with elements of my personal life, although in a way I didn't immediately understand.

The next afternoon I had a long talk with Armenian anthropologist and political activist Levon Abrahamian, who had presented a paper at the conference interpreting Soviet history as a symbolic interplay of father-son conflicts (i.e., Stalin acting as a brutal father figure, Kruschev a buffoonish son, Brezhnev a "false" father, and Gorbachev a mischievous trickster). Our conversation led me to think about my dream as a kind of cultural commentary. In the dream my father drives me around, in control but not in control—endangering me and others with his spastic driving, just as the Soviet military was endangering the people with its spastic grab for power, its tanks clumsily hitting and breaking up the curbs. When I get out of Dad's car, suddenly I'm elated, with the world opened up before me; I can take any class I want, the future is full of possibilities. Likewise, the Russian people had suddenly liberated themselves from the domineering control of the Soviet military, and they could now create their own future, their own world. While I, and they, need some *new* structures to replace the old ones (e.g., the catalog and time schedule), the primary feeling is one of joy and exhilaration.

When I reflected on the dream in this way, I came to believe that at one level the dream was helping me understand that strange, isolating sense of disorientation I felt upon returning from Moscow. The dream seemed to bridge the fear to the elation, helping me integrate the intense yet radically disjointed emotions I had experienced in the past seventy-two hours. If I followed Levon's image of a son's struggle to develop a mature relationship with his father, I could use my own personal experiences with my father to gain at least some insight into the incredible political events swirling about me.

Dreams always bear many gifts, however. As I pursued these reflections I realized that the dream was doing more than interpreting current political events for me. I began to sense that the dream was also suggesting hidden potentials in my future, and perhaps in Russia's future as well. The key fact here is that my father went to college at Stanford, too, and like me he found his time there to be a wonderous, magical period of new possibilities. Despite our many differences and conflicts, he and I nevertheless share a treasured experience of seemingly infinite freedom (what historian of religions Mircea Eliade would call an experience "*in illo tempore*," "in the time of origins"). I thought of how my father and I could perhaps develop a better relationship if we drew more directly on that shared experience, if we talked about the dreams and ideals we formed for ourselves during those enchanting college years.

I also thought of Levon's comments about the patricidal character of the victory celebrations in Moscow following the coup's defeat. Statues of Soviet leaders were being violently torn down, and streets and squares were being hastily renamed, their old Soviet names erased. The Communist Party had already been officially banned. Certainly, when fathers are tyrants, sons must overthrow them. But if the sons forget that even tyrannical fathers once had dreams for the future, and if the sons cast aside those dreams as forcefully as they break free from their shackles, might not the newly liberated sons become tyrannical fathers themselves?

As the end of the conference approached, I started thinking about going back into Moscow one last time. Ever since Wednesday I had been haunted by the image of that broken pavement where the tanks had killed the protesters. I realized that I very much wanted to go there, to *be* at that place now that the crisis had ended. So on Monday, August 26 I left Golitsyno as early as I could and took the long train ride into Moscow. Using the large white balloon flying high above the Russian Parliament building as my beacon, I found my way back to the U.S. Embassy. Then I walked a few blocks down the street, and I was there again.

The spontaneous shrines to the victims of the tanks had grown tremendously in the past few days. Piles of beautiful fresh flowers lay everywhere. At the end of the street, near where the buses had been crushed, a few small fires burned, evidently as part of a continual vigil of mourning. The Russian Orthodox imagery was powerful—crucifixes, images of Jesus and Mary, candles, prayer beads, all emphasizing the martyrdom of the three men who had died there. I saw many adults who had brought their children to the shrines, to see and remember what had happened. I moved slowly through the quiet, reflective crowd, and came to that one place with the broken pavement.

Suddenly, something very unexpected happened. I began to cry. I sat down on the curb, ran my hand over the mangled concrete, and cried.

After a time I stood up and walked slowly over to the main shrine, above which rose a large wooden cross carefully inscribed with the date "8–21–91." People were coming up to the cross and laying down various gifts and offerings—more flowers, icons, food, even money. I wanted to leave an offering, too, but as I patted my pockets I discovered I didn't have anything special with me. Then I realized no, I do have something to offer. I took my green pen from my shirt pocket and laid it down in front of the cross. I said a silent prayer, vowing that my response, my way of honoring the people who had died at this place, would be to write.

Postscript on Dreams, Religion, and Psychological Studies

At the 1997 meeting of the American Academy of Religion a panel discussion was held on "The Future of Religion and Psychological Studies," with the aim of examining the questions of where this field (commonly known as RPS) has come from and where its future may lie. In his introductory comments William Parsons identified six different historical approaches to the field. The first approach, best represented by William James (1958), is the psychology of religion, in which a particular religious phenomenon (such as conversion) is analyzed and explained according to a particular psychological theory. The second approach, typified by the work of Don Browning (1987), is the psychology-theology dialogue, in which the resources of theology are brought into critical conversation with modern cultural voices in art, philosophy, and politics. The third approach, exemplified by Peter Homans (1989), focuses on the intersection of religion and social science, and investigates the complex, multidimensional interactions between individual psychology and broader social structures. The fourth approach, well represented by the work of Diane Jonte-Pace (1993, 1997), takes current thinking about gender and applies it both to the traditional subjects of RPS and to the epistemological bases underlying RPS inquiry itself. The fifth approach, as found in the writings of Sudhir Kakar (1982), is a comparativist one, in which non-Western theories, views, and experiences are brought into the conversation about the relationship between religion and psychology. And the sixth approach, illustrated by M. Scott Peck (1998), develops psychology into a new kind of religion, a religion that while not organized into formal churches or creeds is nevertheless able to address the spiritual yearnings of many people in contemporary society.

129

Visions of the Night does not advocate any one of these views of the RPS field. Rather, I hope that the book illustrates how all of these approaches can provide interesting and fruitful views of the nature, functions, and meanings of dreaming. There are certainly many aspects in the preceding chapters of the psychology of religion and the psychology-theology dialogue, and I have tried to follow the methodological guidance of these two approaches even as I have worked to move beyond the limitations often associated with them (i.e., the problems of psychological reductionism with the former and Protestant exclusivism with the latter). Although I draw less directly on the religion and social science and the gender studies approaches, I believe many elements in this book contribute to the research agendas of those RPS scholars (e.g., with the discussions of the impact of totalitarianism on dreaming in chapter 6 and of the prominent role of women in community dream-sharing groups in chapter 4). I definitely strive to adopt a broadly comparativist approach throughout the book, particularly in the first three chapters, and I make several comments in various chapters about the religious dimensions of contemporary psychological theories about dreaming.

During the panel discussion at the American Academy of Religion meeting, Parsons claimed that "RPS is the most liminal and creative field in religious studies." I hope this book substantiates and justifies his claim by showing that (1) dreaming is the experiential source of many important beliefs (e.g., regarding the nature of the soul, the afterlife, the sacred, morality) and practices (e.g., initiation, healing, mysticism, mourning, artistic creativity) found in the world's religious and spiritual traditions, and (2) the process of sharing and reflecting on dreams with other people is a powerful means of deepening our appreciation of both the common humanity that binds us all and the distinctive qualities that constitute our unique individuality.

Bibliographical Essays

Note: The literature on dreams is so voluminous and continues to grow so rapidly that any bibliography is doomed to be both incomplete and almost immediately outdated. However, having said that, I offer the following annotated survey of the field of dream literature as an aid to readers who want basic information about the current status of dream research literature. These are what I and many others in the field consider to be the most useful books and articles on the study of dreams, organized into several categories.

Freud and Psychoanalysis

Freud's psychological theories are intimately intertwined with his personal life, meaning that any serious attempt to study the former requires attention to the latter. Although Freud relates incidents from his personal life throughout his writings (most revealingly in *The Interpretation of Dreams* [Freud 1965a]), he never wrote a formal autobiography. However, a number of well-researched biographies have been written about Freud. The first was by one of Freud's closest colleagues, the English psychoanalyst Ernest Jones. Jones's three-volume *The Life and Work of Sigmund Freud* (Jones 1953–57) is the basic text on Freud's life. Although Jones paints what later biographers have argued is an excessively favorable and worshipful portrait of Freud, his work remains invaluable for the study of how Freud's life and work interacted.

Two of the best biographies on Freud written after Jones's work are R. W. Clark's *Freud: The Man and the Cause* (Clark 1980) and P. Gay's *Freud: A Life for Our Time* (Gay 1988). Both take a more balanced view of Freud than is found in Jones's book. Clark and Gay examine in some detail Freud's ambivalent feelings about his Jewish heritage, his mixed record in curing his patients, and his political struggles with "defectors" from the psychoanalytic movement.

Valuable biographical information on Freud can be found in two collections of his letters. *The Complete Letters of Sigmund Freud to Wilhelm*

Fliess, 1887–1904 (Masson 1985) presents the correspondence of Freud to his close friend and confidant Wilhelm Fliess. These letters give important insights on the development of Freud's thinking as he began writing *The Interpretation of Dreams*. *The Freud/Jung Letters: The Correspondence between Sigmund Freud and C. G. Jung* (McGuire 1974) gathers the more than 350 letters that Freud and Jung wrote to each other beginning in 1906. The letters chronicle in rich detail the intense friendship, and then the bitter estrangement, of these two psychological pioneers.

Other biographical works focus on particular aspects of Freud's life. H. Ellenberger's excellent *The Discovery of the Unconscious* (Ellenberger 1970) frames Freud's life and work in the broader history of the rise of dynamic psychiatry. Ellenberger's book also includes chapters on the roots of dynamic psychiatry in eighteenth- and nineteenth-century natural philosophy, as well as on the life and work of P. Janet, A. Adler, and C. G. Jung. H. Decker's *Freud, Dora, and Vienna 1900* (Decker 1991) looks at Freud's famous treatment of Dora (Freud 1963a) in the context of the cultural ferment in turn-of-the-century Vienna. P. McCaffrey's *Freud and Dora: The Artful Dream* (McCaffrey 1984) also examines the personal relationship between Freud and his teenage patient as it plays out in his interpretation of Dora's two dreams. K. Frieden's *Freud's Dream of Interpretation* (Frieden 1990) details the connections between Freud's psychoanalytic theory of dream interpretation and the traditional views toward dreams found in classic Jewish religious texts. D. Bakan's *Sigmund Freud and the Jewish Mystical Tradition* (Bakan 1958) also reveals the surprisingly close relations between Freud's psychoanalytic theories and certain trends in Jewish mysticism.

A fascinating book in this area is A. Grinstein's *Sigmund Freud's Dreams* (Grinstein 1980). Grinstein has collected all of the personal dreams of Freud that were reported in his published writings, and gives them as thorough a psychoanalytic interpretation as is possible given the limitations of historical hindsight. One of Grinstein's most interesting findings is that Freud rarely interpreted his own dreams according to the psychoanalytic rules and principles he recommended in his theoretical writings.

Perhaps the most ambitious attempt to understand the life and work of Freud is P. Homan's *The Ability to Mourn: Disillusionment and the Social Origins of Psychoanalysis* (Homans 1989). Homans develops a highly sophisticated sociological approach to the origins of psychoanalysis, arguing that the emergence of Freud's theories can only be understood in the broader historical context of the decline of organized religion in Western culture. *The Ability to Mourn* is in my view the best book available on the personal, cultural, and historical matrix out of which Freud's revolutionary psychological theories emerged.

Freud's principal work on dreams is, of course, *The Interpretation of Dreams* (Freud 1965a). The most commonly used English translation of this work is by J. Strachy; an earlier translation by A. A. Brill is no longer considered adequate. Freud wrote the very brief book *On Dreams* (Freud 1980) a year or so after finishing *The Interpretation of Dreams*. Although everything Freud says in *On Dreams* is consistent with what he presents in *The Interpretation of Dreams*, the former work has none of the rich detail, the sophisticated argumentation, or the sweeping theoretical speculation of the latter. Although it has the virtue of brevity, *On Dreams* should not be taken by anyone, general readers or academic specialists, as a viable substitute for *The Interpretation of Dreams*.

Freud devoted several other major writings to the subject of dreams. As already mentioned, one of the most important of these writings is his case study of a patient named Ida Brauer, whom he called "Dora" in his *Dora: Fragment of an Analysis of a Case of Hysteria* (Freud 1963a). Freud treated Dora in the fall of 1900, just a few months after the publication of *The Interpretation of Dreams*. The core of his treatment of Dora was his interpretation of two of her dreams, which he describes in the book. In his *Introductory Lectures on Psychoanalysis* (Freud 1966), given in 1916–17, Freud devotes a number of lectures to explaining the basic features of his theory of dreams. Two briefer works, "Remarks upon the Theory and Practice of Dream Interpretation" (Freud 1963b) and "Some Additional Notes on Dream Interpretation as a Whole" (Freud 1963c), offer further interesting material on Freud's approach to dreams.

Along with these works, Freud discusses dreams throughout his writings, and readers intent on making a focused study of Freud's dream theory should refer to the twenty-four-volume *Standard Edition of the Complete Psychological Works of Sigmund Freud* (Freud 1953–74).

Virtually everything written on dreams since Freud has been influenced by his theories, making it difficult to identify works that are specifically "psychoanalytic" from those that are not. However, two edited anthologies have been published recently that gather the most important articles written on psychoanalytic dream theory since Freud. The first is *Dream Reader: Psychoanalytic Articles on Dreams* (Alston, Calogeras, and Deserno 1993), and it includes articles on typical and traumatic dreams, transference, manifest content, communicative functions, children's dreams, and symbolization. The second is *Essential Papers on Dreams* (Lansky 1992), and in addition to an excerpt from Freud's lecture on "Revision of the Theory of Dreams" in his *New Introductory Lectures on*

Psychoanalysis (Freud 1965b) it includes articles on synthesis and adaptation, self psychology, trauma and pathology, and current experimental research on psychoanalytic dream theory. Of the two anthologies, Lansky's *Essential Papers on Dreams* is the more useful because it presents significant works from some of the major figures in psychoanalytic psychology—Bertram Lewin, Erik Erikson, Erika Fromm and Thomas French, Hanna Segal, John Mack, Ernest Hartmann, Charles Fisher, J. Allan Hobson—addressing various aspects of psychoanalytic dream theory.

Freud's influence on modern dream psychology is impossible to overestimate. Echoes of his psychoanalytic theories about dreams can be found in almost every article and book of twentieth-century dream research. Unfortunately, many of these articles and books argue against Freud's dream theories even as they assume the truth of much of what Freud said about dreams. Readers who want to study the ongoing influence of Freud on the field of modern dream psychology are thus advised to look not only at what later dream researchers *say* about Freud, but also at what they *do* with Freud's basic theories.

Jung and Analytic Psychology

Like Freud, Jung's psychological theories were closely connected with his personal life experiences. But unlike Freud, Jung spoke openly and at length about these connections. His autobiography, *Memories, Dreams, Reflections* (Jung 1965), is thus the primary reference source for any study of Jung's life and work.

Other biographers have filled out Jung's self-portrait with additional material on his life. In *Jung and the Story of Our Time* (Van der Post 1975) L. Van der Post describes in warm and admiring terms his friendship with Jung and the impact of Jung's thought on modern society. From a much more critical perspective, P. J. Stern's *C. G. Jung: The Haunted Prophet* (Stern 1976) details the more problematic aspects of Jung's life—his political battles with Freud, his sexual infidelities, his political flirtation with the National Socialist movement in Germany in the early 1930s. In a similarly critical vein, R. Noll's *The Jung Cult: Origins of a Charismatic Movement* (Noll 1994) argues that Jung created a quasi-religious cult that rejected egalitarian Christian values for elitist pagan ones. Other notable works include G. Wehr's *Jung: A Biography* (Wehr 1987) and F. McLynn's *Carl Gustav Jung: A Biography* (McLynn 1996).

The most balanced treatment of Jung's life and work is P. Homans's *Jung in Context: Modernity and the Making of a Psychology* (Homans 1979). Homans carefully analyzes the genesis of Jung's psychology in the stern Christian upbringing of his childhood, in his bitterly personal struggles with Freud, and in the general historical decline of religion's influence in modern Western culture. Homans also discusses Jung and his relationship with Freud in *The Ability to Mourn: Disillusionment and the Social Origins of Psychoanalysis* (Homans 1989). Fascinating insights can be gained into Jung's relationship with Freud from the book *The Freud/Jung Letters: The Correspondence between Sigmund Freud and C. G. Jung* (McGuire 1974).

Jung's own dreams heavily influenced his psychological theories about dreams. This makes his autobiography, *Memories, Dreams, Reflections*, all the more important to anyone wanting to understand his views on the nature of dreams. In this work Jung describes dreams that haunted him as a child, dreams that came during his tension-filled relationship with Freud, dreams that gave him practical insights on the treatment of patients, and dreams that directly shaped key features of his psychological theories.

Even more than Freud did, Jung discussed dreams in almost everything he wrote. Readers should thus consult *The Collected Works of C. G. Jung* (Jung 1967) at the beginning of any research project on his dream theories. However, the editors of *The Collected Works* have made the task of researchers much easier by compiling some of Jung's most important works on dreams in a single paperback volume titled *Dreams* (Jung 1974). The volume begins with "The Analysis of Dreams" and "On the Significance of Number Dreams," both of which Jung wrote while still deeply involved with Freud and the psychoanalytic movement. Next come "General Aspects of Dream Psychology," "On the Nature of Dreams," and "The Practical Use of Dream-Analysis." These three excellent articles are among the clearest, most concise statements Jung ever made regarding his theory of dreams. The last article in the book is "Individual Dream Symbolism in Relation to Alchemy," a detailed examination of a series of dreams from one of Jung's patients. This particular work is a good introduction to Jung's thinking about alchemy, mandala symbolism, and the individuation process.

For a less formal, more conversational introduction to Jung's dream theories, readers may consult *Dream Analysis: C. J. Jung Seminars, Vol. 1* (Jung 1984). This book contains transcripts of seminars Jung gave to analytic psychology trainees on the theory and practice of clinical dream interpretation.

Given Jung's great interest in dreams, it comes as no surprise that many of his followers have written books and articles on the subject. What follows is only a selection of the most important and most influential publications on dreams to emerge from the school of analytical psychology.

James Hillman's *The Dream and the Underworld* (Hillman 1979) argues that people should not try to bring their dreams "up" into the waking world of consciousness—rather, Hillman says we should try to bring waking consciousness *down* into the "underworld" of the unconscious as revealed to us in our dreams. His book is one of the few that can rival Jung's work for erudition and scholarship. Marie-Louise Von Franz has written two strong books on dreams: *On Dreams and Death* (Von Franz 1986) and *Dreams* (1991). In the first she explores the archetypal symbolism of death as manifested in people's dreams, while in the second she offers historical analyses of the dreams of Jung, Socrates, Themistocles, Hannibal, Descartes, and the mothers of Saint Augustine, Saint Bernard of Clairvaux, and Saint Dominic. J. Layard's *The Lady of the Hare: A Study in the Healing Power of Dreams* (Layard 1988) recounts Layard's therapeutic work with a woman whose dreams prominently featured hares; Layard gives extensive archetypal interpretations of what these hares symbolized in the woman's dreams. R. Bosnak has written *A Little Course in Dreams* (Bosnak 1988), a brief primer on his Jungian approach to dreams; *Dreaming with an AIDS Patient* (Bosnak 1989), a moving account of the dreams of a gay man dying of AIDS; and *Tracks in the Wilderness of Dreaming* (Bosnak 1996), in which he describes what he learned about dreams from an Australian Aboriginal spirit doctor. M. O. Hill's *Dreaming the End of the World* (Hill 1994) presents dozens of dreams with apocalyptic imagery, which Hill interprets as symbolic rites of passage. R. Hopcke looks at Jungian dream theory as applied to issues of masculinity in *Men's Dreams, Men's Healing* (Hopcke 1990). A. Stevens draws on Jung to provide a sweeping overview of human dreaming experience in his book *Private Myths* (Stevens 1995). The relevance of analytical psychology to issues of race and ethnicity is the subject of M. V. Adams's fascinating work *The Multicultural Imagination: "Race," Color, and the Unconscious* (Adams 1996).

General introductions to Jungian dream theory and practice can be found in M. A. Mattoon's *Understanding Dreams* (Mattoon 1978), J. A. Hall's *Jungian Dream Interpretation* (Hall 1983), E. C. Whitmont and S. B. Perera's *Dreams, A Portal to the Source* (Whitmont and Perera 1989), and the anthology edited by N. Schwartz-Salant and M. Stein titled *Dreams in Analysis* (Schwartz-Salant and Stein 1990).

A good place to start studying contemporary trends in analytical psychology is A. Samuels's *Jung and the Post-Jungians* (Samuels 1985). Samuels divides the post-Jungians into three schools: the developmental school, the classical school, and the archetypal school. One chapter of the book is devoted to the debates among the three post-Jungian schools about Jung's dream theory.

Many books have been written on the connection between Jungian and religious or spiritual approaches to dreams. Among the best of these books are M. Kelsey's *Dreams: A Way to Listen to God* (Kelsey 1978) and *God, Dreams, and Revelation: A Christian Interpretation of Dreams* (Kelsey 1991), J. A. Sanford's *Dreams: God's Forgotten Language* (Sanford 1982), P. O'Connor's *Dreams and the Search for Meaning* (O'Connor 1987), L. M. Savary, P. H. Berne, and S. K. Williams's *Dreams and Spiritual Growth: A Christian Approach to Dreamwork* (Savary, Berne, and Williams 1984), P. H. Berne and L. M. Savary's *Dream Symbol Work* (Berne and Savary 1991), J. D. Clift and W. B. Clift's *Symbols of Transformation in Dreams* (Clift and Clift 1986) and *The Hero Journey in Dreams* (Clift and Clift 1991), and J. A. Hall's *The Unconscious Christian Images of God in Dreams* (Hall 1993).

Alternative Clinical Theories about Dreams

The following citations should give readers a general overview of the various alternative clinical theories about dreams that have arisen after Freud and Jung. Works by single authors, or devoted to a single alternative approach, are described first, followed by anthologies presenting a variety of approaches.

L. Ansbacher and R. R. Ansbacher have done dream researchers a great service by compiling and editing the writings of Alfred Adler into a single volume: *The Individual Psychology of Alfred Adler* (Adler 1956). The book provides a systematic exposition of Adler's major ideas and theories, including a chapter on his basic views about dreams. Excellent material on Adler's life and work can also be found in H. Ellenberger's *The Discovery of the Unconscious* (Ellenberger 1970).

The dream theory of existential psychologist Medard Boss is best expressed in his book *The Analysis of Dreams* (Boss 1958). His other major work on dreams is *I Dreamt Last Night...* (Boss 1977). A number of other important works on dreams from an existentialist perspective deserve mention: L. Binswanger's *Being-in-the-World* (Binswanger 1967), which includes a number of comments about dreams from his philosophical and psychological perspective; M. Foucault's *Dream, Imagination, and Existence* (Foucault 1993), one of the first published writings by the famous postmodern historian; and C. Moustakas's *Existential Psychotherapy and the Interpretation of Dreams* (Moustakas 1994), a detailed account of how dreams are used in existential psychotherapy.

T. French and E. Fromm's *Dream Interpretation: A New Approach* (French and Fromm 1964) lays out an ego psychological approach to the use of dreams in clinical contexts. E. Erikson's earlier paper "The Dream Specimen of Psychoanalysis" (Erikson 1954), a fascinating re-interpretation of Freud's dream of Irma's injection in chapter 2 of *The Interpretation of Dreams*, is similar to French and Fromm's work in look-ing to dreams for evidence of the ego's struggles to gain mastery over internal conflicts and external challenges. R. M. Jones's *Ego Synthesis in Dreams* (Jones 1962) is an underappreciated contribution to the ego psychological approach to dream interpretation. E. Hartmann's *Dreams and Nightmares: The New Theory on the Origin and Meaning of Dreams* (Hartmann 1998) is a remarkably ambitious attempt to explain dream-ing in terms of "boundaries of the mind."

Gestalt Therapy Now (Fagan and Shepherd 1970) gathers the works of a number of Gestalt therapists who describe their methods and techniques. The book includes a lengthy transcript of one of F. Perl's dream seminars. A. Faraday's two books *Dream Power* (Faraday 1972) and *The Dream Game* (Faraday 1974) include good, simple intro-ductions to the Gestalt style of dreamwork, as does J. J. Downing's *Dreams and Nightmares: A Book of Gestalt Therapy Sessions* (1973).

Among the other early alternative responses to Freud's and Jung's dream theories are S. Lowy's *Psychological and Biological Foundations of Dream-Interpretation* (1942), W. Stekel's *The Interpretation of Dreams* (1943), and E. Fromm's *The Forgotten Language* (1951). Lowy and Stekel draw on their extensive clinical experiences to offer alternative views on dream symbolism and the role of dreams in therapy, while Fromm reexamines the universal symbolic language found in dreams as well as in fairy tales and myths. W. Bonime's *The Clinical Use of Dreams* (Bonime 1988), first published in 1962, served as a key instructional text in the training of a whole generation of clinicians. Its combination of a nondogmatic psychoanalytic perspective with an open-minded ap-preciation for the cultural influences on personality development have made Bonime's book an enduring resource for clinical psychologists working with dreams.

More recent alternative clinical approaches are C. E. Hill's *Working with Dreams in Psychotherapy* (Hill 1996), C. Rycroft's *The Innocence of Dreams* (1979) and E. B. Bynum's *Families and the Interpretation of Dreams* (1993). Hill presents a remarkably clear and straightforward ap-proach to the practical use of dream interpretation in psychotherapy. Ry-croft relies on contemporary developments in literary theory to make a compelling argument that dreams are a natural expression of the creative imagination. Bynum combines family systems therapy with African healing traditions to shed new light on the "intimate web" of family dream life.

Two clinicians who have focused on the relationship between dreams and the body are E. Gendlin, in *Let Your Body Interpret Your Dreams* (Gendlin 1986), and A. Mindell, in *Dreambody* (Mindell 1982) and *Working with the Dream Body* (Mindell 1985). Both Gendlin and Mindell argue that most psychological approaches to dreams remain "up in the head"; they argue that dreams offer a powerful means to help people reconnect with the bodily basis of consciousness, health, and healing.

A number of extremely valuable anthologies have been published that bring together many of the leading clinical approaches to dreams. *Dream Interpretation: A Comparative Study* (Fosshage and Loew 1978) takes one woman's dream and interprets it according to six different clinical approaches: Freudian, Jungian, culturalist, object relational, phenomenological, and Gestalt. R. M. Jones's *The New Psychology of Dreaming* (Jones 1978) explores the impact of sleep laboratory research and new interpretive approaches on traditional Freudian dream theory. The book remains one of the best brief introductions to the field. S. Krippner's anthology *Dreamtime and Dreamwork* (Krippner 1990) has a useful section on "Dreams in Therapy and Healing" in which leading practitioners describe Freudian, Jungian, existential, and body-oriented methods of dreamwork. *Dreamtime and Dreamwork* also includes sections on dreams in creativity and education, women, sex, and dreams, cross-cultural dream research, and new frontiers in dreamwork. G. Delaney's *New Directions in Dream Interpretation* (Delaney 1993) collects articles on various approaches to the clinical use and interpretation of dreams. And D. Barrett's *Trauma and Dreams* (Barrett 1996) brings together many of the leading dream psychologists to discuss the value of dreamwork in the clinical treatment of people suffering from various forms of trauma. B. Wolman's *Handbook of Dreams: Research, Theories, and Applications* (Wolman 1979), though now hard to find, is a solid introduction to the different schools of modern psychological dream interpretation.

One of the best sourcebooks for studying alternative clinical approaches to dreams is A. Shafton's *Dream Reader* (Shafton 1995). The book is a vast exposition and synthesis of contemporary dream theories and practices; it is extremely well researched, meticulously documented, and filled with interesting and thought-provoking critical commentary.

Sleep Laboratory Research on REM Sleep and Dreaming

The two papers that initiated the study of REM sleep and dreaming are by E. Aserinsky and N. Kleitman: "Regularly Occurring Periods of Eye Motility, and Concomitant Phenomena, during Sleep" (Aserinsky and Kleitman 1953) and "Two Types of Ocular Motility Occurring in Sleep" (Aserinsky and Kleitman 1955). All subsequent sleep laboratory research on REM sleep and dreaming takes its point of departure from these two articles.

Of the hundreds of highly technical articles written since Aserinsky and Kleitman's original work, a handful stand out as especially important for the understanding of how REM sleep, NREM (non-REM) sleep, and dreaming are related to each other. D. Foulkes's "Dream Reports from Different Stages of Sleep" (Foulkes 1962) made it clear that dreams could not be exclusively identified with REM sleep. Foulkes showed that mental experiences with significant amounts of imagery and emotional content occur in both REM and NREM stages of sleep. A. Rechtschaffen's "The Single-Mindedness and Isolation of Dreams" (Rechtschaffen 1978) argued that the principal characteristic of REM dreams is their "single-mindedness and isolation," distinguishing dreaming consciousness from the more complex forms of self-awareness found in waking consciousness. F. Crick and G. Mitchison's "The Function of Dream Sleep" (Crick and Mitchison 1983) made the controversial claim that REM sleep serves a "reverse learning" function in the brain, which suggests that dreams should not be remembered because doing so might inadvertently retain precisely those parasitic modes of mental activity that REM sleep is trying to eliminate. And R. Cartwright's "Broken Dreams: A Study of the Effects of Divorce and Depression on Dream Content" (Cartwright et al. 1984) provided a model investigation of the connections between sleep physiology, dream content, and the clinical diagnosis and treatment of psychological disturbance.

For readers new to the dream studies field, the best place to start learning about sleep laboratory research on dreams is with books rather than articles. Journal articles by sleep lab researchers generally report to a specialized audience the findings of a particular, often very technical research project. By their very nature, these articles are narrowly focused both in their language and their content. Books, however, give researchers the opportunity to discuss the overall significance of their findings in terms that both specialists and nonspecialists can understand.

A number of excellent books have been written by pioneering sleep lab researchers who explain their basic findings to general audiences. W. Dement's two books *Some Must Watch While Some Must Sleep* (Dement 1972) and *The Sleep Watchers* (Dement 1992) are very accessible introductions to sleep and dream research in the laboratory, written by the person who coined the term "rapid eye movement" or REM sleep. R. Cartwright has written two good introductory texts on sleep-laboratory research. *Night Life* (Cartwright 1979) and *Crisis Dreaming* (Cartwright and Lamberg 1992) both chronicle her long career as a leading scholar in the field, explaining her findings on the dream lives of people who have suffered various psychological crises and traumas. J. A. Hobson's *The Dreaming Brain* (Hobson 1988) is perhaps the most important single book to come out of the area of sleep-laboratory research on dreaming. The first sections of *The Dreaming Brain* give a fascinating historical account of pre-Freudian research on sleep and dreams. In the remainder of the book Hobson elaborates on a theory that he and his colleague R. McCarley first presented in their article "The Brain as a Dream-State Generator: An Activation-Synthesis Hypothesis of the Dream Process" (Hobson and McCarley 1977). For an outstanding collection of articles that discuss and expand upon Hobson and McCarley's Activation-Synthesis hypothesis, readers should look to the special issue of the journal *Consciousness and Cognition,* titled "Dream Consciousness: A Neurocognitive Approach" (Baars and Banks 1994).

Other good books on sleep laboratory research on dreams include the anthology edited by J. Gackenbach, *Sleep and Dreams* (Gackenbach 1987), the anthology edited by S. Ellman, *The Mind in Sleep: Psychology and Psychophysiology* (Ellman 1991), W. Moorcroft's *Sleep, Dreaming, and Sleep Disorders* (Moorcroft 1993), and the anthology edited by A. Moffitt, M. Kramer, and R. Hoffmann, *The Functions of Dreaming* (Moffitt, Kramer, and Hoffman 1993). Each of these works is aimed more at professional researchers than at general audiences, presenting the results of specialized studies and debating the finer points of current knowledge about REM sleep, NREM sleep, and dreaming. Of this group of works, *The Functions of Dreaming* has the virtue of combining high-quality scholarship with a very broad and inclusive understanding of how to investigate the functions of dreaming. Although not an introductory text, it does represent the best picture available of the current state of sleep-laboratory research on dreaming.

Dreaming and Cognition

Much of modern dream research has focused on the question of how the cognitive operations at work in dreaming relate to the operations of the mind during wakefulness. Both Freud (Freud 1965a) and Jung (Jung 1974) speak at length about what their depth psychological studies of dreaming reveal about the nature of the human mind. A number of scholars from the field of sleep-laboratory research have argued that their findings give valuable insights on the relations between the mind and the body (e.g., Hobson 1988, many of the contributors to Moffitt, Kramer, and Hoffmann 1993).

J. Piaget's landmark study of the development of dreaming in childhood, *Play, Dreams, and Imitation in Childhood* (Piaget 1962) showed that experimental psychology could make important contributions to the study of dreaming and cognition that went beyond what clinical psychologists and sleep-laboratory researchers were offering. Among the experimental psychologists who followed Piaget's lead, the most influential figures in the study of dreaming and cognition are D. Foulkes and C. Hall. Foulkes has written three major books: *A Grammar of Dreams* (Foulkes 1978b), *Children's Dreams* (Foulkes 1982), and *Dreaming: A Cognitive-Psychological Analysis* (Foulkes 1985). In each of these books Foulkes draws on his carefully conducted research to argue that dreaming is produced by the same basic cognitive operations that produce waking thought. Hall has also written a number of books: *The Meaning of Dreams* (Hall 1966), *The Content Analysis of Dreams* (Hall and Van de Castle 1966), and *The Individual and His Dreams* (Hall and Nordby 1972). The primary argument Hall develops in all of these books is that dreaming life is continuous with waking life—in their dreams people encounter the same basic settings and people, feel the same basic emotions, and act in the same basic ways as they do in their waking lives.

Some psychologists have looked to computer analogies to help explain the cognitive processes involved in dreaming. Crick and Mitchison's article "The Function of Dream Sleep" (Crick and Mitchison 1983) considers dreaming as comparable to the self-cleaning programs found in many advanced computer systems. S. R. Palombo's book *Dreaming and Memory* (Palombo 1978) makes the most detailed and sophisticated argument for looking at dreaming as a kind of computer-like information processing operation within the mind. C. Evans's *Landscapes of the Night* (Evans 1983) uses this same general computer analogy, but explains it in less technical language than does Palombo.

Two academic journals have devoted special issues to issues relating to dreaming and cognitive psychology. *The Journal of Mind and Behavior* had a special issue on "Cognitive Psychology and Dream Research" (Haskell 1986) with an outstanding collection of articles by H. Fiss, J. S. Antrobus, H. Hunt, F. Crick and G. Mitchison, S. LaBerge, J. Gackenbach, R. Cartwright, M. Ullman, and S. Krippner among others. A special issue of the journal *Consciousness and Cognition*, "Dream Consciousness: A Neurocognitive Approach" (Baars and Banks 1994) gathered articles discussing and expanding on the Activation-Synthesis hypothesis of J. A. Hobson and R. McCarley.

Other experimental psychologists look to literary studies of metaphor and symbolism for insights into the nature of dreaming cognition. H. Hunt's book *The Multiplicity of Dreams* (Hunt 1989) argues that many, many different cognitive operations are at work in dreams. Hunt claims that these operations range from the formal grammatical processes that structure our language to the more emotion-laden imagistic processes that generate novel metaphors and symbols: the various types of dreams people experience reflect, Hunt says, the various possible combinations of these different cognitive operations. G. Globus's *Dream Life, Wake Life* (Globus 1987) is another excellent (though dense) work that uses both psychological and literary-philosophical resources to explore the mental mechanisms responsible for producing the often stunningly creative narratives and images of our dreams. And D. Kuiken has written a number of first-rate articles that examine the emotional and metaphorical bases of dreaming: "Impactful Dreams and Metaphor Generation" (Kuiken and Smith 1991), "The Impact of Dreams on Waking Thoughts and Feelings" (Kuiken and Sikora in Moffitt, Kramer, and Hoffmann 1993), "Dreams and Feeling Realization" (Kuiken 1995).

Another researcher who has devoted careful and sophisticated study to the question of dreaming and cognition is T. Kahan. The particular focus of her research has been on issues of metacognition, that is, one's understanding and awareness of one's own cognitive processes. She has presented the findings of her research in a series of articles, including "Similarities and Differences between Dreaming and Waking Cognition: An Exploratory Study" (Kahan et al. 1997), "Cognition and Metacognition in Dreaming and Waking: Comparisons of First and Third-Person Ratings" (Kahan and LaBerge 1996), "Measuring Dream Self-Reflectiveness: A Comparison of Two Approaches" (Kahan 1994), and "Lucid Dreaming as Metacognition: Implications for Cognitive Science" (Kahan and LaBerge 1994).

A number of scholars from outside the field of psychology have made valuable contributions to psychological knowledge about dreaming and cognition. Linguistic philosopher G. Lakoff's article "How Metaphor Structures Dreams: The Theory of Conceptual Metaphor Applied to Dream Analysis" (Lakoff 1993) brings current philosophical thinking about metaphor generation to the psychological question of how dreams are formed. B. O. States has written two major books, *The Rhetoric of Dreams* (States 1988) and *Dreaming and Storytelling* (States 1993), that explore in great detail the areas of overlap between dream psychology and literary theory on this issue of how the mind creates the imagery, the narratives, and the emotional experiences of dreams. Historian of religion W. D. O'Flaherty's *Dreams, Illusion, and Other Realities* (O'Flaherty 1984) sets modern psychological studies of dreams and the mind in a broader context, comparing Western scientific answers to the answers provided in classic Indian myths and sacred texts. Many anthropologists have made arguments similar to O'Flaherty's, juxtaposing the psychological theories of Freud, Jung, and others to the theories of various non-Western cultures. The best starting point here is the anthology edited by B. Tedlock, *Dreaming: Anthropological and Psychological Interpretations* (Tedlock 1987).

Content Analysis

The content analysis method has become one of the most widely practiced approaches to the systematic study of dreams. It involves the careful analysis of dream reports into different categories (the five major categories are setting, characters, emotions, activities, and objects); each dream is scored in terms of these categories, and its scores are then compared to the scores of other dreams from the same dreamer or to the scores of dreams from other groups of people. This allows researchers to gain a more precise view of the patterns of dream content across a series of dreams from one individual and among various groups of people.

The content analysis method was first developed by C. Hall and R. Van de Castle in their book *The Content Analysis of Dreams* (Hall and Van de Castle 1966). In addition to describing the method's scoring techniques, Hall and Van de Castle offer the results of their study of five hundred dream reports from one hundred European-American female college students and five hundred dream reports from one hundred European-American male students, all between the ages of eighteen and twenty-five. The dream content frequencies derived from this study have become the "norms" by which other content analysis studies are evaluated.

Hall published two major books that summarized and explained to general audiences the principal findings of his research: *The Meaning of Dreams* (Hall 1966), first published in 1953 and then revised and expanded in 1966, and *The Individual and His Dreams* (Hall and Nordby 1972). Hall also coauthored the books *Dreams, Life, and Literature: A Study of Franz Kafka* (Hall and Lind 1970) and *The Personality of a Child Molester: An Analysis of Dreams* (Bell and Hall 1971), and wrote with G. W. Domhoff the article "The Dreams of Freud and Jung" (Hall and Domhoff 1968).

R. Van de Castle's book *Our Dreaming Mind* (Van de Castle 1994) offers an accessible introduction to the techniques and findings of the content analysis method by one of its founders. The most comprehensive statement and defense of the content analysis method comes from G. W. Domhoff in *Finding Meaning in Dreams: A Quantitative Approach* (Domhoff 1996). Domhoff surveys all the published works using the content analysis method, describes several unpublished studies by Hall and others, and provides a beginner's manual for learning how to perform a content analysis study. Anyone interested in what content analysis is, what it has discovered, and how to do it oneself, should read Domhoff's outstanding book before looking at anything else.

A number of articles have used the content analysis method to examine various populations of college students. Among these are P. Stairs and K. Blick's "A Survey of Emotional Content of Dreams Recalled by College Students" (Stairs and Blick 1979), V. Tonay's "California Women and Their Dreams: A Historical and Sub-Cultural Comparison of Dream Content" (Tonay 1990–91), C. Kane and colleagues's "Differences in the Manifest Dream Content of Mexican-American and Anglo-American Women: A Research Note" (Kane et al. 1993), and L. Dudley and J. Fungaroli's "The Dreams of Students in a Women's College: Are They Different?" (Dudley and Fungaroli 1987). Other articles have performed content analysis studies to examine the dream content patterns of different age groups. These include H. Zepelin's "Age Differences in Dreams: I. Men's Dreams and Thematic Apperceptive Fantasy" (Zepelin 1980–81) and "Age Differences in Dreams: II. Distortion and Other Variables" (Zepelin 1981), C. Brenneis's "Developmental Aspects of Aging in Women: A Comparative Study of Dreams" (Brenneis 1975), and C. Hall and G. W. Domhoff's "Aggression in Dreams" (Hall and Domhoff 1963b) and "Friendliness in Dreams" (Hall and Domhoff 1964).

An extensive literature has developed around the application of the content analysis method to the dreams of people living in cultures outside the United States. Among the best of these articles are D. Waterman, M. De Jong, and R. Magdelijns's study of dreams in the Netherlands, "Gender, Sex Role Orientation and Dream Content" (Waterman, De Jong, and Magdelijns 1988), M. Lortie-Lussier's two studies of dreams and gender in Canada, "Working Mothers versus Homemakers: Do Dreams Reflect the Changing Roles of Women?" (Lortie-Lussier et al. 1985) and "Beyond Sex Differences: Family and Occupational Roles' Impact on Women's and Men's Dreams" (Lortie-Lussier et al. 1992), S. P. Urbina and A. Grey's study of dreams in Peru, "Cultural and Sex Differences in the Sex Distribution of Dream Characters" (Urbina and Grey 1975), A. Grey and D. Kalsched's study of dreams in

India, "Oedipus East and West: An Exploration Via Manifest Dream Content" (Grey and Kalsched 1971), T. Yamanaka, Y. Morita, and J. Matsumoto's report on dreams in Japan, "Analysis of the Dream Contents in Japanese College Students by REM-Awakening Technique" (Yamanaka, Morita, and Matsumoto 1982), and T. Gregor's study of dreams among the Mehinaku people of the Brazilian rain forest, "A Content Analysis of Mehinaku Dreams" (Gregor 1981b).

Nightmares

Both Freud and Jung devote considerable attention to explaining nightmares. Freud said that most nightmares were the result of repressed unconscious wishes breaking through the deceptive dream façade created by the censor, thus generating the intense fear so common in nightmares. He also said that some nightmares were the fulfillment of masochistic wishes (Freud 1965a). In his later writings Freud revised his view of nightmares slightly, allowing that frightening dreams that vividly replay traumatic experiences are expressing wishes from the ego (rather than from the id) to master the trauma (Freud 1965b). Jung, by contrast, said that nightmares were the result of consciousness becoming unbalanced and one-sided; when consciousness fails to recognize and integrate important elements of the unconscious, those elements are forced to demand the attention of consciousness by means of frightening nightmares (Jung 1974).

E. Jones's book *On the Nightmare* (Jones 1951) is an explanation and elaboration of Freud's view of nightmares. Jones combines clinical case studies with folklore, mythology, and historical data to argue that the creatures so prevalent in nightmares—vampires, werewolves, witches, and so forth—symbolize the repressed sexual wishes found in all people. Another book on nightmares in the psychoanalytic tradition is J. Mack's *Nightmares and Human Conflict* (Mack 1970). Though not as stridently Freudian as Jones is, Mack follows the same path of examining nightmares as expressions of basic human conflicts that usually remain deeply repressed in the unconscious.

The study of nightmares changed significantly with the publication of E. Hartmann's *The Nightmare: The Psychology and Biology of Terrifying Dreams* (Hartmann 1984). Hartmann brought clinical and historical material together with the latest findings of the sleep laboratory to give a remarkably detailed portrait of what different forms nightmares take, what conditions give rise to them, and who is most likely to suffer from them. He offers the notion of "boundaries of the mind" to explain why some people (those with "thin boundaries") suffer frequent nightmares while others have few or none (those with "thick boundaries"). Hartmann has expanded on this notion in his book *Boundaries of the Mind* (Hartmann 1991a). Many other researchers have followed Hartmann's lead in exploring the relationship between nightmares and boundaries of the mind. Two of the better articles are Levin, Galin, and Zywiak's "Nightmares, Boundaries, and Creativity" (Levin, Galin, and Zywiak 1991) and C. Bearden's "The Nightmare: Biological and Psychological Origins" (Bearden 1994).

Other researchers have focused on the relationship between nightmares and trauma. W. H. R. Rivers drew upon the dreams of World War I veterans in his book *Conflict and Dream* (Rivers 1923). M. Cuddy and K. Belicki have done extensive research on the nightmares of victims of physical and sexual abuse, which they report in "Nightmare Frequency and Related Sleep Disturbance as Indicators of a History of Sexual Abuse" (Cuddy and Belicki 1992) and "The 55–Year Secret: Using Nightmares to Facilitate Psychotherapy in a Case of Childhood Sexual Abuse" (Cuddy and Belicki 1996). Similar research is described by B. Krakow and his colleagues in "Nightmares and Sleep Disturbance in Sexually Assaulted Women" (Krakow et al. 1995). Krakow and J. Neidhardt's *Conquering Bad Dreams and Nightmares* (Krakow and Neidhardt 1992) is a book aimed at introducing general readers to some basic information about nightmares. Krakow and Neidhardt summarize current research findings and outline a self-help program to help people suffering from highly disturbing dreams. H. Kellerman's anthology *The Nightmare: Psychological and Biological Foundations* (Kellerman 1987) offers an excellent compendium of research, clinical data, and theoretical reflections on the phenomenon of nightmares.

The major work on the relation of dreams to trauma is D. Barrett's *Trauma and Dreams* (1996). In this anthology Barrett collects several fascinating articles by E. Hartmann, A. Siegel, J. King, R. J. Lifton, O. Sacks, R. Bosnak, P. Garfield, A. Zadra, K. Belicki, and M. Cuddy among others. Barrett's work will likely be the standard reference for many years to come for clinicians and researchers interested in the dreaming-trauma connection.

An alternative understanding of nightmares is posited by M. Kramer in "The Nightmare: A Failure in Dream Function" (Kramer 1991). Kramer argues that nightmares occur when the dreamer is suddenly incapable of integrating the emotional surge that regularly accompanies REM sleep; it is not the specific content that produces the nightmare, but what Kramer calls the "hyperresponsiveness" of the dreamer under the distinct emotional conditions created by REM sleep.

Posttraumatic stress nightmares can occur after any severe trauma (e.g., wartime combat, physical or sexual abuse, an auto accident, a natural disaster) and may persist for a long time after the trauma. These nightmares are distinguished from other types by their vivid, graphic reproductions of the trauma. Hartmann's *The Nightmare* (Hartmann 1984), Cartwright and Lamberg's *Crisis Dreaming* (Cartwright and Lamberg 1992), and Krakow and Neidhardt's *Conquering Bad Dreams and Nightmares* (Krakow and Neidhardt 1992) all offer clear information on what psychological researchers have learned about posttraumatic stress nightmares and what clinicians and psychotherapists have found most effective in treating victims of severe traumas who are suffering from such nightmares. Other valuable works on posttraumatic stress nightmares are H. A. Wilmer's "Vietnam and Madness: Dreams of Schizophrenic Veterans" (Wilmer 1982), "Combat Nightmares: Toward a Therapy of Violence" (Wilmer 1986a), and "The Healing Nightmare: A Study of the War Dreams of Vietnam Combat Veterans" (Wilmer 1986b), S. S. Brockway's "Group Treatment of Combat Nightmares in Post-Traumatic Stress Disorder" (Brockway 1987), and M. R. Lansky and C. R. Bley's "Exploration of Nightmares in Hospital Treatment of Borderline Patients" (Lansky and Bley 1990).

Children's Dreams

Although Freud, Jung, and many other clinical psychologists mention children's dreams, no one made this subject the focus of sustained, high-quality research until cognitive psychologist J. Piaget wrote *Play, Dreams, and Imitation in Childhood* (Piaget 1962). Piaget's careful observations, his familiarity with both Freudian and Jungian theory, and his masterly understanding of cognitive development all combine to make this book a landmark in the study of the form and content of children's dreams.

D. Foulkes greatly expanded the scope of Piaget's work by using sleep laboratory technology to aid in the investigation of children's dreaming. His *Children's Dreams: Longitudinal Studies* (Foulkes 1982a) is an outstanding work that traces the development of dreaming from its first appearance among preschool children all the way through to adolescence. Foulkes thoroughly documents his long-term sleep laboratory research on children's dreams, and this makes his book difficult for nonspecialists. But patient readers who want to know more about this subject will find *Children's Dreams* to be an invaluable resource.

Foulkes has also authored a number of articles and book chapters that provide briefer accounts of his research on children's dreams. These include "Dreams of a Male Child: Four Case Studies" (Foulkes 1967), "Longitudinal Studies of Dreams in Children" (Foulkes 1971), "Dreams of Innocence" (Foulkes 1978a), "Children's Dreams" (Foulkes 1979), and "Two Studies of Childhood Dreaming" (Foulkes et al. 1969).

Many content analysis studies of dreams include data on the dreams of children and adolescents. As part of a developmental study of characters, aggressions, and friendliness, C. Hall and G. W. Domhoff gathered and analyzed 217 dream reports from 119 boys and 274 reports from 133 girls in the two to twelve age range. Their results were published in "A Ubiquitous Sex Difference in Dreams" (Hall and Domhoff 1963a), "Aggression in Dreams" (Hall and Domhoff 1963b), and "Friendliness in Dreams" (Hall and Domhoff 1964). Domhoff summarizes and expands on the findings of these content analysis studies in his book *Finding Meaning in Dreams: A Quantitative Approach* (Domhoff 1996). R. Van de Castle also has a section on children's dreams in *Our Dreaming Mind* (Van de Castle 1994).

Freud's major comments on children's dreams come in chapter 3 of *The Interpretation of Dreams* (Freud 1965a), in which he says that children's dreams are relatively simpler and less disguised than are the dreams of adults. The wishes expressed in children's dreams are transparent, which in theoretical terms demonstrates the fundamentally wish-fulfilling function of all dreams. For the more practical purposes of clinical psychology, this means that children's dreams can be valuable aids in the therapeutic treatment of children with any number of emotional troubles.

Many psychoanalysts and psychoanalytically oriented psychotherapists have followed Freud's practical insights and examined the role of dreams in therapy with children. Among the best of these studies are S. Catalano's *Children's Dreams in Clinical Practice* (Catalano 1990), D. Gensler's "Soliciting Dreams in Child Psychotherapy: The Influence of the Therapist's Interest" (Gensler 1994), C. Medici de Steiner's "Children and Their Dreams" (Medici de Steiner 1993), S. Roll and L. Millen's "The Friend as Represented in the Dreams of Late Adolescents: Friendship without Rose-Colored Glasses" (Roll and Millen 1979), L. M. Jokipaltio's "Dreams in Child Psychoanalysis" (Jokipaltio 1982), M. Harley's "The Role of the Dream in the Analysis of a Latency Child" (Harley 1962), R. Ekstein's "Some Thoughts Concerning the Clinical Use of Children's Dreams" (Ekstein 1981), N. N. Root's "Some Remarks on Anxiety Dreams in Latency and Adolescence" (Root 1962), S. Spiegel's "An Alternative to Dream Interpretation with Children"

(Spiegel 1994), D. G. Singer and M. L. Lenahan's "Imagination Content in Dreams of Deaf Children" (Singer and Lenahan 1976), A. Samuels and M. Taylor's "Children's Ability to Distinguish Fantasy Events from Real-Life Events" (Samuels and Taylor 1994), and S. L. Ablon and J. E. Mack's "Children's Dreams Reconsidered" (Ablon and Mack 1980).

Several good popular psychology books have been written about children's dreams. P. Garfield's *Your Child's Dreams* (Garfield 1985) summarizes the findings of Piaget, Foulkes, Hall and Domhoff, and other psychologists and combines their research with her own studies of the dreams of children from the United States and from other countries. D. Beaudet's *Encountering the Monster: Pathways in Children's Dreams* (Beaudet 1990) is an excellent study of the dreams of a small group of five- to seven-year-old schoolchildren that she worked with in a Canadian classroom. For a number of weeks Beaudet asked the children to share their dreams with her and to draw pictures of them. Her book examines the recurring motif of monsters in the children's dreams, and draws on Jungian psychology to understand the unfolding imaginal lives of these children as revealed in their monster dreams. A. S. Wiseman's *Nightmare Help* (Wiseman 1986) is presented in a coloring book format as a way of encouraging children to use artistic media like drawing and painting to express and understand their dreams. A. Siegel and K. Bulkeley's *Dreamcatching: Every Parents Guide to Understanding and Exploring Children's Dreams and Nightmares* (Siegel and Bulkeley 1998) offers a guide to parents interested in stimulating the creative energies that emerge through children's dreams.

Like Beaudet's book, F. Wickes's *The Inner World of Childhood: A Study in Analytical Psychology* (Wickes 1988) takes a Jungian approach to children's dreams. Wickes's work has chapters on dreams, imaginary friends, early relationships, and many other facets of childhood experience that reveal the first upsurges of archetypal material from the collective unconscious into the child's maturing consciousness.

Some anthropological studies of dreams include fascinating material on children's dreams in other cultures. Among these studies are R. A. Shweder and R. A. Levine's "Dream Concepts of Hausa Children: A Critique of the 'Doctrine of Invariant Sequence'" (Shweder and Levine 1975), K. Stewart's "Dream Theory in Malaya" (Stewart 1969), G. Straker's "Integrating African and Western Healing Practices in South Africa" (Straker 1994), and a number of the articles in B. Tedlock's anthology *Dreaming: Anthropological and Psychological Interpretations* (Tedlock 1987) and in M. C. Jedrej and R. Shaw's anthology *Dreaming, Religion, and Society in Africa* (Jedrej and Shaw 1992). J. Levine's article

"The Role of Culture in the Representation of Conflict in Dreams: A Comparison of Bedouin, Irish, and Israeli Children" (Levine 1991) is an extremely interesting analysis of the influence of culture on both the form and content of children's dreams.

Gender and Sexuality

Most psychological research studies on dreams (especially those published in the past 10–15 years) provide data on the dreams of both male and female subjects. Likewise, most popular psychology books include sections on the different dream patterns of women and men. Thus, readers interested in studying the subject of dreams and gender have ample resources available to them, even before they begin examining those books and articles focused specifically on this subject.

The subject of dreams and sexuality is inevitably connected to the subject of dreams and gender. I will discuss here works on both topics, even though the two are not identical and some authors sharply disagree about how the relationship between the two topics should be understood.

One of Freud's major legacies to dream psychology is the insight that dreams frequently express sexual wishes, desires, and conflicts that have been repressed in the unconscious. He first describes his theory about dreams and sexuality in *The Interpretation of Dreams* (Freud 1965a). He offers a more concrete demonstration of his theory in his interpretation of the two dreams of Dora, an adolescent girl who was briefly a patient of Freud's, as recounted in *Dora: Fragment of an Analysis of a Case of Hysteria* (Freud 1963a). Freud's treatment of Dora has become a primary focus of studies by later scholars of his views on dreams, gender, and sexuality. Good representatives of these studies are H. Decker's *Freud, Dora, and Vienna 1900* (Decker 1991) and the anthology edited by C. Bernheimer and C. Kahane, *In Dora's Case: Freud— Hysteria—Feminism* (Bernheimer and Kahane 1985).

Jung's contribution to the study of dreams and gender derives primarily from his account of the anima and animus archetypes, those psychic structures that represent the energies of the opposite sex in each human being. Jung discusses the appearance of anima and animus archetypes in people's dreams at great length in many of the articles gathered in *Dreams* (Jung 1974).

Three Jungian analysts have written excellent works on the relations of dreams, gender, and sexuality. R. Bosnak's *Dreaming with an AIDS Patient* (Bosnak 1989) is a deeply moving portrait of the dreams of one of Bosnak's patients, a young gay man, as he was slowly dying of AIDS. R. H. Hopcke's *Men's Dreams, Men's Healing* (Hopcke 1990) offers a detailed account of Hopcke's years of therapeutic work with two men, one heterosexual and one homosexual, as they struggled with pressing issues facing contemporary men (e.g., fear of intimacy, authority issues, the experience of fatherhood). And K. A. Signell's *Wisdom of the Heart: Working with Women's Dreams* (Signell 1990) explores themes in dreams, myths, and fairy tales regarding the nature of femininity, and discusses the relevance of personal dream study for women living in modern society. Another notable Jungian treatment of dreams and gender is Naomi Goldenberg's "Dreams and Fantasies as Sources of Revelation: Feminist Appropriation of Jung" (Goldenberg 1979).

Popular psychologists have written many good books on dreams, gender, and sexuality. P. Garfield has two books in this area. *Pathway to Ecstasy: The Way of the Dream Mandala* (Garfield 1989) describes her experiences with powerfully sexual lucid dreams and relates those dream experiences to the spiritual revelations that are reported in various religions around the world. *Women's Bodies, Women's Dreams* (Garfield 1988) examines the many ways in which women's dreams are different from men's dreams, largely because of the different physical realities of being male or being female. Chapters in this book include "Growing-Up and Menstrual Dreams," "Love and Sex Dreams," "Wedding Dreams," "Career Dreams," "Divorce Dreams," and "Menopausal Dreams." Similar to Garfield's book is L. Goodison's *The Dreams of Women: Exploring and Interpreting Women's Dreams* (Goodison 1995), in which she looks at dreams in the context of the distinctive physical, psychological, and social factors shaping women's lives in contemporary society. P. Maybruck's book *Pregnancy and Dreams* (Maybruck 1989) focuses on the specific topic of the dreams of expectant parents. She argues that the increase in nightmares that so many expectant mothers experience during pregnancy can actually help ease the pregnancy, labor, and delivery process by bringing forth the natural anxieties that accompany pregnancy. Maybruck's other book, *Romantic Dreams: How to Enhance Your Romantic Relationship by Understanding and Sharing Your Dreams* (Maybruck 1991) contains extensive accounts of dreams and their complex relationship with gender and sexuality. G. Delaney's *Sensual Dreaming: How to Understand and Interpret the Erotic Content of Your Dreams* (Delaney 1994) is a careful study of the sexual dreams of both men and women and how they relate to people's waking-life sexual experiences, desires, and conflicts.

A sizable literature has developed in recent years around the topic of dreams, gender, and sexual trauma. M. Cuddy and K. Belicki's article "Nightmare Frequency and Related Sleep Disturbance as Indicators of a History of Sexual Abuse" (Cuddy and Belicki 1992) is one of the best articles in this literature, as is their article "The Fifty-five-Year Secret: Using Nightmares to Facilitate Psychotherapy in a Case of Childhood Sexual Abuse" (Cuddy and Belicki 1996). Another excellent article on this theme is by B. Krakow and his colleagues, "Nightmares and Sleep Disturbance in Sexually Assaulted Women" (Krakow et al. 1995). Articles that focus on less violent gender-related stressors and dreams are R. Armitage's "Gender Differences and the Effect of Stress on Dream Recall: A Thirty-Day Diary Report" (Armitage 1992) and R. Cartwright's "Broken Dreams: A Study of the Effects of Divorce and Depression on Dream Content: (Cartwright et al. 1984). A fuller account of Cartwright's work on dreams, gender, and sexuality comes in her book *Crisis Dreaming* (Cartwright and Lamberg 1992).

Content analysis research has provided extensive information on the different contents of men's and women's dreams. Three key articles here are C. Hall and G. W. Domhoff's "A Ubiquitous Sex Difference in Dreams" (Hall and Domhoff 1963a), Hall's "The Dreams of College Men and Women in 1950 and 1980: A Comparison of Dream Contents and Sex Differences" (Hall 1982), and Hall's "'A Ubiquitous Sex Difference in Dreams' Revisited" (Hall 1984). The "Ubiquitous Sex Difference" described in these articles refers to the finding of content analysis that men's dreams contain twice as many male characters as female characters, while women's dreams contain an equal number of male and female characters. The evidence supporting this finding and discussion of its implications can be found in R. Van de Castle's *Our Dreaming Mind* (Van de Castle 1994) and G. W. Domhoff's *Finding Meaning in Dreams: A Quantitative Approach* (Domhoff 1996).

Important quantitative research on dreams and gender has also been done by M. Lortie-Lussier and her colleagues, as reported in the articles "Working Mothers versus Homemakers: Do Dreams Reflect the Changing Roles of Women?" (Lortie-Lussier et al. 1985) and "Beyond Sex Differences: Family and Occupational Roles' Impact on Women's and Men's Dreams" (Lortie-Lussier et al. 1992).

From a literary-humanities perspective, the leading researcher in the area of dreams, gender, and sexuality is C. S. Rupprecht. In the anthology she edited with E. Lauter, *Feminist Archetypal Theory: Interdisciplinary Re-Visions of Jungian Thought* (Rupprecht and Lauter 1985), she has an article titled "The Common Language of Women's Dreams: Colloquy of Mind and Body" in which she draws together many strands of psychological dream research with feminist theory to explore the power of dreams to help women in the process of "unconsciousness raising." Another anthology she edited, *The Dream and the Text: Essays on Literature and Language* (Rupprecht 1993), includes a number of essays that explore dreams, gender, and sexuality as they are portrayed in various literary texts. And her essay "Sex, Gender, and Dreams: From Polarity to Plurality" (Rupprecht 1996) is one of the best works available for understanding this area of dream research.

Popular Psychology

Many researchers in the field of dream studies have written books aimed largely or exclusively at popular audiences. These books translate specialized, highly technical research findings into language that broader audiences of general readers can understand and appreciate.

One set of popular books offers sweeping historical reviews of the various roles that dreams have played in cultures all over the world. One of the earliest of these books is F. Seafield's *The Literature and Curiosities of Dreams: A Commonplace Book of Speculations Concerning the Mystery of Dreams and Visions, Records of Curious and Well-Authenticated Dreams, and Notes on The Various Modes of Interpretation Adopted in Ancient and Modern Times* (Seafield 1877). As the long subtitle indicates, Seafield's book includes a vast amount of historical material on dreams, much of it no longer available in any other readily available book.

Turning to more recent times, a highly influential historical work is N. MacKenzie's *Dreams and Dreaming* (MacKenzie 1965). Although the book suffers the serious flaw of providing no reference notes or citations (thus creating an unfortunate ripple effect in those later books that cite MacKenzie's work as a reference source), it does give a good narrative account of how dreams have been regarded in Western cultural history. R. De Becker's *The Understanding of Dreams, and Their Influence on the History of Man* (De Becker 1968) is even more ambitious than MacKenzie's book in surveying humankind's fascination with the experience of dreams. Well written and fully documented, De Becker's work has long served as a key historical resource for dream psychologists. A wonderful anthology edited by S. Brook, *The Oxford Book of Dreams* (Brook 1987) gathers together quotations about dreams from an amazing variety of sources: from literary, religious, and psychological texts, from private letters and diaries, from ancient hieroglyphics and modern scientific research. R. L. Woods and H. B. Greenhouse's *The New World of Dreams* (Woods and Greenhouse 1974) also presents a selection of important and fascinating writings on dreams from various sources and texts. R. Van de Castle's *Our Dreaming Mind* (Van de Castle 1994) is the latest work in this genre of dream psychology. His book possesses the great advantage of being written by someone who has been actively involved in dream research for more than thirty years and knows from the inside how the field has developed.

Another set of books presents various articles that aim at giving an introductory survey of major theories, trends, and approaches in the psychology of dreaming. The articles in B. Wolman's *Handbook of Dreams: Research, Theories, and Applications* (Wolman 1979) cover many of the primary fields of dream research and clinical practice. M. Ullman and C. Limmer's *The Variety of Dream Experience: Expanding Our Ways of Working with Dreams* (Ullman and Limmer 1987) has articles on group dreamwork, on applications of dream psychology to clinical psychotherapy, and on the relation of dreams to religion, literature, and history. R. Russo's *Dreams Are Wiser Than Men* (Russo 1987) includes several articles exploring the creative interplay between dreams, psychology, literature, and spirituality. S. Krippner's *Dreamtime and Dreamwork: Decoding the Language of the Night* (Krippner 1990) has articles on dreams in therapy and healing, dreams in creativity and education, women, sex and dreams, and historical and cross-cultural dream research. G. Delaney's *New Directions in Dream Interpretation* (Delaney 1993) introduces general readers to the basic clinical modes of dream interpretation. And K. Bulkeley's *Among All These Dreamers: Essays on Dreaming and Modern Society* (Bulkeley 1996) offers essays on the relevance of dream research for addressing various social and cultural problems (e.g., child education, sexual abuse, racial conflict, environmental awareness, the denial of death, criminal justice, etc.).

Many of the field's leading scientific researchers have written general audience books recounting their investigations. W. C. Dement's *Some Must Watch While Some Must Sleep: Exploring the World of Sleep* (Dement 1972) is one of the best introductions available to the history and practice of contemporary sleep laboratory research. J. A. Hobson's *The Dreaming Brain: How the Brain Creates Both the Sense and the Nonsense of Dreams* (Hobson 1988) is also an excellent historical survey of scientific research on the nature of sleep, dreaming, and consciousness. R. Cartwright and L. Lamberg's *Crisis Dreaming: Using Your Dreams to Solve Your Problems* (Cartwright and Lamberg 1992) tells the story of Cartwright's long career as a sleep laboratory researcher. And D. Koulack's *To Catch a Dream: Explorations of Dreaming* (Koulack 1991) is a remarkably accessible description of how experimental psychologists have over the past several decades studied various aspects of dreams and dreaming.

There are dozens, and perhaps hundreds, of popular psychology books that describe a particular method of understanding and interpreting dreams. The following list includes only relatively recent books that have had a significant impact on the broad field of dream psychology.

A. Faraday's *Dream Power* (Faraday 1972) and *The Dream Game* (Faraday 1974) were in large part responsible for the current wave of interest in dreams among the general public. Likewise, P. Garfield's *Creative Dreaming* (Garfield 1974) and G. Delaney's *Living Your Dreams* (Delaney 1979) also spurred widespread attention to the dreams of ordinary people outside of the clinician's office and the scientist's sleep laboratory. M. Ullman's *Working with Dreams* (Ullman and Zimmerman 1979) and J. Taylor's *Dream Work* (Taylor 1983) and *Where People Fly and Water Runs Uphill* (Taylor 1992) gave people instructions on how to organize dreamsharing groups. C. Rycroft's *The Innocence of Dreams* (Rycroft 1979) combines Freudian psychoanalysis with contemporary literary theory and philosophy to argue that dreaming is a form of imaginative creativity. S. K. Williams's *Jungian-Senoi Dreamwork Manual* (Williams 1980) combines principles from Jungian psychology and K. Stewart's reports on Senoi dream practices. H. Reed's *Getting Help from Your Dreams* (Reed 1985) is a friendly, down-to-earth primer on personal dream interpretation, with detailed instructions on how to make dream pillows and dream shields, how to create dream poetry and dream theater, and how to engage in a dream quest ritual. A. Mindell's *Dreambody: The Body's Role in Revealing the Self* (Mindell 1982) and *Working with the Dream Body* (Mindell 1985) describe methods of exploring the bodily dimensions of dream experience and dream interpretation. Similarly, E. Gendlin's *Let Your Body Interpret Your Dreams* (Gendlin 1986) explores the role of "felt sense" as a powerful nonrational guide in interpreting dreams. R. Bosnak's *A Little Course in Dreams* (Bosnak 1988) draws on both Jungian theory and body work to view dreams as a self-created environment. A. Siegel's *Dreams That Can Change Your Life* (Siegel 1990) focuses on the significance of dreams that occur at key "turning points" in life (e.g., during adolescence, marriage, childbirth, job change, divorce, death, etc.). R. E. Guiley's *Dreamwork for the Soul: A Spiritual Guide to Dream Interpretation* (Guiley 1998) and R. Moss's *Dreamgates: An Explorer's Guide to the Worlds of Soul, Imagination, and Life Beyond Death* (Moss 1998) both offer spiritually oriented approaches to understanding dreams. The focus of K. Sullivan's excellent work *Recurring Dreams: A Journey to Wholeness* is the special significance of recurrent images and themes in dreams. E. B. Bynum's *Families and the Interpretation of Dreams: Awakening the Intimate Web* (Bynum 1993) brings together family-systems theory and an African-based "Kemitic" philosophy to look at the powerful role dreams can play in family relationships. V. Tonay's *The Art of Dreaming* (Tonay 1995) draws on her psychological research on the dreams of creative artists to outline methods ordinary people can use to develop the creative potentials of their own dreams. In R. Moss's *Conscious Dreaming* (Moss 1996) shamanic dreamwork techniques from Australian Aborigines and Native Americans are offered to people as means of enhancing their own spiritual dream experiences. W. Phillips wrote *Every Dreamer's Handbook* (1994) as a simple, easy-to-follow guide for people who want to learn how to remember, record, and understand their dreams.

Again, the list of popular dream books could go on and on. Although some of these books repeat the same basic ideas and methods, and although a few of them contain serious errors of fact regarding current knowledge about dreams, they remain valuable to dream researchers for their first-hand narrative accounts of people's actual dream experiences.

Lucid Dreaming

Lucid dreaming is the phenomenon of becoming aware within the dream state that one is dreaming. One of the earliest personal accounts of lucid dream experiences is from the Marquis Hervey de Saint-Denys, a French professor of ethnography who in 1867 published a book, *Les Rêves et les Moyens de les Diriger*, which was translated into English in 1982 and published as *Dreams and How to Guide Them* (Saint-Denys 1982). The person most widely credited with coining the term "lucid dream" is Frederick Van Eeden, a Dutch psychiatrist who from 1898 to 1912 gathered reports of lucid dreams and performed experiments on his own abilities to have lucid dream experiences. He presented his findings to the Society for Psychical Research in the article "A Study of Dreams" (Van Eeden 1913). Mary Arnold-Forster's book *Studies in Dreams* (Arnold-Forster 1921) is another early study of personal dream experiences that often had dimensions of lucidity to them.

The English parapsychologist Celia Green's book *Lucid Dreams* (Green 1968a) was the first work to provide a scholarly review and examination of the available data on lucid dreaming. Although her book was met with skepticism by many academic psychologists, it generated great interest among people who had experienced lucid dreaming themselves. This interest was stimulated all the more by the reprinting in C. Tart's anthology *Altered States of Consciousness* (Tart 1969) of K. Stewart's article "Dream Theory in Malaya" (Stewart 1969). Stewart's portrait of the Senoi people as skilled practitioners of lucid dreaming techniques encouraged many readers in the West to try and develop their own abilities to experience lucid dreams.

Most of the popular psychology books on dreams published in the 1970s and early 1980s included lengthy descriptions of lucid dream experiences and detailed instructions for learning how to become a lucid dreamer. A Faraday's *Dream Power* (Faraday 1972) and *The Dream Game* (Faraday 1974), P. Garfield's *Creative Dreaming* (Garfield 1974), G. Delaney's *Living Your Dreams* (Delaney 1979), S. K. William's *Jungian-Senoi Dreamwork Manual* (Williams 1980), and J. Taylor's *Dream Work* (Taylor 1983) all drew on the reports from Stewart, Green, and others to offer lucid dreaming as an exciting new frontier of dream consciousness.

The researcher who has done the most to bring lucid dreaming to the attention of both academic investigators and members of the general public is S. LaBerge. His book *Lucid Dreaming: The Power of Being Awake and Aware in Your Dreams* (LaBerge 1985) is based on his doctoral research at the sleep laboratory of Stanford University. *Lucid Dreaming* contains a historical review of reports of lucid dreams, a summary of LaBerge's research findings, and a program for developing the ability to have lucid dreams in the service of physical, psychological, and spiritual well-being. LaBerge's book is without question the primary reference source in any study of lucid dreaming.

Another pioneering psychologist in the area of lucid dreaming research is J. Gackenbach. Even more than LaBerge, Gackenbach has worked to develop a broad and diverse community of researchers concentrating on the study of lucid dreaming. For ten years Gackenbach edited *Lucidity Letter*, a biannual journal publishing both technical research papers and personal reports of lucid dream experiences. She and LaBerge coedited the anthology *Conscious Mind, Sleeping Brain: Perspectives on Lucid Dreaming* (Gackenbach and LaBerge 1988), an outstanding compendium of current investigations, theories, and techniques related to lucid dreaming. She coauthored the book *Control Your Dreams* (Gackenbach and Bosveld 1989), a general audience book teaching people how to induce lucid dreams. And she wrote "Frameworks for Understanding Lucid Dreaming: A Review" (Gackenbach 1991), an excellent scholarly review article that surveys the various methodological approaches researchers have taken toward studying and understanding lucid dreaming.

Two important articles on lucid dreaming have been written by D. Barrett. One, "Flying Dreams and Lucidity: An Empirical Study of

Their Relationship" (Barrett 1991) explores the often-remarked connection between flying dreams and lucid dreams and discusses this connection in terms of possible psychological and physiological commonalities between the two phenomena. The other, "Just How Lucid Are Lucid Dreams?" (Barrett 1992) questions the precise definition of "lucidity" used by researchers in this area. She conducted an empirical study to investigate the question, and found that most lucid dreams are only "partly" lucid, that is, lacking absolutely full and clear self-awareness of being in the dream state.

Many other influential works have been published recently on the nature and potential values of lucid dreaming. K. Kelzer's *The Sun and the Shadow* (Kelzer 1987) is in the tradition of Saint-Denys, Van Eeden, Arnold-Forster, and Green in giving a detailed personal account of Kelzer's own lucid dream experiences. H. Hunt's *The Multiplicity of Dreams* (Hunt 1989) offers a highly sophisticated cognitive psychological model for understanding how lucid dreams are formed and how they relate to other "intensified" types of dream experience. G. Gillespie's "Light in Lucid Dreams: A Review" (Gillespie 1992) examines the widely reported experience of brilliant light imagery in association with lucid dreaming. A. L. Zadra, D. C. Donderi, and R. O. Pihl's article "Efficacy of Lucid Dream Induction for Lucid and Non-Lucid Dreamers" (Zadra, Donderi, Pihl 1992) reports on the efficacy of certain techniques for inducing lucid dreaming.

A critical perspective on lucid dreaming is provided by W. Doniger, a historian of religions with a specialization in Hindu culture. Her article "Western Dreams about Eastern Dreams" (Doniger 1996) argues that Westerners like LaBerge who look to lucid dreaming as a way of experiencing the same kinds of spiritual insights gained in Eastern religious traditions are ignoring the tremendous cultural differences between ancient Eastern religions and modern Western society. A similar argument is made by N. Norbu, a Tibetan master of the Dzogchen tradition, in *Dream Yoga and the Practice of Natural Light* (Norbu 1992). While he encourages Westerners to explore the religious traditions of the East, Norbu cautions them that lucid dreaming is not an end in itself and should not be isolated from the other practices involved in any authentic yoga discipline.

Perhaps the most creative scholarly research on lucid dreaming is being done by T. Kahan (Kahan 1994; Kahan and LaBerge 1996; Kahan and LaBerge 1994; Kahan, LaBerge, Levitan, and Zimbardo 1997). She has been investigating the metacognitive dimensions of lucid dreaming, and using the findings from carefully performed experiments to address broader psychological and even spiritual questions about consciousness, cognition, and self-awareness. Her research offers important material for reflection on how dreaming can reveal the deepest processes of the human mind.

Paranormal Dreams

As R. Van de Castle defines the term in *Our Dreaming Mind* (Van de Castle 1994), "paranormal" dreams include three different types of dreams: (1) *precognitive* dreams correctly represent or anticipate unlikely future events (e.g., accidents, deaths); (2) *telepathic* dreams involve the dreamer becoming aware of someone else's current mental state; and (3) in *clairvoyant* dreams the dreamer gains information about some distant physical object directly (i.e., not through someone else's mind). Paranormal dreams have been reported by people throughout history, and for just as long they have been the object of intense debate. Readers interested in this topic of dream research are encouraged to enter its study with an open mind and a willingness to examine carefully all the evidence before making any final judgements.

Freud devoted considerable attention to the question of paranormal dreams. He wrote of his views in a number of papers: "Psychoanalysis and Telepathy" (Freud 1953a), "Dreams and Telepathy" (Freud 1953b), "The Occult Significance of Dreams" (Freud 1953c), and "Dreams and Occultism" (in Freud 1965b). In these papers Freud expresses a general scientific skepticism toward claims that dreams have paranormal powers, but also a willingness to examine any particular case with the calm objectivity that science brings to its study of all phenomena.

Jung's autobiography *Memories, Dreams, Reflections* (Jung 1965) includes a number of reports of paranormal dreams experienced by him and by his patients. Jung is much more definite than Freud is in endorsing the reality of such dreams, and he believes that they occur far more frequently than most scientifically minded Westerners believe. Further accounts of Jung's views on paranormal dreams can be found *Dreams* (Jung 1974) and in many sections of *The Collected Works of C. G Jung* (Jung 1967).

The most elaborate and carefully conducted investigation of paranormal dreams was conducted in the early 1960s by M. Ullman and S. Krippner in the dream laboratory at Maimonides Hospital in Brooklyn, New York. This study was designed as follows: one person, the "percipient," slept in the lab and had his or her sleep stages monitored by an electroencephalograph (EEG) machine; another person, the "agent," attempted from another room to "send" a target stimulus (the image of a randomly chosen art reproduction) to the sleeping percipient; while a third person, the "monitor," watched the EEG machine to track the percipient's REM periods. When the percipient went into REM sleep, the monitor would signal the agent to begin concentrating on the target picture. After ten to fifteen minutes the monitor would awaken the percipient and ask for a dream report. The next morning the percipient was shown eight art reproductions, one of which was the target picture, and asked to rank them from the most likely target picture to the least likely. The dreams and the rankings were then given to outside judges for evaluation. Of the thirteen studies they conducted, Ullman and Krippner found that in nine of them the percipient's dreams related to the target picture at a rate significantly higher than chance. They describe their research and findings in their book *Dream Telepathy* (Ullman, Krippner, and Vaughan 1989).

Many books in clinical, experimental, and popular psychology include sections on paranormal dreams. M. Boss's *The Analysis of Dreams* (Boss 1958) has a chapter on "The Possibilities of 'Extra-Sensory' Relationship in Dreams. A Faraday's *The Dream Game* (Faraday 1974) offers a chapter on "Through the Dream Gates: ESP and Altered States of Consciousness in Dreams." Two chapters in G. Delaney's *Living Your Dreams* (Delaney 1979) discuss paranormal dreams: "The Twilight Zone: Psychic Dreaming; ESP; Past-Life, Other-Life, and Afterlife Dreams" and "Startrekking: Conscious Dreaming, Astral Travel, and Exploring Other Levels of Reality." H. Hunt's *The Multiplicity of Dreams* (Hunt 1989) discusses the various cognitive processes that appear to generate various types of paranormal dreams. S. Krippner's anthology *Dreamtime and Dreamwork* (Krippner 1990) presents chapters on psychic dreams and shared dreams.

One of the most extensive treatments of the subject of paranormal dreams is D. Ryback and L. Sweitzer's *Dreams That Come True: Their Psychic and Transforming Powers* (Ryback and Sweitzer 1988). In this book Ryback and Sweitzer discuss the literal and symbolic elements of paranormal dreams and give lengthy case studies of particular individuals who have experienced several precognitive dreams.

The best single source of general information on paranormal dreams is Van de Castle's *Our Dreaming Mind* (Van de Castle 1994). In addition to clear summaries of most of the major studies on the subject, Van de Castle recounts his own extensive experience as a subject in paraphyschological experiments. He is currently the leading authority on this topic, and readers wanting to study paranormal dreams in further detail should look first to Van de Castle's book.

An outstanding source of historical information about paranormal dreams is the work of Hendrika Vande Kemp on dream beliefs and practices in nineteenth-century America and Europe. Readers can consult her meticulously researched doctoral dissertation, "The Dream in Periodical Literature: 1860–1910" (Vande Kemp 1977). She has also written a two-part article, "Psycho-Spiritual Dreams in the Nineteenth Century" (Vande Kemp 1994a, 1994b) that focuses specifically on the more extraordinary types of dream experience, with part I dealing with dreams of death and part II addressing dreams, metaphysics, and immortality.

Most studies of paranormal dreams avoid the question of how exactly such dreams occur, focusing instead on what impact the dreams have on the people who have them. A noteworthy exception here is E. B. Bynum's fascinating book *Families and the Interpretation of Dreams: Awakening the Intimate Web* (Bynum 1993). Bynum notes that the majority of paranormal dream experiences involve people who are family members (for example, a son dreaming that his mother, 2,000 miles away, has just had an auto accident; when he wakes up he gets a phone call from the hospital informing him that such an accident did in fact occur that night, just as he had dreamed it.) Bynum argues that dreams like these emerge out of the "family unconscious," a shared field of psychological energy that is generated between and among family members. Through dreams prompted by the family unconscious people may become aware of threats of crises that endanger the lives of loved ones.

Performing precise, scientifically controlled experiments in the area of paranormal dreams is of course very difficult. Despite the generally positive results of the Maimonides experiments, the ever-growing number of anecdotal reports, and the theoretical explanations put forth by researchers like Bynum, there continues to be widespread debate about this area of dream psychology.

Cross-Cultural Studies of Dreaming

The first cross-cultural studies of dreaming were conducted by anthropologists who were trained in psychoanalytic theory and who used this theory to evaluate the dream experiences and practices of people in non-Western cultures. J. S. Lincoln's *The Dream in Primitive Cultures* (Lincoln 1935) brings together a vast amount of anthropological material on dreams and subjects it all to a Freudian analysis, arguing that oedipal themes and symbols are pervasive not just in Western but in non-Western dream experience. Similarly, G. Roheim's *The Gates of the Dream* (Roheim 1952) interprets anthropological data in terms of Freudian categories, using cross-cultural dream reports as evidence that these categories are universal. Roheim claims that all human dreams, no matter what cultures they come from, are instances of "the basic dream," which he defines as a regressive wish to return to the mother's womb. Although Lincoln's and Roheim's books are filled with fascinating anthropological material, both writers insist so vigorously on the absolute correctness of Freudian theory that they become vulnerable to the charge of psychoanalytic reductionism.

A more persuasive effort to combine psychoanalytic and anthropological methods of studying dreams is G. Devereux's *Reality and Dream: Psychotherapy of a Plains Indian* (Devereux 1969). The book recounts the efforts of Devereux, who is both a trained psychoanalyst and an anthropologist, to treat a Plains Indian man who was suffering from various neurotic symptoms. Devereux is careful to examine the subtle cultural influences on the man's condition and to work toward the development of a "transcultural technique of psychotherapy" that rejects all reductionistic, ethnocentric models of understanding the psychological experiences of people from other cultures. Devereux has also written *Dreams in Greek Tragedy: An Ethno-Psychoanalytic Study* (Devereux 1975), which uses psychoanalysis to interpret the dreams portrayed in the plays of Sophocles, Aeschylus, and Euripides.

An important new development in the cross-cultural study of dreams came with the publication in the 1950s of several articles by anthropologist D. Eggan. She rejected the psychoanalytic model's quest for hidden "latent content" dreams, and focused instead on what the "manifest content" of people's dreams could reveal about their personalities, their cultures, and the interactions between the two. In "The Manifest Content of Dreams: A Challenge to Social Science" (Eggan 1952), "The Personal Use of Myth in Dreams" (Eggan 1955), and "Hopi Dreams and a Life History Sketch" (Eggan 1957) she charted a new course for the cross-cultural study of dreams, maintaining contact with psychological theories but refusing to abide by the unduly polemical strictures of orthodox psychoanalysis.

The landmark publication in the cross-cultural study of dreams is the anthology edited by G. E. Van Grunebaum and R. Callois, *The Dream and Human Societies* (Von Grunebaum and Callois 1966). This book collects several excellent articles from leading psychologists, anthropologists, and scholars from many other fields, all focusing on the complex relations between dreams and cultural reality. Although other outstanding books on the cross-cultural study of dreams have been written since *The Dream and Human Societies* was first published, Von

Grunebaum and Callois's book remains the most distinguished and most valuable work in this area of dream research.

The two most recent major additions to the literature here are B. Tedlock's *Dreaming: Anthropological and Psychological Interpretations* (Tedlock 1987) and M. D. Jedrej and R. Shaw's *Dreaming, Religion, and Society in Africa* (Jedrej and Shaw 1992). Both books are anthologies that gather scholarly articles that skillfully combine first-rate anthropological field research with sophisticated psychological analysis. Most of the articles in Tedlock's book discuss the dream theories and practices of indigenous cultures in Central and South America, while all the articles in Jedrej and Shaw's book focus on the role of dreams in various African cultures. Readers interested in broadening their understanding of the psychology of dreaming will find these two books to be filled with new perspectives and insights. Although the articles in each book are primarily addressed to professional anthropologists, they have tremendous value for anyone studying the formation, function, and interpretation of dreams.

Two books use anthropological methods to study the use of dreams in the therapeutic practices of contemporary Western mental health professionals. M. Dombeck's *Dreams and Professional Personhood: The Contexts of Dream Telling and Dream Interpretation among American Psychotherapists* (Dombeck 1991) presents very interesting findings about the ideas, attitudes, and practices regarding dreams among two groups of mental-health professionals working at community health centers in the Northeastern United States. Dombeck uses anthropological theories on the nature of the self and personhood to evaluate the often ambivalent feelings these professional psychotherapists had about dreams. And I. Edgar's *Dreamwork, Anthropology and the Caring Professions* (Edgar 1995) also draws on current anthropological theorizing about language and metaphor to develop a social anthropology of dreamwork that the author applied in the context of modern mental-health care. These works by Dombeck and Edgar offer highly stimulating perspectives that should be of interest to anyone who does clinical work with dreams.

Two other works on dreams from an anthropological perspective are C. W. O'Nell's *Dreams Culture, and the Individual* (O'Nell 1976) and S. Parman's *Dreams and Culture: An Anthropological Study of the Western Intellectual Tradition* (Parman 1991). Although both books contain much valuable information, they have to date proven less useful to dream researchers than have other anthropological works.

Below are some of the most significant anthropological articles devoted specifically to dreaming, grouped by geographic regions.

North American Cultures

P. Radin's "Ojibwa and Ottawa Puberty Dreams" (Radin 1936) described the dream fast rituals used to initiate adolescents into Ojibwa and Ottawa culture. A. I. Hallowell's "The Role of Dreams in Ojibwa Culture" (Hallowell 1966) also discusses the dream fast rituals of the Ojibwa. W. Morgan's "Navaho Dreams" (Morgan 1932), G. Toffelmeir and K. Luomala's "Dreams and Dream Interpretation of the Diegueno Indians of Southern California" (Toffelmeir and Luomala 1936), and R. Flannery and M. E. Chambers's "Each Man Has His Own Friends: The Role of Dream Visitors in Traditional East Cree Belief and Practice" (Flannery and Chambers 1985) analyze the many important roles dreams play in particular Native American cultures. A. F. C. Wallace's article "Dreams and Wishes of the Soul: A Type of Psychoanalytic Theory among the Seventeenth Century Iroquois" (Wallace 1958) and his book *The Death and Rebirth of the Seneca* (Wallace 1969) both use psychoanalytic theory to study the functions of dreams in Iroquois culture. L. Irwin's *The Dream Seekers: Native American Visionary Traditions of the Great Plains* (Irwin 1994) describes the importance of visionary dreams to the religious beliefs and practices of the Plains Indians.

South American Cultures

W. Kracke has written three important articles describing the dream beliefs and practices of the Kagwahiv people of the Brazilian rain forests: "Dreaming in Kagwahiv: Dream Beliefs and Their Psychic Uses in an Amazonian Indian Culture" (Kracke 1979), "Kagwahiv Mourning: Dreams of a Bereaved Father" (Kracke 1981), and "Myths in Dreams, Thought in Images: An Amazonian Contribution to the Psychoanalytic Theory of Primary Process" (Kracke 1987). From T. Gregor come a number of articles examining the roles of dreams in the culture of the Mehinaku Indians, also from the Brazilian rain forests: "'Far, Far Away My Shadow Wandered. . . . ': The Dream Symbolism and Dream Theories of the Mehinaku Indians of Brazil" (Gregor 1981a), "A Content Analysis of Mehinaku Dreams" (Gregor 1981b), and "Dark Dreams About the White Man" (Gregor 1983). Both Kracke and Gregor are thoroughly familiar with current thinking in dream psychology, and they each offer valuable reflections on the relations between psychological and anthropological approaches to dreams. P. Descola is another psychoanalytically minded anthropologist, whose book *The Spears of Twilight: Life and Death in the Amazon Jungle* (Descola 1993) offers fascinating information on the dream life of the Achuar tribespeople.

Asia

B. Laufer's "Inspirational Dreams in Eastern Asia" (Laufer 1931) describes how dreams have been used in medical, political, religious, and artistic contexts in East Asian cultures. K. Ewing's "The Dream of Spiritual Initiation and the Organization of Self Representations among Pakistani Sufis" (Ewing 1989) examines the role of dreams in Sufi initiations, while A. Wayman's "Significance of Dreams in India and Tibet" (Wayman 1967) looks primarily at the teachings about dreams found in Indian and Tibetan religious and mythological texts. Similarly, W. D. O'Flaherty's *Dreams, Illusion, and Other Realities* (O'Flaherty 1984) explores traditional Indian ideas about dreams and compares them to both classical and modern Western dream theories. R. K. Dentan and L. G. McClusky's "'Pity the Bones by Wandering River Which Still in Lovers' Dreams Appear as Men'" (Dentan and McClusky 1993) is a very careful analysis of dreams in Chinese culture. A good source on Chinese dream theory is R. K. Ong's extensively documented book *The Interpretation of Dreams in Ancient China* (Ong 1985). G. Tanabe's *Myoe the Dreamkeeper: Fantasy and Knowledge in Early Kamakura Buddhism* (Tanabe 1992) describes how the twelfth-century Buddhist leader Myoe Shonin drew upon his dreams and his visions during meditation to revitalize traditional Buddhism in Japan. The leading scholar in the area of Eastern dream theory is S. Young, whose works include "Dream Practices in Medieval Tibet" (Young 1998), "Dream Rituals from Tangyur" (Young, in press), and *Dreaming in the Lotus: Innovation and Continuity in Buddhist Sacred Biography* (Young, forthcoming).

Africa

Many good articles have been written on dreams in the many cultures of Africa: S. R. Charsley's "Dreams in an Independent African Church" (Charsley 1973) and "Dreams and Purposes: An Analysis of Dream Narratives in an Independent African Church" (Charsley 1987), V. Crapanzano's "Saints, Jnun, and Dreams" An Essay in Moroccan Ethnopsychology" (Crapanzano 1975), R. T. Curley's "Dreams of Power: Social Process in a West African Religious Movement (Curley 1983), J. Fabian's "Dreams and Charisma: 'Theories of Dreams' in the Jamaa-Movement (Congo)" (Fabian 1966), and R. A. Shweder and R. A. LeVine's "Dream Concepts of Hausa Children: A Critique of the 'Doctrine of Invariant Sequence'" (Shweder and LeVine 1975). Most of these articles discuss the clash between traditional African dream beliefs and the modern Western beliefs imported into African cultures by colonial and missionary forces.

Oceania

Good sources in the cross-cultural study of dreams in Oceanic cultures include R. Firth's "The Meaning of Dreams in Tikopia" (Firth 1934), M. Stephen's "Dreams of Change: The Innovative Role of Altered States of Consciousness in Traditional Melanesian Religion" (Stephen 1979), and *A'Aisa's Gifts: A Study of Magic and the Self* (Stephen 1995), R. Tonkinson's "Aboriginal Dream-Spirit Beliefs in a Contact Situation: Jigalong, Western Australia" (Tonkinson 1970), and especially G. W. Trompf's *Melanesian Religion* (Trompf 1990). D. M. Schneider and L. Sharp's *The Dream Life of a Primitive People: The Dreams of the Yir Yoront of Australia* (Schneider and Sharp 1969), although difficult to find, is a wonderful collection of dreams of people from an Australian Aboriginal culture. R. Bosnak's *Tracks in the Wilderness of Dreaming* (Bosnak 1996) recounts the experiences Bosnak, a Jungian analyst, had in discussing dreams with an Aboriginal spirit doctor.

A surprisingly large number of works in the field of anthropology contain fascinating information on dreams and dreaming. Readers who want to explore the cross-cultural study of dreams can learn a great deal simply by going to the anthropology section of a library and perusing book indexes and journal abstracts.

Dreams, Psychology, and the Humanities

Many scholars in the humanities have studied dreams and dreaming and have developed very interesting and important new perspectives that are relevant to dream psychology. Below are some of the most significant of these works from the fields of philosophy, literature, and history.

N. Malcolm's *Dreaming* (Malcolm 1959) is the major philosophical examination of dreaming written in the past several decades. C. Dunlop's anthology *Philosophical Essays on Dreaming* (Dunlop 1977) has several articles responding to Malcolm's ideas in *Dreaming* as well as articles investigating questions of knowledge, memory, experience, skepticism, and consciousness. G. Globus's *Dream Life, Wake Life: The Human Condition through Dreams* (Globus 1987) draws on philosophical phenomenology to explore the nature of being and consciousness in both waking and dreaming modes of existence. None of these difficult, densely reasoned books are aimed at general readers, but they nevertheless contain thought-provoking reflections on how we understand the nature of dreaming. Two of the more accessible works connecting dream psychology to current trends in philosophy and literary theory are C. Rycroft's *The Innocence of Dreams* (Rycroft 1979) and G. Lakoff's "How Metaphor Structures Dreams: The Theory of Conceptual Metaphor Applied to Dream Analysis" (Lakoff 1993).

Dreams have been of growing interest to literary critics in recent years. The scholar who has done the most to integrate literary and psychological approaches to dreams is C. S. Rupprecht. She has written several works aimed at developing an interdisciplinary framework for understanding the narrative creativity found in dream experience. She coedited with E. Lauter the anthology *Feminist Archetypal Theory: Interdisciplinary Re-Visions of Jungian Thought* (Rupprecht and Lauter 1985), in which she wrote the article "The Common Language of Women's Dreams: Colloquy of Mind and Body." She has written the historical article "Our Unacknowledged Ancestors: Dream Theorists of Antiquity, the Middle Ages, and the Renaissance" (Rupprecht 1990) and the more specifically literary article "The Drama of History and Prophecy: Shakespeare's Use of Dream in *2 Henry VI*" (Rupprecht 1993). Her major contribution to this area of dream study is the anthology *The Dream and the Text: Essays on Literature and Language* (Rupprecht 1993). The book contains essays on dreams and literary theory, on the historical and cultural contexts of dreaming, and on the role of dreams in particular literary texts. *The Dream and the Text* is an invaluable resource for readers interested in pursuing the complex interrelations between dreaming, psychology, and literature.

Another literary scholar who has devoted considerable attention to dreams is B. O. States. In *The Rhetoric of Dreams* (States 1988), *Dreaming and Storytelling* (States 1993), "Authorship in Dreams and Fictions" (States 1994), and "Dreaming 'Accidentally' of Harold Pinter: The Interplay of Metaphor and Metonymy in Dreams" (States 1995) he engages in lengthy reflections on the ways in which studies of literary creativity can shed new light on the process of dream formation. By his direct engagement with the research projects of experimental psychologists like D. Foulkes and H. Hunt, States has helped raise the literary study of dreams to a new level of sophistication and significance.

A recent double issue of the journal *Dreaming* was devoted to the subject of poet, author, and philosopher Samuel Taylor Coleridge's views of dreams and dreaming. Coedited by D. S. Miall and D. Kuiken (1997), the two special issues contain several excellent articles addressing the relationship between Coleridge's literary art and his own personal dream experiences, the historical and philosophical context of his deep interest in dreams, and the implications of his ideas for contemporary dream theory. As a model of how literature and psychology can work together in the field of dream studies, these two issues of the journal *Dreaming* deserve special attention.

An important work in the area of dreams, psychology and the humanities that is aimed at general audiences but has relevance to academic specialists as well is N. Epel's *Writers Dreaming: Twenty-six Writers Talk about Their Dreams and the Creative Process* (Epel 1993). The book recounts Epel's interviews with prominent contemporary writers of fiction (e.g., Isabel Allende, Maya Angelou, Stephen King, John Sayles, Amy Tan, John Barth, Anne Rice, Elmore Leonard, William Styron), in which she asks them how dreams have shaped, influenced, and informed their writing. The answers Epel elicits from these writers are fascinating to read, and the material she gathers in *Writers Dreaming* should be of value to scholars from many different areas of dream psychology.

Along the same lines as Epel's work, two books have come out recently that present the dream journals of important literary artists: Graham Greene, *A World of My Own: A Dream Diary* (Greene 1992), and William S. Burroughs, *My Education: A Book of Dreams* (Burroughs 1995). Both books offer fascinating insights into the dreaming imaginations of people whose contributions to twentieth-century literary culture have been enormous. An earlier literary dream journal is that of Jack Kerouac: *Book of Dreams* (Kerouac 1981).

Other good works examining the relations between dreams, psychology, and literature are C. B. Hieatt's *Realism of Dream Vision: The Poetic Exploitation of the Dream Experience in Chaucer and His Contemporaries* (Hieatt 1967), M. Weidhorn's *Dreams in Seventeenth-Century English Literature* (Weidhorn 1970), M. B. Garber's *Dream in Shakespeare: From Metaphor to Metamorphosis* (Garber 1974), A. C. Spearing's *Medieval Dream-Poetry* (Spearing 1976), M. Skura's *The Literary Use of the Psychoanalytic Process* (Skura 1981), K. Stockholder's *Dream Works: Lovers and Families in Shakespeare's Plays* (Stockholder 1987), R. Russo's anthology *Dreams Are Wiser Than Men* (Russo 1987), K. L. Lynch's *The High Medieval Dream Vision: Poetry, Philosophy, and Literary Form* (Lynch 1988), J. Van Meurs and J. Kidd's *Jungian Literary Criticism, 1920–1980: An Annotated, Critical Bibliography of Works in English* (Van Meurs and Kidd 1988), R. Kagan's *Lucrecia's Dreams: The Politics of Prophesy in Sixteenth-Century Spain* (Kagan 1990), and D. B. Wilson's *The Romantic Dream: Wordsworth and the Poetics of the Unconscious* (Wilson 1993).

Many popular psychology books include discussions of dreams and artistic creativity. Both S. Brook's *The Oxford Book of Dreams* (Brook 1987) and C. Navratil's *In the House of Night: A Dream Reader*

(Navratil 1997) present dozens of excerpts from famous literary texts and from the personal writings of famous artists relating to dreams. N. MacKenzie's *Dreams and Dreaming* (MacKenzie 1965) presents wonderful reproductions of dream-inspired art from various eras of Western history, while both R. De Becker's *The Understanding of Dreams* (De Becker 1968) and R. Van de Castle's *Our Dreaming Mind* (Van de Castle 1994) have lengthy chapters on the role of dreams in art, literature, and culture. M. L. Von Franz's *Dreams* (Von Franz 1991) includes a series of studies of dreams in the lives of major Western cultural figures. M. Ullman and C. Limmer's anthology *The Variety of Dream Experience* (Ullman and Limmer 1987) presents several articles on dreams, creativity, and history. S. Krippner's anthology *Dreamtime and Dreamwork* (Krippner 1990) devotes a whole section to dreams in creativity and education.

Dreams, Psychology, and Religion

The relationship between dreams, psychology, and religion is filled with ambiguity. On the one hand, religion is in historical terms the "original" field of dream study with continuing relevance to modern psychological investigations, a point discussed in W. Doniger and K. Bulkeley's "Why Study Dreams? A Religious Studies Perspective" (Doniger and Bulkeley 1993). On the other hand, many of the leading researchers in the psychology of dreaming have sharply distinguished modern psychological approaches to dreams from traditional religious approaches (e.g., Freud 1965a, Hall and Van de Castle 1966, Foulkes 1985, Hobson 1988). As a result, a great deal of controversy and debate fills this particular area of dream study.

Many excellent works have been written on the historical and cross-cultural dimensions of the relationship between dreams, psychology, and religion. K. Frieden's *Freud's Dream of Interpretation* (Frieden 1990) examines the roots of Freud's dream theory in traditional Jewish religious teachings about dreams. M. Harris's *Studies in Jewish Dream Interpretation* (Harris 1994) is a detailed investigation of those rich traditional Jewish teachings, as is J. Covitz's *Visions of the Night: A Study of Jewish Dream Interpretation* (Covitz 1990). A. Leo Oppenheim's "The Interpretation of Dreams in the Ancient Near East with a Translation of an Assyrian Dream-Book" (Oppenheim 1956) remains the most detailed account of the many important roles dreams played in the religions of the ancient Near East. M. Kelsey's *God, Dreams, and Revelation: A Christian Interpretation of Dreams* (Kelsey 1974) provides an outstanding survey of Christian teachings about dreams. P. C. Miller's "'A Dubious Twilight': Reflections on Dreams in Patristic Literature" (Miller 1986) and *Dreams in Late Antiquity: Studies in the Imagination of a Culture* (Miller 1994) discuss the extensive attention given to dreams by early Christian theologians. S. M. Oberhelman's translation of *The Oneirocriticon of Achmet: A Medieval Greek and Arabic Treatise on the Interpretation of Dreams* (Oberhelman 1991) includes a good introductory discussion of the religious role of dreams in antiquity.

A. Wayman's "Significance of Dreams in India and Tibet" (Wayman 1967) discusses dreams in the religious and mythological texts of Indian and Tibetan culture. W. D. O'Flaherty's *Dreams, Illusion, and Other Realities* (O'Flaherty 1984) offers a wide-ranging survey of Hindu teachings on dreams. M. C. Jedrej and R. Shaw's *Dreaming, Religion, and Society in Africa* (Jedrej and Shaw 1992) has several anthropological articles analyzing the religious significance of dreams in various African cultures. G. E. Von Grunebaum and R. Callois's *The Dream and Human Societies* (Von Grunebaum and Callois 1966) includes articles on dreams in many of the world's religions, with many of the articles focusing on dreams and Islam. L. Irwin's *The Dream Seekers: Native American Visionary Traditions of the Great Plains* (Irwin 1994) describes the many important roles dreams and visions played in the religious traditions of the Plains Indians. G. Tanabe's *Myoe the Dreamkeeper: Fantasy and Knowledge in Early Kamakura Buddhism* (Tanabe 1992) discusses how dreams were a key spiritual resource in the efforts of the twelfth-century Buddhist leader Myoe Shonin to revitalize Buddhist religion in Japan. E. Swedenborg's *Journal of Dreams* (Van Dusen 1986) provides a record of the dreams and visions that helped transform Swedenborg from a scientist into a religious mystic; Van Dusen's commentary on the journal draws on Jungian psychology to evaluate Swedenborg's dream-fueled journey of spiritual discovery. K. P. Kramer's *Death Dreams: Unveiling Mysteries of the Unconscious Mind* (Kramer 1993) looks at how many different religious and philosophical traditions have understood the relationship between dreaming and death. K. Bulkeley's *Spiritual Dreaming: A Cross-Cultural and Historical Journey* (Bulkeley 1995) offers a survey of the most important roles dreams have played in the world's religious traditions. J. Campbell's edited anthology *Myths, Dreams, and Religion* (Campbell 1970) includes several good articles directly related to the relationship between dreams, religion, and psychology.

Almost every article cited in the bibliographic essay "Cross-Cultural Studies in Dreams" touches on the relationship of dreams and religion, and many of the articles address that relationship in great detail.

Readers interested in the area of dreams, psychology, and religion should look closely at the cross-cultural literature on dreams.

Although some modern psychologists are skeptical about the relevance of religion to the psychological study of dreams, others insist that the connection is extremely important. C. G. Jung regards psychology as a modern transformation of religion, and in *Memories, Dreams, Reflections* (Jung 1965) and *Dreams* (Jung 1974) he argues that dreams are one of the best ways for modern, secularized Westerners to reconnect with the essentially religious yearnings of the psyche. Many other books have been written on the connection between Jungian and religious or spiritual approaches to dreams: M. Kelsey's *Dreams: A Way to Listen to God* (Kelsey 1978) and *God, Dreams, and Revelation: A Christian Interpretation of Dreams* (Kelsey 1991), J. Sanford's *Dreams: God's Forgotten Language* (Sanford 1982), L. M. Savary, P. H. Berne, and S. K. Williams's *Dreams and Spiritual Growth: A Christian Approach to Dreamwork* (Savary, Berne, and Williams 1984), P. H. Berne and L. M. Savary's *Dream Symbol Work* (Berne and Savary 1991), P. O'Connor's *Dreams and the Search for Meaning* (O'Connor 1987), J. D. Clift and W. B. Clift's *Symbols of Transformation in Dreams* (Clift and Clift 1986) and *The Hero Journey in Dreams* (Clift and Clift 1991), and J. A. Hall's *The Unconscious Christian: Images of God in Dreams* (Hall 1993).

In *The Analysis of Dreams* (Boss 1958) M. Boss describes a number of dreams from his patients that disclose profound religious truths, powers, and realities. E. Fromm's *The Forgotten Language: An Introduction to the Understanding of Dreams, Fairy Tales, and Myths* (Fromm 1951) describes the common symbolic language spoken by both ancient religions and modern psychological theories. J. Taylor's *Dream Work* (Taylor 1983) and *Where People Fly and Water Runs Uphill* (Taylor 1992) show how dreamsharing groups create the kind of spiritual community and mutual understanding that all religions strive to achieve. H. Hunt's *The Multiplicity of Dreams* (Hunt 1989) investigates the many types of dreams reported from cultures around the world and suggests that the more "intensified" types (which often have religious qualities) can be explained as the product of certain cognitive processes interacting in especially powerful and creative ways. Very similar to Hunt's book is J. B. Arden's *Consciousness, Dreams, and Self: A Transdisciplinary Approach* (Arden 1996), which integrates biological, philosophical, and psychophysiological perspectives to argue that dreaming reveals better than anything else the contextual, fluid nature of human consciousness. E. B. Bynum's *Families and the Interpretation of Dreams: Awakening the Intimate Web* (Bynum 1993) reveals the connections between traditional African religious teachings and modern psychological dream research.

Much of the literature on lucid dreaming specifically addresses the religious dimensions of lucid-dream experience. S. LaBerge's *Lucid Dreaming* (LaBerge 1985) describes lucid dreaming as a means by which Westerners can experience the kinds of spiritual insights gained in the practice of Buddhist yogic and meditational traditions. Similarly, J. Gackenbach and J. Bosveld's *Control Your Dreams* (Gackenbach and Bosveld 1989) compare lucid dreaming to various Eastern religious practices. Criticism of this view of lucid dreaming can be found in W. Doniger's "Western Dreams about Eastern Dreams" (Doniger 1996) and N. Norbu's *Dream Yoga and the Practice of Natural Light* (Norbu 1992), both of which argue that lucid dreaming cannot be a shortcut for Westerners who want to experience an Eastern form of religious enlightenment.

Two works have been written that focus on dreams as a key intersection in the contemporary dialogue between religion and psychology. J. Gollnick's *Dreams in the Psychology of Religion* (Gollnick 1987) uses the psychology of William James to evaluate and explore the religious dimensions of dreams. K. Bulkeley's *The Wilderness of Dreams: Exploring the Religious Meanings of Dreams in Modern Western Culture* (Bulkeley 1994) integrates the major dream theories of the twentieth century with a hermeneutically informed theory of religious meaning.

Many books on dreams by popular psychologists include sections on the religious or spiritual dimensions of dreams. Because this aspect of dreams is of such great interest to members of the general public, readers who are interested in this area of dream study should give special attention to popular psychological texts.

Key Resources in the Study of Dreams

Whether the reader is a high school student or an advanced academic specialist, the following resources can offer valuable assistance in any research project in the study of dreaming.

• *Standard Edition of The Complete Psychological Works of Sigmund Freud* (Freud 1953–74). Freud's theories remain central to the modern psychology of dreaming, and the *Standard Edition* collects all of Freud's works into a well-organized, readily accessible set of volumes.
• *The Collected Works of C. G. Jung* (Jung 1974). Jung's theories may be even more influential than Freud's on current developments in dream psychology. *The Collected Works* presents Jung's prolific writings on dreams, symbolism, and consciousness (although Jung's vitally important

autobiography, *Memories, Dreams, Reflections* [Jung 1965], is not in-cluded among the 20 volumes).

• *Encyclopedia of Sleep and Dreaming* (Carskadon 1993). The *Encyclopedia* covers a vast range of topics in the study of sleep and dream-ing, drawing on the basic findings of biological, medical, and psycho-logical research. The information is presented clearly, in a form that both general readers and academic specialists will find helpful.

• SUNY Series in Dream Studies, edited by R. Van de Castle. Since 1991 the State University of New York Press has been publishing a series of books, under the general editorship of R. Van de Castle, on the study of dreams. This series has helped to stimulate an ever-growing dialogue among dream researchers from many different academic fields and theoretical backgrounds. Books published so far in the SUNY Se-ries in Dream Studies include D. Koulack's *To Catch a Dream: Explora-tions of Dreaming* (Koulack 1991), M. T. B. Dombeck's *Dreams and Pro-fessional Personhood: The Contexts of Dream Telling and Dream Interpretation among American Psychotherapists* (Dombeck 1991), A. Moffitt, M. Kramer, and R. Hoffmann's *The Functions of Dreaming* (Moffitt, Kramer, and Hoffmann 1993), C. S. Rupprecht's *The Dream and the Text: Essays on Language and Literature* (Rupprecht 1993), G. Delaney's *New Directions in Dream Interpretation* (Delaney 1993), K. Bulkeley's *The Wilderness of Dreams: Exploring the Religious Meanings of Dreams in Modern Western Culture* (Bulkeley 1994), A. Shafton's *Dream Reader: Contemporary Approaches to the Understanding of Dreams* (Shaf-ton 1995), and K. Bulkeley's *Among All These Dreamers: Essays on Dreaming and Modern Society* (Bulkeley 1996).

• *Dreaming: The Journal of the Association for the Study of Dreams.* First appearing in 1991, the quarterly, peer-reviewed journal *Dreaming* is the leading periodical devoted exclusively to the study of dreams. It publishes articles that cover the full spectrum of dream research, from clinical case studies to sleep laboratory investigations, from anthropo-logical field research to literary criticism, from cognitive psychology to group dreamsharing techniques.

• The Association for the Study of Dreams (ASD). The ASD is a nonprofit, international, multidisciplinary organization dedicated to the pure and applied investigation of dreams and dreaming. Its pur-poses are to promote an awareness and appreciation of dreams in both professional and public arenas, to encourage research into the nature, function, and significance of dreaming, to advance the application of the study of dreams, and to provide a forum for the eclectic and inter-disciplinary exchange of ideas and information. In addition to sponsor-ing the journal *Dreaming*, the ASD hosts an annual five-day conference at which hundreds of the world's foremost dream researchers gather to share their work; publishes a quarterly magazine, *Dream Time*, with interviews, research reports, bibliographic summaries, and debates on cutting-edge issues in the field; sponsors regional meetings and symposia in many different parts of the world; and fosters the further growth and development of the study of dreams in all its diversity. Anyone interested in studying the psychology of dreaming, from any perspective or background, will find the ASD to be an invaluable source of information, support, and encouragement. Details on the ASD's programs are available by contacting the central office: The Association for the Study of Dreams, P.O. Box 1600, Vienna, VA, 22183, phone: 703-242-0062, fax: 703-242-8888, e-mail: ASDreams@aol.com; website: http://www.ASDreams.org.

Bibliography

Ablon, S. L., and Mack, J. E. 1980. Children's Dreams Reconsidered. *Psychoanalytic Study of the Child* 35:179–217.

Adams, M. V. 1996. *The Multicultural Imagination: "Race," Color, and the Unconscious*. London: Routledge.

Adler, Alfred. 1956. *The Individual Psychology of Alfred Adler*. Edited by H. L. A. and R. R. Ansbacher. New York: Harper Torchbooks.

Alston, T., Calogeras, R., and Deserno, H., eds. 1993. *Dream Reader: Psychoanalytic Articles on Dreams*. Madison, Conn.: International Universities Press.

Arden, J. B. 1996. *Consciousness, Dreams, and Self: A Transdisciplinary Approach*. Madison, Conn.: Psychosocial Press.

Aristotle. 1941a. *On Dreams*. Translated and edited by R. McKeon. New York: Random House.

———. 1941b. On Prophesying by Dreams. In *The Collected Works of Aristotle*, edited by R. McKeon. New York: Random House.

Armitage, R. 1992. Gender Differences and the Effect of Stress on Dream Recall: a Thirty-Day Diary Report. *Dreaming* 2(3): 137–42.

Arnold-Forster, M. 1921. *Studies in Dreams*. London: Allen & Unwin.

Artemidorus. 1975. *Oneirocriticon*. Translated by Robert J. White. Park Ridge, N.J.: Noyes Press.

Aserinsky, E. and Kleitman, N. 1953. Regularly Occurring Periods of Eye Motility, and Concomitant Phenomena, during Sleep. *Science* 118:273–74.

177

———. Two Types of Ocular Motility Occurring in Sleep. *Journal of Applied Physiology* 8:1–10.

Baars, B., and Banks, W., eds. 1994. "Dream Consciousness: A Neurocognitive Approach." (Special Issue of *Consciousness and Cognition,* vol. 3, no. 1). San Diego, Calif.: Academic Press.

Bakan, D. 1958. *Sigmund Freud and the Jewish Mystical Tradition.* Boston: Beacon Press.

Barrett, D. 1991. Flying Dreams and Lucidity: An Empirical Study of Their Relationship. *Dreaming* 1(2): 129–34.

———. 1992. Just How Lucid Are Lucid Dreams? *Dreaming* 2(4): 221–28.

———. 1994. Dreams in Dissociative Disorders. *Dreaming* 4(3): 165–76.

———. 1996. *Trauma and Dreams.* Cambridge: Harvard University Press.

Bearden, C. 1994. The Nightmare: Biological and Psychological Origins. *Dreaming* 4(2): 139–52.

Beaudet, D. 1990. *Encountering the Monster: Pathways in Children's Dreams.* New York: Continuum.

Bellah, R., Madsen, R., Sullivan, W. M., Swidler, A., and Tipton, S. M. 1985. *Habits of the Heart: Individualism and Commitment in American Life.* Berkeley: University of California Press.

Belicki, K. 1986. Recalling Dreams: An Examination of Daily Variation and Individual Differences. In *Sleep and Dreams: A Sourcebook,* edited by J. Gackenbach. New York: Garland.

Bell, A., and Hall, C. 1971. *The Personality of a Child Molester: An Analysis of Dreams.* Chicago: Aldine Atherton.

Beradt, C. 1966. *The Third Reich of Dreams.* Translated by A. Gottwald. Chicago: Quadrangle Books.

Berger, P. 1967. *The Sacred Canopy: Elements of a Sociological Theory of Religion.* Garden City, N.Y.: Doubleday.

Berlyne, D. E. 1960. *Conflict, Arousal, and Curiosity.* New York: McGraw-Hill.

Berne, P., and Savary, L. 1991. *Dream Symbol Work.* Mahwah, N.J.: Paulist Press.

Bernheimer, C., and Kahane, C., eds. 1985. *In Dora's Case: Freud—Hysteria—Feminism.* New York: Columbia University Press.

Binswanger, L. 1967. *Being in the World: Selected Papers of Ludwig Binswanger.* Translated by J. Needleman. New York: Harper Torchbooks.

———. 1993. Dream and Existence. In *Dream and Existence*, edited by K. Hoeller. Atlantic Highlands, N.J.: Humanities Press.

Blagrove, M. 1992. Dreams as the Reflection of our Waking Concerns and Abilities: A Critique of the Problem-Solving Paradigm in Dream Research. *Dreaming* 2(4): 205–20.

Bonime, W., with Bonime, F. 1988. *The Clinical Use of Dreams.* New York: DeCapo Press.

Bosnak, R. 1988. *A Little Course in Dreams.* Boston: Shambhala.

———. 1989. *Dreaming with an AIDS Patient: An Intimate Look Inside the Dreams of a Gay Man with AIDS by His Analyst.* Boston: Shambhala.

———. 1996. *Tracks in the Wilderness of Dreaming: Exploring Interior Landscape through Practical Dreamwork.* New York: Delacorte Press.

Boss, M. 1958. *The Analysis of Dreams.* New York: Philosophical Library.

———. 1977. *I Dreamt Last Night . . .* New York: Gardner.

Breger, L. 1967. Function of Dreams. *Journal of Abnormal Psychology*, monograph 72.

Brenneis, C. 1975. Developmental Aspects of Aging in Women: A Comparative Study of Dreams. *Archives of General Psychiatry* 32:429–34.

Brockway, S. S. 1987. Group Treatment of Combat Nightmares in Post-Traumatic Stress Disorder. *Journal of Contemporary Psychotherapy* 17:270–84.

Brook, S., ed. 1987. *The Oxford Book of Dreams*. Oxford: Oxford University Press.

Browning, D. 1987. *Religious Thought and the Modern Psychologies: A Critical Conversation in the Theology of Culture*. Philadelphia: Fortress Press.

Bruner, J., Jolly, A., and Sylva, K. eds., 1976. *Play: Its Role in Development and Evolution*. New York: Basic Books.

Bulkeley, K. 1994. *The Wilderness of Dreams: Exploring the Religious Meanings of Dreams in Modern Western Culture*. Albany: State University of New York Press.

———. 1995. *Spiritual Dreaming: A Cross-Cultural and Historical Journey*. Mahwah, N.J.: Paulist.

———. ed. 1996. *Among All These Dreamers: Essays on Dreaming and Modern Society*. Albany: State University of New York Press.

———. 1997. *An Introduction to the Psychology of Dreaming*. Westport, Conn.: Praeger.

Burridge, K. 1960. *Mambu: A Melanesian Millennium*. London: Methuen.

Burroughs, W. S. 1995. *My Education: A Book of Dreams*. New York: Viking.

Bynum, E. B. 1993. *Families and the Interpretation of Dreams: Awakening the Intimate Web*. New York: Harrington Park Press.

Campbell, J., ed. 1970. *Myths, Dreams, and Religion*. New York: E. P. Dutton.

Carskadon, M., ed. 1993. *Encyclopedia of Sleep and Dreaming*. New York: Macmillan.

Cartwright, R. 1979. *Night Life: Explorations in Dreaming*. Englewood Cliffs, N.J.: Prentice Hall.

———. 1991. Dreams That Work: The Relation of Dream Incorporation to Adaptation to Stressful Events. *Dreaming* 1 (1): 3–10.

———. 1993. Who Needs Their Dream? The Usefulness of Dreams in Psychotherapy. *Journal of the American Academy of Psychoanalysis* 21(4): 539–47.

Cartwright, R., and Lamberg, L. 1992. *Crisis Dreaming: Using Your Dreams to Solve Your Problems*. New York: Harper Collins.

Cartwright, R., Lloyd, S., Knight, S., and Trenholme, I. 1984. Broken Dreams: A Study of the Effects of Divorce and Depression on Dream Content. *Psychiatry* 47:251–59.

Catalano, S. 1990. *Children's Dreams in Clinical Practice*. New York: Plenum Press.

Charsley, S. R. 1973. Dreams in an Independent African Church. *Africa: Journal of the International African Institute* 43(3): 244–57.

———. 1987. Dreams and Purposes: An Analysis of Dream Narratives in an Independent African Church. *Africa: Journal of the International African Institute* 57(3): 281–96.

Clark, R. W. 1980. *Freud: The Man and the Cause*. New York: Random House.

Clift, J. D., and Clift, W. B. 1986. *Symbols of Transformation in Dreams*. New York: Crossroad.

———. 1991. *The Hero Journey in Dreams*. New York: Crossroad.

Cooper, J. 1987. *The Nightmare on Elm Street Companion*. New York: St. Martin's Press.

Covitz, J. 1990. *Visions of the Night: A Study of Jewish Dream Interpretation*. Boston: Shambhala.

Crapanzano, V. 1975. Saints, Jnun, and Dreams: An Essay in Moroccan Ethnopsychology. *Psychiatry* 38:145–59.

Crick, F., and Mitchison, G. 1983. The Function of Dream Sleep. *Nature* 304:111–14.

Cuddy, M. A., and Belicki, K. 1992. Nightmare Frequency and Related Sleep Disturbance as Indicators of a History of Sexual Abuse. *Dreaming* 2(1): 15–22.

———. 1996. The Fifty-five-Year Secret: Using Nightmares to Facilitate Psychotherapy in a Case of Childhood Sexual Abuse. In *Among All These Dreamers: Essays on Dreaming and Modern Society*, edited by K. Bulkeley.

Curley, R. T. 1983. Dreams of Power: Social Process in a West African Religious Movement. *Africa: Journal of the International African Institute* 53(3): 20–37.

Dahlenberg, R., Christensen, O. J., and Moore, J. C. 1996. The Effect of Group Dreamwork on Spiritual Well-Being. *Journal of Psychology and Theology* 24:54–61.

Davis, W. 1980. *Dojo: Magic and Exorcism in Modern Japan*. Stanford, Calif.: Stanford University Press.

Dawkins, R. 1995. *River out of Eden: A Darwinian View of Life*. New York: Basic Books.

De Becker, R. 1968. *The Understanding of Dreams and Their Influence on the History of Man*. New York: Hawthorn Books.

Decker, H. 1991. *Freud, Dora, and Vienna 1900*. New York: Free Press.

Delaney, G. 1979. *Living Your Dreams*. New York: Harper and Row.

———. 1991. *Breakthrough Dreaming: How to Tap the Power of Your Twenty-four-Hour Mind*. New York: Bantam.

————. ed. 1993. *New Directions in Dream Interpretation.* Albany: State University of New York Press.

————. 1994. *Sensual Dreaming: How to Understand and Interpret the Erotic Content of Your Dreams.* New York: Fawcett Columbine.

Dement, W. 1960. The Effect of Dream Deprivation. *Science* 131: 1705–1707.

————. 1972. *Some Must Watch While Some Must Sleep: Exploring the World of Sleep.* New York: W.W. Norton.

————. 1992. *The Sleepwatchers.* Stanford: Stanford Alumni Association.

Dement, W., Kahn, E., and Roffwarg, H. 1965. The Influence of the Laboratory Situation on the Dreams of the Experimental Subject. *Journal of Nervous and Mental Disease* 149:119–31.

Dentan, R. K., and McClusky, L. J. 1993. "Pity the Bones by Wandering River which Still in Lovers' Dreams Appear as Men." In *The Functions of Dreaming.* Edited by A. Moffitt, R. Hoffmann, and M. Kramer. Albany: State University of New York Press.

Derr, D. B., and Zimpfer, D. G. 1996. Dreams in Group Therapy: A Review of Models. *International Journal of Group Psychotherapy* 46:501–15.

Descola, P. 1993. *The Spears of Twilight: Life and Death in the Amazon Jungle.* New York: The New Press.

Devereux, G., ed. 1953. *Psychoanalysis and the Occult.* New York: International Universities Press.

————. 1969. *Reality and Dream: Psychotherapy of a Plains Indian.* Rev. ed. New York: Doubleday Anchor.

————. 1975. *Dreams in Greek Tragedy: An Ethno-Psychoanalytic Study.* Berkeley: University of California Press.

Dombeck, M. T. 1991. *Dreams and Professional Personhood: The Contexts of Dream Telling and Dream Interpretation among American Psycho-therapists.* Albany: State University of New York Press.

Domhoff, G. W. 1985. *The Mystique of Dreams: A Search for Utopia Through Senoi Dream Theory.* Berkeley: University of California Press.

———. 1996. *Finding Meaning in Dreams: A Quantitative Approach.* New York: Plenum.

Doniger, W., 1996. Western Dreams about Eastern Dreams. In *Among All These Dreamers: Essays on Dreaming and Modern Society,* edited by K. Bulkeley. Albany: State University of New York Press.

Doniger, W., and Bulkeley, K. 1993. Why Study Dreams? A Religious Studies Perspective. *Dreaming* 3 (1): 69–74.

Downing, J. J. 1973. *Dreams and Nightmares: A Book of Gestalt Therapy Sessions.* New York: Harper and Row.

Dudley, L., and·Fungaroli, J. 1987. The Dreams of Students in a Women's College: Are They Different? *ASD Newsletter* 4(6): 6–7.

Dunlop, C., ed. 1977. *Philosophical Essays on Dreaming.* Ithaca, N.Y.: Cornell University Press.

Ebert, R. 1997. *Roger Ebert's Book of Film.* New York: W. W. Norton.

Edgar, I. 1995. *Dreamwork, Anthropology, and the Caring Professions.* Aldershot, England: Avebury.

Eggan, D. 1952. The Manifest Content of Dreams: A Challenge to Social Science. *American Anthropologist* 54:469–85.

———. 1955. The Personal Use of Myth in Dreams. *Journal of American Folklore* 68:445–63.

———. 1957. Hopi Dreams and a Life History Sketch. *Primary Records in Culture and Personality* 2(16): 1–147.

Ekstein, R. 1981. Some Thoughts Concerning the Clinical Use of Children's Dreams. *Bulletin of the Menninger Clinic.* 45(2):115–24.

Ellenberger, H. 1970. *The Discovery of the Unconscious: The History and Evolution of Dynamic Psychiatry*. New York: Basic Books.

Ellman, S., ed. 1991. *The Mind in Sleep: Psychology and Psychophysiology*. 2d ed. New York: John Wiley & Sons.

Epel, N. 1993. *Writers Dreaming: Twenty-six Writers Talk About Their Dreams and the Creative Process*. New York: Crown.

Erikson, E. 1954. The Dream Specimen of Psychoanalysis. *Journal of the American Psychoanalytical Association* 2:5–56.

———. 1963. *Childhood and Society*. New York: W. W. Norton.

Evans, C. 1983. *Landscapes of the Night: How and Why We Dream*. London: V. Gollancz.

Ewing, K. 1989. The Dream of Spiritual Initiation and the Organization of Self Representations among Pakistani Sufis. *American Ethnologist* 16:56–74.

Fabian, J. 1966. Dreams and Charisma: "Theories of Dreams" in the Jamaa-Movement (Congo). *Anthropos* 61:544–60.

Fagan, Joen, and Shepherd, Irma Lee, eds. 1970. *Gestalt Therapy Now: Theory, Techniques, Applications*. New York: Harper Colophon.

Faraday, A. 1972. *Dream Power*. New York: Berkeley Books.

———. 1974. *The Dream Game*. New York: Harper and Row.

Firth, R. 1934. The Meaning of Dreams in Tikopia. In *Essays Presented to C. G. Seligman*, edited by E. E. Evans-Pritchard. London: Kegan Paul.

Fisher, H. J. 1979. Dreams and Conversion in Black Africa. In *Conversion to Islam*, edited by N. Levtzion. New York: Holmes and Meier.

Flannery, R., and Chambers, M. E. 1985. Each Man Has His Own Friends: The Role of Dream Visitors in Traditional East Cree Belief and Practice. *Arctic Anthropology* 22(1):1–22.

Fosshage, J. L. 1983. The Psychological Function of Dreams: A Revised Psychoanalytic Perspective. *Psychoanalysis and Contemporary Thought* 6(4): 641–70.

Fosshage, J. L., and Loew, C. A., eds. 1978. *Dream Interpretation: A Comparative Study*. New York: Spectrum.

Foucault, M. 1993. Dream, Imagination, and Existence. In *Dream and Existence*, edited by K. Hoeller. Atlantic Highlands, N.J.: Humanities Press.

Foulkes, D. 1962. Dream Reports from Different Stages of Sleep. *Journal of Abnormal and Social Psychology* 65:14–25.

————. 1967. Dreams of a Male Child: Four Case Studies. *Journal of Child Psychology and Psychiatry* 8:81–98.

————. 1971. Longitudinal Studies of Dreams in Children. *Science and Psychoanalysis.* 19:48–71.

————. 1978a. Dreams of Innocence. *Psychology Today* (December): 78–88.

————. 1978b. *A Grammar of Dreams*. New York: Basic Books.

————. 1979. Children's Dreams. In *Handbook of Dreams: Research, Theories, and Applications*, edited by B. B. Wolman. New York: Van Nostrand Reinhold.

————. 1982a. *Children's Dreams: Longitudinal Studies*. New York: Wiley.

————. 1982b. A Cognitive-Psychological Model of REM Dream Production. *Sleep* 5(2): 169–87.

————. 1985. *Dreaming: A Cognitive-Psychological Analysis*. Hillsdale, N.J.: L. Erlbaum.

Foulkes, D., Larson, J. D., Swanson, E. M., and Rardin, M. 1969. Two Studies of Childhood Dreaming. *American Journal of Orthopsychiatry* 39: 627–43.

French, T., and Fromm, E. 1964. *Dream Interpretation: A New Approach*. New York: Basic Books.

Freud, S. 1953–74. *Standard Edition of the Complete Psychological Works of Sigmund Freud*. Edited by J. Strachey. 24 vols. London: Hogarth Press.

———. 1953a. Psychoanalysis and Telepathy. In *Psychoanalysis and the Occult*, edited by G. Devereux. New York: International Universities Press.

———. 1953. Dreams and Telepathy. In *Psychoanalysis and the Occult*, edited by G. Devereux. New York: International Universities Press.

———. 1953c. The Occult Significance of Dreams. In *Psychoanalysis and the Occult*, edited by G. Devereux. New York: International Universities Press.

———. 1961. *Civilization and its Discontents*. Translated by J. Strachey. New York: W. W. Norton.

———. 1963a. *Dora: Fragment of an Analysis of a Case of Hysteria*. Translated by P. Rieff. New York: Collier Books.

———. 1963b. Remarks upon the Theory and Practice of Dream Interpretation. In *Therapy and Technique*, edited by P. Rieff. New York: Collier Books.

———. 1963c. Some Additional Notes on Dream Interpretation as a Whole. In *Therapy and Technique*, edited by P. Rieff. New York: Collier Books.

———. 1963d. *The Future of an Illusion*. Translated by J. Strachey. New York: W. W. Norton.

———. 1965a. *The Interpretation of Dreams*. Translated by J. Strachey. New York: Avon.

———. 1965b. *New Introductory Lectures on Psychoanalysis*. Translated by J. Strachey. New York: W. W. Norton.

————. 1966. *Introductory Lectures on Psychoanalysis*. Translated by J. Strachey. New York: W. W. Norton.

————. 1980. *On Dreams*. Translated by J. Strachey. New York: W. W. Norton.

Frieden, K. 1990. *Freud's Dream of Interpretation*. Albany: State University of New York Press.

Fromm, E. 1951. *The Forgotten Language: An Introduction to the Understanding of Dreams, Fairy Tales, and Myths*. New York: Grove Press.

Gabbard, K. and Gabbard, G. O. 1987. *Psychiatry and the Cinema*. Chicago: University of Chicago Press.

Gackenbach, J. 1991. Frameworks for Understanding Lucid Dreaming: A Review. *Dreaming* 1(2): 109–28.

————. ed. 1987. *Sleep and Dreams: A Source Book*. New York: Garland.

Gackenbach, J., and Bosveld, J. 1989. *Control Your Dreams*. New York: Harper and Row.

Gackenbach, J., and LaBerge, S., eds. 1988. *Conscious Mind, Sleeping Brain: Perspectives on Lucid Dreaming*. New York: Plenum Press.

Garber, M. B. 1974. *Dream in Shakespeare: From Metaphor to Metamorphosis*. New Haven, Conn.: Yale University Press.

Gardner, J., and Maier, J. trans. 1984. *Gilgamesh*. New York: Random House.

Garfield, P. 1974. *Creative Dreaming*. New York: Ballantine.

————. 1985. *Your Child's Dreams*. New York: Ballantine.

————. 1988. *Women's Bodies, Women's Dreams*. New York: Ballantine.

————. 1989. *Pathway to Ecstasy: The Way of the Dream Mandala*. 2d ed. New York: Prentice Hall.

———. 1991. *The Healing Power of Dreams*. New York: Fireside Books.

Gay, P. 1988. *Freud: A Life for Our Time*. New York: W. W. Norton.

Gedo, J., and Goldberg, A. 1973. *Models of the Mind: A Psychoanalytic Theory*. Chicago: University of Chicago Press.

Gendlin, E. 1986. *Let Your Body Interpret Your Dreams*. Wilmette, Ill.: Chiron.

Gensler, D. 1994. Soliciting Dreams in Child Psychotherapy: The Influence of the Therapist's Interest. *Contemporary Psychoanalysis* 30(2): 367–83.

Gillespie, G. 1992. Light in Lucid Dreams: A Review. *Dreaming* 2(3): 167–80.

Globus, G. 1987. *Dream Life, Wake Life: The Human Condition Through Dreams*. Albany: State University of New York Press.

Goldenberg, N. M. 1979. Dreams and Fantasies as Sources of Revelation: Feminist Appropriation of Jung. In *Womanspirit Rising: A Feminist Reader in Religion*, edited by C. P. Christ and J. Plaskow. San Francisco: Harper & Row.

Gollnick, J. 1987. *Dreams in the Psychology of Religion*. New York: Edwin Mellen Press.

Goodison, L. 1995. *The Dreams of Women: Exploring and Interpreting Women's Dreams*. New York: W. W. Norton.

Gorlitz, D., and Wohlwill, J. F., eds. 1987. *Curiosity, Imagination, and Play*. Hillsdale, N.J.: Lawrence Erlbaum.

Green, C. 1968a. *Lucid Dreams*. London: Hamish Hamilton.

———. 1968b. *Lucid Dreams*. Oxford, England: Institute of Psychophysical Research.

Greenberg, Jay R., and Mitchell, Stephen A. 1983. *Object Relations in Psychoanalytic Theory*. Cambridge: Harvard University Press.

Greenberg, R., Pillard, R., and Pearlman, C. 1972. The Effect of Dream (REM) Deprivation on Adaptation to Stress. *Psychosomatic Medicine* 34:257–62.

Greene, G. 1992. *A World of My Own: A Dream Diary*. New York: Viking.

Gregor, T. 1981a. "Far, Far Away My Shadow Wandered. . .": The Dream Symbolism and Dream Theories of the Mehinaku Indians of Brazil. *American Ethnologist* 8(4): 709–29.

———. 1981b. A Content Analysis of Mehinaku Dreams. *Ethos* 9:353–90.

———. 1983. Dark Dreams about the White Man. *Natural History* 92(1): 8–14.

Grey, A., and Kalsched, D. 1971. Oedipus East and West: An Exploration via Manifest Dream Content. *Journal of Cross-Cultural Psychology* 2:337–52.

Grinstein, A. 1980. *Sigmund Freud's Dreams*. New York: International Universities Press.

Guiley, R. E. 1998. *Dreamwork for the Soul: A Spiritual Guide to Dream Interpretation*. New York: Berkley Books.

Hall, C. 1966. *The Meaning of Dreams*. Rev. ed. New York: McGraw-Hill.

———. 1967. Representation of the Laboratory Setting in Dreams. *Journal of Nervous and Mental Disease* 144:198–206.

———. 1982. The Dreams of College Men and Women in 1950 and 1980: A Comparison of Dream Contents and Sex Differences. *Sleep* 5:188–94.

———. 1984. "A Ubiquitous Sex Difference in Dreams" Revisited. *Journal of Personality and Social Psychology* 46:1109–17.

Hall, C., and Domhoff, G. W. 1963a. A Ubiquitous Sex Difference in Dreams. *Journal of Abnormal and Social Psychology* 66:278–80.

————. 1963b. Aggression in Dreams. *International Journal of Social Psychiatry* 9:259–67.

————. 1964. Friendliness in Dreams. *Journal of Social Psychology* 62:309–14.

————. 1968. The Dreams of Freud and Jung. *Psychology Today.*

Hall, C., and Lind, R. 1970. *Dreams, Life, and Literature: A Study of Franz Kafka.* Chapel Hill: University of North Carolina Press.

Hall, C., and Nordby, V. 1972. *The Individual and His Dreams.* New York: Signet Books.

Hall, C., and Van de Castle, R. 1966. *The Content Analysis of Dreams.* New York: Appleton-Century-Crofts.

Hall, J. A. 1983. *Jungian Dream Interpretation.* New York: Inner City Books.

————. 1993. *The Unconscious Christian: Images of God in Dreams.* Mahwah, N.J.: Paulist Press.

Hall, L. J. 1994. Experiential Dream Group Work from a Lay Perspective. *Dreaming* 4(4): 231–36.

Hallowell, A. I. 1966. The Role of Dreams in Ojibwa Culture. In *The Dream and Human Societies*, edited by G. E. Von Grunebaum and R. Callois. Berkeley: University of California Press.

Harley, M. 1962. The Role of the Dream in the Analysis of a Latency Child. *Journal of the American Psychoanalytic Association.* 10(2):271–88.

Harris, M. 1994. *Studies in Jewish Dream Interpretation.* Northvale, N.J.: Jason Aronson.

Hartmann, E. 1984. *The Nightmare: The Psychology and Biology of Terrifying Dreams.* New York: Basic Books.

————. 1991a. *Boundaries of the Mind: A New Psychology of Personality.* New York: Basic Books.

————. 1991b. Introductory Statement. *Dreaming* 1(1): 1–2.

————. 1995. Making Connections in a Safe Place: Is Dreaming Psychotherapy? *Dreaming* 5(4): 213–28.

————. 1998. *Dreams and Nightmares: The New Theory on the Origin and Meaning of Dreams.* New York: Plenum Trade.

Hartmann, E., Elkin, R., and Garg, M. 1991c. Personality and Dreaming: The Dreams of People with Very Thick or Very Thin Boundaries. *Dreaming* 1(4): 311–24.

Haskell, R. E. 1986. Cognitive Psychology and Dream Research: Historical, Conceptual, and Epistemological Considerations. *The Journal of Mind and Behavior* 7(2–3): 131–59.

Heidel, A. 1963. *The Gilgamesh Epic and Old Testament Parallels.* Chicago: University of Chicago Press.

Hieatt, C. B. 1967. *Realism of Dream Vision: The Poetic Exploitation of the Dream Experience in Chaucer and His Contemporaries.* The Hague: Moton.

Hill, C. E. 1996. *Working with Dreams in Psychotherapy.* New York: Guilford Press.

Hill, M. O. 1994. *Dreaming the End of the World: Apocalypse as a Rite of Passage.* Dallas, Tex.: Spring Publications.

Hillman, J. 1979. *The Dream and the Underworld.* New York: Harper and Row.

Hobson, J. A. 1988. *The Dreaming Brain: How the Brain Creates Both the Sense and the Nonsense of Dreams.* New York: Basic Books.

Hobson, J. A. and McCarley, R. W. 1977. The Brain as a Dream-State Generator: An Activation-Synthesis Hypothesis of the Dream Process. *American Journal of Psychiatry* 134:1335–68.

Hoeller, K., ed. 1993. *Dream and Existence.* Atlantic Highlands, N.J.: Humanities Press.

Homans, P. 1979. *Jung in Context: Modernity and the Making of a Psychology.* Chicago: University of Chicago Press.

————. 1989. *The Ability to Mourn: Disillusionment and the Social Origins of Psychoanalysis.* Chicago: University of Chicago Press.

Homer. 1961. *The Odyssey.* Translated by R. Fitzgerald. New York: Anchor Books.

Hopcke, R. H. 1990. *Men's Dreams, Men's Healing: A Psychotherapist Explores a New View of Masculinity through Jungian Dreamwork.* Boston: Shambhala.

Huizinga, J. 1955. *Homo Ludens: A Study of the Play Element in Culture.* Boston: Beacon Press.

Hunt, H. 1989. *The Multiplicity of Dreams: Memory, Imagination, and Consciousness.* New Haven, Conn.: Yale University Press.

Irwin, L. 1994. *The Dream Seekers: Native American Visionary Traditions of the Great Plains.* Norman: University of Oklahoma Press.

James, W. 1910. A Suggestion about Mysticism. *Journal of Philosophy, Psychology and Scientific Methods* 7: 5–92.

————. 1958. *The Varieties of Religious Experience.* New York: Mentor Books.

Jedrej, M. C., and Shaw, R., eds. 1992. *Dreaming, Religion, and Society in Africa.* Leiden, the Netherlands: E.J. Brill.

Jokipaltio, L. M. 1982. Dreams in Child Psychoanalysis. *Scandanavian Psychoanalytic Review.* 5(1):31–47.

Jones, E. 1951. *On the Nightmare.* New York: Liveright.

————. 1953–57. *The Life and Work of Sigmund Freud.* 3 vols. New York: Basic Books.

Jones, R. M. 1962. *Ego Synthesis in Dreams.* Cambridge, Mass.: Schenkman Publishing.

——. 1978. *The New Psychology of Dreaming*. New York: Penguin Books.

Jonte-Pace, D. 1993. Psychoanalysis after Feminism. *Religious Studies Review* 19(2):110–15.

——. 1997. New Directions in Feminist Psychology of Religion: An Introduction. *Journal of Feminist Studies in Religion* 13(1): 63–74.

Jung, C. G. 1965. *Memories, Dreams, Reflections.* Translated by R. Winston and C. Winston. New York: Vintage Books.

——. 1966. *The Practice of Psychotherapy.* Translated by R. F. C. Hull. 2d ed. Princeton, N.J.: Princeton University Press.

——. 1974. *The Collected Works of C. G. Jung.* Translated by R. F. C. Hull. Edited by W. McGuire. 20 vols. Princeton, N.J.: Princeton University Press.

——. 1974. *Dreams*. Translated by R. F. C. Hull. Princeton, N.J.: Princeton University Press.

——. ed. 1979. *Man and His Symbols*. New York: Dell Publishing.

——. 1984. *Dream Analysis: C. G. Jung Seminars, Vol. 1.* Translated by R. F. C. Hull. Princeton, N.J.: Princeton University Press.

Kagan, R. 1990. *Lucrecia's Dreams: The Politics of Prophesy in Sixteenth Century Spain*. Berkeley: University of California Press.

Kahan, T. L. 1994. Measuring Dream Self-Reflectiveness: A Comparison of Two Approaches. *Dreaming* 4(3): 177–94.

Kahan, T. L., and LaBerge, S. 1994. Lucid Dreaming as Metacognition:Implications for Cognitive Science. *Consciousness and Cognition* 3:246–64.

——. 1996. Cognition and Metacognition in Dreaming and Waking: Comparisions of First and Third-Person Ratings. *Dreaming* 6(4): 235–49.

Kahan, T. L., LaBerge, S., Levitan, L., and Zimbardo, P. 1997. Similarities and Differences between Dreaming and Waking Cognition: An Exploratory Study. *Consciousness and Cognition* 6: 108–14.

Kakar, S. 1982. *Shamans, Mystics, and Doctors: A Psychological Inquiry into India and its Healing Traditions.* Boston: Beacon Press.

Kane, C. R., Mellen, P., Patton, P., and Samano, I. 1993. Differences in the Manifest Dream Content of Mexican-American and Anglo-American Women: A Research Note. *Hispanic Journal of Behavioral Sciences* 5:134–39.

Karon, B. P. 1996. On Being Abducted by Aliens. *Psychoanalytic Psychology* 13:417–18.

Kellerman, H., ed. 1987. *The Nightmare: Psychological and Biological Foundations.* New York: Columbia University Press.

Kelsey, M. 1981. *God, Dreams, and Revelation: A Christian Interpretation of Dreams.* Minneapolis, Minn.: Augsburg Publishing.

———. 1978. *Dreams: A Way to Listen to God.* Mahwah, N.J.: Paulist Press.

Kelzer, K. 1987. *The Sun and the Shadow.* New York: A.R.E. Press.

Kerouac, J. 1981. *Book of Dreams.* San Francisco: City Lights.

King, J., and Bulkeley, K. 1994. ASD Historical Committee Report. *ASD Newsletter* 11(4): 14–15, 22.

Koulack, D. 1991. *To Catch a Dream: Explorations of Dreaming.* Albany: State University of New York Press.

Kracke, W. 1979. Dreaming in Kagwahiv: Dream Beliefs and Their Psychic Uses in an Amazonian Indian Culture. *The Psychoanalytic Study of Society* 8:119–71.

———. 1981. Kagwahiv Mourning: Dreams of a Bereaved Father. *Ethos* 9(4): 258–75.

———. 1987. Myths in Dreams, Thought in Images: An Amazonian Contribution to the Psychoanalytic Theory of Primary Process. In *Dreaming: Anthropological and Psychological Interpretations*, edited by B. Tedlock. New York: Cambridge University Press.

Krakow, B., and Neidhardt, J. 1992. *Conquering Bad Dreams and Nightmares*. New York: Berkley Books.

Krakow, B., Tandberg, D., Barey, M., and Scriggins, L. 1995. Nightmares and Sleep Disturbance in Sexually Assaulted Women. *Dreaming* 5(3): 199–206.

Kramer, K. P. 1993. *Death Dreams: Unveiling Mysteries of the Unconscious Mind*. Mahwah, N.J.: Paulist Press.

Kramer, M. 1991. The Nightmare: A Failure in Dream Function. *Dreaming* 1(4): 277–86.

Krippner, S., ed. 1990. *Dreamtime and Dreamwork: Decoding the Language of the Night*. Los Angeles: Jeremy Tarcher.

Krippner, S., and Dillard, J. 1988. *Dreamworking: How to Use Your Dreams for Creative Problem-Solving*. Buffalo: Bearly.

Krippner, S., Gabel, S., Green, S., and Rubien, R. 1994. Community Applications of an Experiential Group Approach to Teaching Dreamwork. *Dreaming* 4(4): 215–22.

Kuiken, D. 1995. Dreams and Feeling Realization. *Dreaming* 5(3): 129–58.

Kuiken, D., and Smith, L. 1991. Impactful Dreams and Metaphor Generation. *Dreaming* 1(2): 135–46.

LaBerge, S. 1985. *Lucid Dreaming: The Power of Being Awake and Aware in Your Dreams*. Los Angeles: Jeremy Tarcher.

Lakoff, G. 1993. How Metaphor Structures Dreams: The Theory of Conceptual Metaphor Applied to Dream Analysis. *Dreaming* 3(2): 77–98.

Lakoff, G., and Johnson, M. 1980. *Metaphors We Live By*. Chicago: University of Chicago Press.

Lansky, M., ed. 1992. *Essential Papers on Dreams*. New York: New York University Press.

Lansky, M. R., and Bley, C. R. 1990. Exploration of Nightmares in Hospital Treatment of Borderline Patients. *Bulletin of the Menninger Clinic* 54:466–77.

Lanternari, V. 1975. Dreams as Charismatic Significants: Their Bearing on the Rise of New Religious Movements. In *Psychological Anthropology*, edited by T. R. Williams. Paris: Mouton.

Laufer, B. 1931. Inspirational Dreams in Eastern Asia. *Journal of American Folk-Lore* 44:208–16.

Lauter, E., and Rupprecht, C. S., eds. 1985. *Feminist Archetypal Theory: Interdisciplinary Re-visions of Jungian Thought*. Knoxville: University of Tennessee Press.

Lavie, P., and Kaminer, H. 1991. Dreams That Poison Sleep: Dreaming in Holocaust Survivors. *Dreaming* 1(1): 11–22.

Layard, J. 1988. *The Lady of the Hare: A Study in the Healing Power of Dreams*. Boston: Shambhala.

Levin, R. 1990. Psychoanalytic Theories on the Function of Dreaming: A Review of the Empirical Dream Research. In *Empirical Studies of Psychoanalytic Theories*, vol. 3. Edited by J. Masling. New York: Analytic Press.

Levin, R., Galin, J., and Zywiak, B. 1991. Nightmares, Boundaries, and Creativity. *Dreaming* 1(1): 63–74.

Levine, J. 1991. The Role of Culture in the Representation of Conflict in Dreams: A Comparison of Bedouin, Irish, and Israeli Children. *Journal of Cross Cultural Psychology* 22(4): 472–90.

Lincoln, J. S. 1935. *The Dream in Primitive Cultures*. London: University of London.

Lortie-Lussier, M., Simond, S., Rinfret, N., and De Koninck, J. 1985. Working Mothers versus Homemakers: Do Dreams Reflect the Changing Roles of Women? *Sex Roles* 12:1009–21.

Lortie-Lussier, M., Simond, S., Rinfret, N., and De Koninck, J. 1992. Beyond Sex Differences: Family and Occupational Roles's Impact on Women's and Men's Dreams. *Sex Roles* 26:79–96.

Lowy, Samuel. 1942. *Psychological and Biological Foundations of Dream-Interpretation*. London: Kegan Paul, Trench, and Trubner.

Lynch, Kathryn L. 1988. *The High Medieval Dream Vision: Poetry, Philosophy, and Literary Form*. Stanford, Calif.: Stanford University Press.

Mack, J. E. 1970. *Nightmares and Human Conflict*. New York: Columbia University Press.

MacKenzie, N. 1965. *Dreams and Dreaming*. New York: Vanguard.

Malcolm, N. 1959. *Dreaming*. London: Routledge & Kegan Paul.

Marcus, S. 1985. Freud and Dora: Story, History, Case History. In *In Dora's Case: Freud—Hysteria—Feminism*. Edited by C. Bernheimer and C. Kahane. New York, NY: Columbia University Press.

Masson, J. M., ed. 1985. *The Complete Letters of Sigmund Freud to Wilhelm Fliess, 1887–1904*. Cambridge, Mass.: Belknap Press.

Mattoon, M. A. 1978. *Understanding Dreams*. Dallas, Tex.: Spring Publications.

Maybruck, P. 1989. *Pregnancy and Dreams*. Los Angeles: Jeremy Tarcher.

———. 1991. *Romantic Dreams: How to Enhance Your Romantic Relationship by Understanding and Sharing Your Dreams*. New York: Pocket Books.

McCaffrey, P. 1984. *Freud and Dora: The Artful Dream*. New Brunswick, N.J.: Rutgers University Press.

McDonald, P. 1987. *Dreams: Night Language of the Soul*. New York: Continuum.

McFague, S. 1982. *Metaphorical Theology: Models of God in Religious Language*. Philadelphia: Fortress Press.

McGuire, W., ed. 1974. *The Freud/Jung Letters: The Correspondence between Sigmund Freud and C. G. Jung*. Princeton, N.J.: Princeton University Press.

McLynn, F. 1996. *Carl Gustav Jung: A Biography*. New York: St. Martins Griffin.

Medici de Steiner, C. 1993. Children and Their Dreams. *International Journal of Psychoanalysis* 74(2): 359–70.

Meier, C. A. 1967. *Ancient Incubation and Modern Psychotherapy*. Translated by M. Curtis. Evanston, Ill.: Northwestern University Press.

Miall, D. S., and Kuiken, D. 1997. Coleridge and Dreams: An Introduction. *Dreaming* 7(1): 1–12.

Miller, P. C. 1986. "A Dubious Twilight": Reflections on Dreams in Patristic Literature. *Church History* 55(2): 153–64.

———. 1994. *Dreams in Late Antiquity: Studies in the Imagination of a Culture*. Princeton, N.J.: Princeton University Press.

Mindell, A. 1982. *Dreambody: The Body's Role in Revealing the Self*. London: Routledge & Kegan Paul.

———. 1985. *Working with the Dream Body*. New York: Mathuen Press.

Moffitt, A., and Hoffman, R. 1987. On the Single-Mindedness and Isolation of Dream Psychophysiology. In *Sleep and Dreams: A Sourcebook*. Edited by Jayne Gackenbach. New York: Garland Publishing.

Moffitt, A., Kramer, M., and Hoffmann, R., eds. 1993. *The Functions of Dreaming*. Albany: State University of New York Press.

Moorcroft, W. 1993. *Sleep, Dreaming, and Sleep Disorders*. Second ed. Lanham, Md.: University Press of America.

Morgan, W. 1932. Navaho Dreams. *American Anthropologist* 34:390–405.

Moss, R. 1996. *Conscious Dreaming: A Spiritual Path for Everyday Life.* New York: Crown.

———. 1998. *Dreamgates: An Explorer's Guide to the Worlds of Soul, Imagination, and Life Beyond Death.* New York: Three Rivers Press.

Moustakas, C. 1994. *Existential Psychotherapy and the Interpretation of Dreams.* Northvale, N.J.: Jason Aronson.

Muff, J. 1996. From the Wings of the Night: Dream Work with People Who Have Acquired Immunodeficiency Syndrome. *Holistic Nursing Practice* 10:69–87.

Navratil, C., ed. 1997. *In the House of Night: A Dream Reader.* San Francisco: Chronicle Books.

Noll, R. 1994. *The Jung Cult: Origins of a Charismatic Movement.* Princeton, N.J.: Princeton University Press.

Norbu, N. 1992. *Dream Yoga and the Practice of Natural Light.* Ithaca, N.Y.: Snow Lions Publications.

O'Flaherty, W. D. 1984. *Dreams, Illusion, and Other Realities.* Chicago: University of Chicago Press.

O'Nell, C. W. 1976. *Dreams, Culture, and the Individual.* San Francisco: Chandler and Sharp.

Oberhelman, S. M., ed. 1991. *The Oneirocriticon of Achmet: A Medieval Greek and Arabic Treatise on the Interpretation of Dreams.* Lubbock: Texas Tech University Press.

Obeyesekere, G. 1981. *Medusa's Hair: An Essay on Personal Symbols and Religious Experience.* Chicago: University of Chicago Press.

O'Connor, P. 1986. *Dreams and the Search for Meaning.* Mahwah, N.J.: Paulist Press.

Ong, R. K. 1985. *The Interpretation of Dreams in Ancient China.* Bochum, Germany: Studienverlag Brockmeyer.

Oppenheim, A. L. 1956. The Interpretation of Dreams in the Ancient Near East with a Translation of an Assyrian Dream-Book. *Transactions of the American Philosophical Society* 46(3): 179–343.

Osborne, K. E. 1970. A Christian Graveyard Cult in the New Guinea Highlands. *Practical Anthropologist* 17:10–15.

Palombo, S. R. 1978. *Dreaming and Memory: A New Information-Processing Model.* New York: Basic Books.

Parman, S. 1991. *Dream and Culture: An Anthropological Study of the Western Intellectual Tradition.* New York: Praeger.

Peck, M. S. 1998. *The Road Less Travelled: A New Psychology of Love, Traditional Values, and Spiritual Growth.* 2d edition. New York: Simon and Schuster.

Perls, F. 1970a. Dream Seminars. In *Gestalt Therapy Now*, edited by J. Fagan and I. L. Shepherd. New York: Harper Colophon.

———. 1970b. Four Lectures. In *Gestalt Therapy Now*, edited by J. Fagan and I. L. Shepherd. New York: Harper Colophon.

Phillips, W. 1994. *Every Dreamer's Handbook.* Altamonte Springs, Fla.: Totonada Press.

Piaget, J. 1962. *Play, Dreams, and Imitation in Childhood.* Translated by C. Gattegno and F. M. Hodgson. New York: W. W. Norton.

Radin, P. 1936. Ojibwa and Ottawa Puberty Dreams. In *Essays in Anthropology Presented to A. L. Kroeber.* Berkeley: University of California Press.

Ramas, M. 1985. *Freud's Dora, Dora's Hysteria.* In *In Dora's Case: Freud—Hysteria—Feminism.* Edited by C. Bernheimer and C. Kahane. New York: Columbia University Press.

Rambo, L. 1993. *Understanding Religious Conversion.* New Haven, Conn.: Yale University Press.

Rechtschaffen, A. 1978. The Single-Mindedness and Isolation of Dreams. *Sleep* 1:97–109.

Reed, H. 1985. *Getting Help from Your Dreams*. Virginia Beach, Va.: Inner Vision.

Ricoeur, P. 1970. *Freud and Philosophy: An Essay on Interpretation*. Translated by D. Savage. New Haven, Conn.: Yale University Press.

———. 1974. *The Conflict of Interpretations: Essays in Hermeneutics*. Translated by D. Ihoe. Evanston, Ill.: Northwestern University Press.

———. 1981. *Hermeneutics and the Human Sciences: Essays on Language, Action, and Interpretation*. Translated by J. Thompson. New York: Cambridge University Press.

Rieff, P. 1966. *The Triumph of the Therapeutic: Uses of Faith after Freud*. New York: Harper and Row.

Rivers, W. H. R. 1923. *Conflict and Dream*. London: Kegan Paul, Trench, Trubner.

Roheim, G. 1952. *The Gates of the Dream*. New York: International Universities Press.

Roll, S., and Millen, L. 1979. The Friend as Represented in the Dreams of Late Adolescents: Friendship Without Rose-Colored Glasses. *Adolescence* 14:255–75.

Root, N. N. 1962. Some Remarks on Anxiety Dreams in Latency and Adolescence. *Journal of the American Psychoanalytic Association* 10(2):303–22.

Rubin, K. H., Fein, G., and Vandenberg, B. 1983. Play. In *Handbook of Child Psychology*, edited by P. H. Mussen. New York: John Wiley & Sons.

Rupprecht, C. S. 1990. Our Unacknowledged Ancestors: Dream Theorists of Antiquity, the Middle Ages, and the Renaissance. *Psychiatric Journal of the University of Ottawa* 15(2): 117–22.

———. 1993. The Drama of History and Prophecy: Shakespeare's Use of Dream in *2 Henry VI*. *Dreaming* 3(3):211–28.

————, ed. 1993. *The Dream and the Text: Essays on Literature and Language*. Albany: State University of New York Press.

————. 1996. Sex, Gender, and Dreams: From Polarity to Plurality. In *Among All These Dreamers: Essays on Dreaming and Modern Society*, edited by K. Bulkeley. Albany: State University of New York Press.

Russo, R., ed. 1987. *Dreams Are Wiser Than Men*. Berkeley, Calif.: North Atlantic Books.

Ryback, D., with Sweitzer, Letitia. 1988. *Dreams That Come True: Their Psychic and Transforming Powers*. New York: Ivy Books.

Rycroft, C. 1979. *The Innocence of Dreams*. New York: Pantheon Books.

Saint Denys, Hervey de. 1982. *Dreams and How to Guide Them*. Translated by N. Fry. London: Duckworth.

Samuels, A. 1985. *Jung and the Post-Jungians*. Boston: Routledge & Kegan Paul.

Samuels, A., and Taylor, M. 1994. Children's Ability to Distinguish Fantasy Events from Real-Life Events. *British Journal of Developmental Psychology* 12:417–27.

Sanford, J. 1982. *Dreams: God's Forgotten Language*. New York: Crossroads.

Savary, L. M., Berne, P. H., and Williams, S. K. 1984. *Dreams and Spiritual Growth: A Christian Approach to Dreamwork*. Mahwah, N.J.: Paulist.

Scales, B., Almy, M., Nicolopoulou, A., and Ervin-Tripp, S. 1991. *Play and the Social Context of Development in Early Care and Education*. New York: Teachers College, Columbia University.

Schneider, D. M., and Sharp, L. 1969. *The Dream Life of a Primitive People: The Dreams of the Yir Yoront of Australia*. Washington, D.C.: American Anthropological Association.

Schroeder, H. W. 1996. Seeking the Balance: Do Dreams Have a Role in Natural Resource Management? In *Among All These Dreamers:*

Essays on Dreaming and Modern Society, edited by K. Bulkeley. Albany: State University of New York Press.

Schwartz-Salant, N. and Stein, M., eds. 1990. *Dreams in Analysis*. Wilmette, Ill.: Chiron Publications.

Seafield, F. 1877. T*he Literature and Curiosities of Dreams: A Commonplace Book of Speculations Concerning the Mystery of Dreams and Visions, Records of Curious and Well-Authenticated Dreams, and Notes on the Various Modes of Interpretation Adopted in Ancient and Modern Times*. 2d ed. rev. London: Crosby, Lockwood, and Co.

Shafton, A. 1995. *Dream Reader: Contemporary Approaches to the Understanding of Dreams*. Albany: State University of New York Press.

Shastri, H. P., trans. 1953. *The Ramayana of Valmiki*. London: Shyantisdan.

Shweder, R. A. and Levine, R. A. 1975. Dream Concepts of Hausa Children: A Critique of the "Doctrine of Invariant Sequence." *Ethos* 3:209–30.

Siegel, A. B. 1990. *Dreams That Can Change Your Life*. Los Angeles: Jeremy Tarcher.

Siegel, A. B., and Bulkeley, K. 1998. *Dreamcatching: Every Parent's Guide to Understanding and Exploring Children's Dreams and Nightmares*. New York: Three Rivers Press.

Signell, K. A. 1990. *Wisdom of the Heart: Working with Women's Dreams*. New York: Bantam Books.

Singer, D. G., and Lenahan, M. L. 1976. Imagination Content in Dreams of Deaf Children. *American Annals of the Deaf* 121(1): 44–48.

Skura, M. 1981. *The Literary Use of the Psychoanalytic Process*. New Haven, Conn.: Yale University Press.

Smith, C. 1993. REM Sleep and Learning: Some Recent Findings. In *The Functions of Dreaming*, edited by A. Moffitt, M. Kramer, and R. Hoffmann. Albany: State University of New York Press.

Spearing, A. C. 1976. *Medieval Dream-Poetry*. New York: Cambridge University Press.

Spiegel, S. 1994. An Alternative to Dream Interpretation with Children. *Contemporary Psychoanalysis*. 30(2):384–95.

Stairs, P., and Blick, K. 1979. A Survey of Emotional Content of Dreams Recalled by College Students. *Psychological Reports* 45:839–42.

States, B. O. 1988. *The Rhetoric of Dreams*. Ithaca, N.Y.: Cornell University Press.

———. 1993. *Dreaming and Storytelling*. Ithaca, N.Y.: Cornell University Press.

———. 1994. Authorship in Dreams and Fictions. *Dreaming* 4(4): 237–54.

———. 1995. Dreaming "Accidentally" of Harold Pinter: The Interplay of Metaphor and Metonymy in Dreams. *Dreaming* 5(4): 229–46.

Stekel, W. 1943. *The Interpretation of Dreams: New Developments and Technique*. 2 vols. New York: Liveright.

Stephen, M. 1979. Dreams of Change: The Innovative Role of Altered States of Consciousness in Traditional Melanesian Religion. *Oceania* 50(1): 3–22.

———. 1995. *A'Aisa's Gifts: A Study of Magic and the Self*. Berkeley: University of California Press.

Stern, P. J. 1976. *C. G. Jung: The Haunted Prophet*. New York: Delta.

Stevens, A. 1995. *Private Myths: Dreams and Dreaming*. Cambridge: Harvard University Press.

Stewart, K. 1969. Dream Theory in Malaya. In *Altered States of Consciousness*, edited by C. Tart. New York: HarperCollins.

Stockholder, K. 1987. *Dream Works: Lovers and Families in Shakespeare's Plays*. Toronto: University of Toronto Press.

Straker, G. 1994. Integrating African and Western Healing Practices in South Africa. *American Journal of Psychotherapy* 48(3): 455–67.

Sullivan, K. 1998. *Recurring Dreams: A Journey to Wholeness*. Freedom, Calif.: The Crossing Press.

Sundkuler, Bengt G. M. 1961. *Bantu Prophets in South Africa*. 2d ed. London: Oxford University Press.

Tanabe, G. J. Jr. 1992. *Myoe the Dreamkeeper: Fantasy and Knowledge in Early Kamakura Buddhism*. Cambridge: The Council on East Asian Studies, Harvard University.

Tart, C. T. ed. 1969. *Altered States of Consciousness*. New York: Harper Collins.

Taylor, J. 1983. *Dream Work: Techniques for Discovering the Creative Power in Dreams*. Mahwah, N.J.: Paulist Press.

———. 1992. *Where People Fly and Water Runs Uphill: Using Dreams to Tap the Wisdom of the Unconscious*. New York: Warner Books.

———. 1995. Debate on the Legacy of the Senoi. *ASD Newsletter* 12(2): 30–34.

———. 1998. *The Living Labyrinth: Exploring Universal Themes in Myths, Dreams, and the Symbolism of Waking Life*. Mahwah, N.J.: Paulist Press.

Tedlock, B., ed. 1987. *Dreaming: Anthropological and Psychological Interpretations*. New York: Cambridge University Press.

———. 1991. The New Anthropology of Dreaming. *Dreaming* 1(2): 161–78.

Tigay, J. H. 1987. *The Evolution of the Gilgamesh Epic*. Philadelphia: University of Philadelphia Press.

Tillich, P. 1952. *The Courage to Be*. New Haven, Conn.: Yale University Press.

Toffelmeir, G. and Luomala, K. 1936. Dreams and Dream Interpretation of the Diegueno Indians of Southern California. *The Psycho-analytic Quarterly* 5:195–225.

Tonay, V. 1990–91. California Women and Their Dreams: A Historical and Sub-Cultural Comparison of Dream Content. *Imagination, Cognition, and Personality* 10:83–97.

———. 1995. *The Art of Dreaming*. Berkeley, Calif.: Celestial Arts.

Tonkinson, R. 1970. Aboriginal Dream-Spirit Beliefs in a Contact Situation: Jigalong, Western Australia. In *Australian Aboriginal Anthropology*, edited by R. M. Berndt. Sidney: University of Western Australia Press.

Tracy, D. 1975. *Blessed Rage for Order: The New Pluralism in Theology*. Minneapolis, Minn.: Seabury Press.

Trafzer, C. E. and Beach, M. A. 1985. Smohalla, the Washani, and Religion as a Factor in Northwestern Indian History. *American Indian Quarterly* 9(3): 309–24.

Trompf, G. W. 1990. *Melanesian Religion*. Cambridge: Cambridge University Press.

Turner, V. 1969. *The Ritual Process: Structure and Anti-Structure*. Ithaca, N.Y.: Cornell University Press.

Ullman, M. 1994. The Experiential Dream Group: Its Application in the Training of Therapists. *Dreaming* 4(4): 223–30.

Ullman, M., and Krippner, S. with Vaughan, A. 1989. *Dream Telepathy: Experiments in Nocturnal ESP*. 2d ed. Jefferson, N.C.: McFarland & Co.

Ullman, M., and Limmer, C., eds. 1987. *The Variety of Dream Experience: Expanding Our Ways of Working with Dreams*. New York: Continuum.

Ullman, M., and Zimmerman, N. 1979. *Working with Dreams*. Los Angeles: Jeremy Tarcher.

Urbina, S. P., and Grey, A. 1975. Cultural and Sex Differences in the

Sex Distribution of Dream Characters. *Journal of Cross-Cultural Psychology* 6:358–64.

Van de Castle, R. 1994. *Our Dreaming Mind.* New York: Ballantine Books.

Vande Kemp, H. 1977. "The Dream in Periodical Literature: 1860–1910. From Oneirocriticon to Die Traumdeutung via the Questionaire." Doctoral dissertation, University of Massachusetts.

———. 1994a. Psycho-Spiritual Dreams in the Nineteenth Century. I. Dreams of Death. *Journal of Psychology and Theology* 22:97–108.

———. 1994b. Psycho-Spiritual Dreams in the Nineteenth Century. II. Metaphysics and Immortality. *Journal of Psychology and Theology* 22:109–119.

Van der Post, L. 1975. *Jung and the Story of Our Time.* New York: Vintage Books.

Van Dusen, W., ed. 1986. *Emanuel Swedenborg's Journal of Dreams.* New York: Swedenborg Foundation.

Van Eeden, F. 1913. A Study of Dreams. *Proceedings of the Society for Psychical Research* 26:431–61.

Van Meurs, J., with Kidd, J. 1988. *Jungian Literary Criticism, 1920–1980: An Annotated, Critical Bibliography of Works in English.* New York: Scarecrow Press.

Von Franz, M. L. 1986. *On Dreams and Death.* Boston: Shambhala.

———. 1991. *Dreams.* Boston: Shambhala.

Von Grunebaum, G. E. and Callois, R., eds. 1966. *The Dream and Human Societies.* Berkeley, Calif.: University of California Press.

Wallace, A. F. C. 1958. Dreams and Wishes of the Soul: A Type of Psychoanalytic Theory among the Seventeenth Century Iroquois. *American Anthropologist* 60:234–48.

———. 1969. *The Death and Rebirth of the Seneca.* New York: Vintage Books.

Wallace, W. J. 1947. The Dream in Mohave Life. *Journal of American Folklore* 60:252–58.

Waterman, D., De Jong, M., and Magdelijns, R. 1988. Gender, Sex Role Orientation, and Dream Content. In *Sleep '86*. New York: Gustav Fischer Verlag.

Wayman, A. 1967. Significance of Dreams in India and Tibet. *History of Religions* 7:1–12.

Weber, M. 1976. *The Protestant Ethic and the Spirit of Capitalism*. Translated by T. Parsons. London: Unwin Paperbacks.

Wehr, G. 1987. *Jung: A Biography*. Boston: Shambhala.

Weidhorn, M. 1970. *Dreams in Seventeenth-Century English Literature*. Paris: Mouton.

Whitman, R., et al. 1962. The Dreams of the Experimental Subject. *Journal of Nervous and Mental Disease* 134:431–39.

Whitmont, E. C. and Perera, S. B. 1989. *Dreams, a Portal to the Source*. New York: Routledge.

Wickes, F. G. 1988. *The Inner World of Childhood: A Study in Analytical Psychology*. 3d ed. Boston: Sigo Press.

Williams, S. K. 1980. *Jungian-Senoi Dreamwork Manual*. Berkeley, Calif.: Journey Press.

Wilmer, H. A. 1982. Vietnam and Madness: Dreams of Schizophrenic Veterans. *Journal of the American Academy of Psychoanalysis* 10:47–65.

———. 1986a. Combat Nightmares: Toward a Therapy of Violence. *Spring*: 120–39.

———. 1986b. The Healing Nightmare: A Study of the War Dreams of Vietnam Combat Veterans. *Quadrant* 19(1): 47–61.

Wilson, D. B. 1993. *The Romantic Dream: Wordsworth and the Poetics of the Unconscious*. Lincoln: University of Nebraska Press.

Winget, C., and Kramer, M. 1979. *Dimensions of Dreams*. Gainesville, Fla.: University Presses of Florida.

Winnicott, D. W. 1960. *The Maturational Process and the Facilitating Environment*. London: Hogarth Press.

———. 1971. *Playing and Reality*. London: Tavistock Publications.

———. 1986a. *The Family and Individual Development* London: Tavistock Publications.

———. 1986b. *Holding and Interpretation*. New York: Grove Press.

———. 1987. *The Child, the Family, and the Outside World*. Reading, Mass.: Addison Wesley Publishing.

Wiseman, A. S. 1986. *Nightmare Help: For Children, From Children*. Berkeley, Calif.: Ten Speed Press.

Wolman, B. B., ed. 1979. *Handbook of Dreams: Research, Theories, and Applications*. New York: Van Nostrand Reinhold.

Woods, R. L., and Greenhouse, H. B., eds. 1974. *The New World of Dreams*. New York: Macmillan.

Wuthnow, R. 1994. *Sharing the Journey: Support Groups and America's New Quest for Community*. New York: Free Press.

Yamanaka, T., Morita, Y., and Matsumoto, J. 1982. Analysis of the Dream Contents in Japanese College Students by REMP-Awakening Technique. *Folia Psychiatrica et Neurological Japonica* 36:33–52.

Yawkey, T. D., and Pellegrini, A. D. eds. 1984. *Child's Play: Developmental and Applied*. Hillsdale, N.J.: Lawrence Erlbaum.

Young, S. 1998. Dream Practices in Medieval Tibet. *Dreaming: The Journal of the Association for the Study of Dreams* 8(3):145–55.

———. In press. Dream Rituals from the Tangyur. In *Tantra in Practice*, edited by David White. Princeton: Princeton University Press.

———. Forthcoming. *Dreaming in the Lotus: Innovation and Continuity in Buddhist Sacred Biography.*

Zadra, A. L., Donderi, D. C., and Pihl, R. O. 1992. Efficacy of Lucid Dream Induction for Lucid and Non-Lucid Dreamers. *Dreaming* 2(2): 85–94.

Zepelin, H. 1980–81. Age Differences in Dreams: I. Men's Dreams and Thematic Apperceptive Fantasy. *International Journal of Aging and Human Development* 12:171–86.

———. 1981. Age Differences in Dreams: II. Distortion and Other Variables. *International Journal of Aging and Human Development* 13:37–41.

Zimmerman, M. E. 1988. Quantum Theory, Intrinsic Value, and Panenthcism. *Environmental Ethics* 10(1): 3–30.

Index

213